because

of

her

sex

kate figes

The myth of

equality

for women

in Britain

PAN BOOKS

First published 1994 by Macmillan London Ltd
This edition published 1995 by Pan Books Ltd
an imprint of Macmillan General Books
25 Eccleston Place, London SW1W 9NF
and Basingstoke

Associated companies throughout the world

ISBN 0-330-32849-2

9 8 7 6 5 4 3 2 1

A CIP catalogue record for this book is available from the British Library

Photoset by Parker Typesetting Service, Leicester
Printed and bound in Great Britain by
Cox & Wyman Ltd, Reading, Berkshire

For my daughters
Eleanor and Grace

contents

Kate Figes was born in 1957 and studied Arabic and Russian at the Polytechnic of Central London. She worked for six years for the publishers Pandora Press and is now Fiction Editor for *Cosmopolitan* magazine. She also reviews fiction regularly for BBC radio. She lives with her husband and two small children in north London.

acknowledgements

My mother's book *Patriarchal Attitudes* was published when I was thirteen. Many of the issues were discussed at school where other girls forced me to defend arguments; I usually had to climb on a chair to make sure they got the point. Thanks have to go to Eva, for without her early influence this book undoubtedly would not have been written.

The idea for this book came from Felicity Rubinstein. She wanted to know the answers to some basic questions about women's lives today and her persistent arm twisting, enthusiasm and sound editorial judgement ensured its completion.

Thanks are due to Cassia Kidron for her superb and incisive interviewing and to Jane Wood and Sue Moore for editorial advice. I have many other men and women to thank for helping me with ideas, expertise and access to research papers: Frank Spencer, Alice Leonard, Sheila Wild and David Perfect from the EOC; academics Heather Joshi, Lynn Ashburner, Angela Dale and Angela Coyle and the many dedicated campaigners and lobbyists working for pressure groups trying to improve the position of women.

I am deeply grateful for the generosity and honesty of the hundreds of men and women who have been interviewed for this book. Some are named, but I have used pseudonyms for those who are more vulnerable.

Finally, special thanks to Cher Cawley for helping to look after and teach my daughter Eleanor and to my husband Christopher Wyld for, among millions of other things, making me laugh.

chapter one

there
is a
difference

When my eldest child was pulled feet first from me into the world, the doctor forgot to tell me whether it was a boy or a girl. It had been a complicated labour, culminating in surgery, and he was busy rushing the baby to a hotplate on the other side of the room. But once the drama and pain of labour were over, I needed to lose no time in knowing exactly which I had. I tentatively asked the question as I peered up at the doctor's back over a gaping hole where my abdomen had been. 'Oh, it's a girl,' he said absentmindedly, as if he was telling me what make of car he had. The gender of the baby in his hands was secondary to his need as a professional to ensure that the child was healthy.

While the sex of my child meant little to the doctor, it meant the world to me. I had a daughter. We were to share a common gender, if nothing else. I knew already that she was destined to struggle harder than any man if she was to succeed in her chosen field, that she was likely to plummet to the depths of depression, anger and disappointment and soar occasionally to the heights of rapture and passion. Such is the female experience. But until I began researching for this book I had no idea how hard that struggle was still likely to be for her in the golden age of 'equal opportunity'. For, unlike the doctor who helped bring my daughter into the world, most people still define each other primarily by gender and therefore by the prejudices associated with that gender. We still see only men or women, rather than individuals with distinct needs, differences and contributions to make to society. And as a society we still do not afford women equal citizenship with men.

But if the reality of 'equal opportunity' remains largely denied to women, the rhetoric has been hugely successful. Young people can be forgiven for growing up believing that we now have equality between the sexes – that every male privilege or opportunity is also available to any woman and that she simply has to be brave enough to grab it. Women can now work at whatever they choose: as chief executives, or engineers, or as Prime Minister. They can drive fast cars, go where they please, live where and with whom they like and use contraceptives to limit their fertility. If they don't achieve their ambitions, women have only themselves to blame, now that society is supposed to have altered sufficiently to accommodate their every need.

The myth of equal opportunity has bred other falsehoods about the working woman, which are even harder to discredit now that the media finds feminism unfashionable, deploying the word 'postfeminism' to pronounce it dead. Women no longer need men, we're told, now that they have every right and privilege once exclusive to men. Consequently it is men, not women, who are in 'crisis': rendered sexually and economically redundant by women, the argument continues, they have become more rapacious and violent than ever. The rise in the number of unemployed men is often linked – inaccurately – with the increase in working women, the assumption being that there is one large pot of labour, ladled out in equal measure. In fact there are two separate labour markets, segregated by sex, with one sector paid considerably more than the other. The real reason for rising male unemployment in Britain has been the steady shrinking of manufacturing since the 1950s. Meanwhile the service sector has grown, with mothers and married women actively sought after because they are cheaper to employ. The new wisdom claims that, having taken over the majority of recently created jobs, it is women who will become the breadwinners. In fact the kind of jobs done by women are often the only ones on offer, and rarely pay enough to support one person let alone her children.

Women are being educated for work, and they want and need to work for all the same reasons, psychological, social, intellectual and economic, as men. Yet they are still denied access to the better jobs, or paid inadequately for valuable work in teaching, health care and the rest of our service industries. These days women cannot afford not to work. Yet it is they who are blamed for the rising divorce rate; it is their changing roles, we are told, rather than male reluctance to change, which have upset the balance between the sexes. Now that a high divorce rate means that marriage cannot be relied upon as a meal ticket for all time, many women are reluctant or simply unable to give up their means of earning a living for a romantic notion of how family life once was. 'I've always worked; we could live in a smaller flat and I could work less hard,' says Jackie, who drives a London black cab and has two children, 'but I feel that at forty-two I want something to show for my hard work. If Kevin did leave me for another woman, at least I'd still have my life, but if I had no work, I'd have nothing.'

Even for women married to a man in full-time employment, giving up paid work is no longer an option. The average salary in Britain in 1994 was £19,000 with two-thirds of wage earners paid the average or below. It is estimated that a man needs to earn £20,000 or more in order to support a wife and two children. Less than 10 per cent of families in Britain are now supported solely by their fathers. Families need the income of women, however small; but there has been no legislation to prevent this need being exploited, and no establishment of a childcare policy. Instead, the age-old fallacy that a woman's income is secondary to that of a male primary breadwinner has been used repeatedly in recent years to reinforce women's dependency on men and encourage the exploitation of women as a cheap source of labour.

This book is about the reality of women's lives in the 1990s, of life as it is actually lived, for discrimination against a woman because of her sex not only survives but is worse than ever. We have become preoccupied with the social and cultural manifestations of feminism, with representations of women in the media, with language, with sexuality and with the so-called war between the sexes. Fascinating though these issues can be, they are not the heart of the matter. They are reflections, consequences of the basic economic and political imbalance between the sexes. Women are still dependent on the hazard of finding a well-intentioned man as their provider. They remain unable to stand beside him as an equal citizen because our entire system of political, economic and social policymaking still favours the earner and taxpayer over the dependant. While a woman is supported by a man she is invisible and can be ignored. But once she becomes dependent on the state she is a pariah, a parasite who is somehow to blame for her dependency on the taxpayer. There is little willingness to see her as the victim of a society which prevents her, because of her sex, from participating fully by earning her own living.

Within the home, neglect and abuse threaten many women who lack full economic independence. Those who do not earn their own living consistently put their wants behind the needs of their families. Should they suffer rape, abuse or other violence, they have limited means of escape from the men on whom they depend. The state is happy to relinquish clearing up after such acts of squalor to a dedicated group of women in the refuges and rape crisis centres of the poorly funded voluntary sector. Like the outcast unmarried mothers of yesteryear, victims of mistreatment by men are given charity, rather than the means to stand alongside men as equal citizens.

In the arts and advertising, as in pornography, represent-ations of women as weak and subjugated reflect a culture which still places a lower value on a woman. If, through its economic policies, society says often enough that women matter less, then women themselves come to believe this – and so do men. A woman's status within the home will be dictated by her role in the world at large. Women who are seen routinely to earn less for the work they do, or to be channelled into unpaid domestic labour, are more likely to be perceived by their menfolk as sexually passive: there for the taking. The borderline between wife and possession is still hazy. When women become wives and mothers, they can still disappear as citizens. It was not until 1991 that the Lord Chief Justice, Lord Lane, ruled that rape in marriage should be perceived as a crime: 'We take the view that the time has now arrived when the law should declare that a rapist remains a rapist irrespective of his relationship with the victim.' With this utterance he established for the first time in British law that marriage for a woman does not diminish the right to protection from violence. But such a judgment can do little to reduce violence against women while society still assaults them metaphorically, by undervaluing their contribu-tions as unpaid carers of the young, the sick and the elderly; and by exploiting them as cheap labour.

Young women expect and want to do paid work. 'You can't not work these days,' says seventeen-year-old Stella, 'so you might as well try and get a good job.' In 1992 more girls than boys gained five good grades as GCSE, and in subject areas such as maths and science where they lag behind boys, they are catching up fast. Often though, they do so in vain: the job opportunities available to them prove severely limited in a mar-ket that has not altered its base sufficiently to welcome them or to cater for their biological difference.

Today, young women have more confidence than ever. They expect more from life, and, while the women's movement has no address, feminism has raised the expectations of a whole new generation. They may have no idea what feminism means, but they expect to be able to have a baby and continue with their careers, and they want relationships with men who provide love and companionship rather than housekeeping money. Reasonable though these expectations are, society has done nothing to help women meet them, neither giving the family due support nor allowing men and women to find a more equitable basis for their relationships. Individual men and women try hard to get on with each other, and the idea that the sexes are somehow at war is a myth. Many try to live as equals within a loving partnership, but in vain given that the only model the state sees fit to support is the nearly extinct nuclear family, provided for solely by a male breadwinner.

If our education system does betray this country's young women, it does so by failing to warn them. Most have no idea how difficult it will be, as mothers, to maintain their working lives while the world of work is moulded entirely around the male model and makes few concessions to female needs. Women who want to pursue their careers, maintain intellectual stimulation or simply earn a living must behave like men. Even then they are punished for it – labelled 'tokens' or 'men in skirts'.

A false sense of security swaddles many women, who believe that their interests are protected by the existence of equality legislation. Only when a woman experiences discrimination first hand – when she finds her attempts at promotion blocked, when she becomes a mother and cannot continue working in exactly the same way as a man, or when she discovers that she is not being paid the same rate as a male contemporary – does she land with a bump on the floor of reality, bruised and bewildered to find how personal experience differs from the theory of equality.

We have bought the rhetoric of equal opportunity hook, line

and sinker. Its policies, and our equality legislation, have been bolted on to a structure of institutionalized discrimination which still keeps women economically dependent on men and sees motherhood as a luxury rather than a necessity. The rhetoric of equal opportunity has merely forced such discrimination to become covert where once it was unabashed and easier to detect. It has also deflected attention from a host of measures in recent years which have made it harder, rather than easier, for a woman to achieve economic independence and thereby equal citizenship.

Myth suggests that the kept wife is becoming a thing of the past. Statistics show otherwise. Among women of working age, 72 per cent do have paid employment; nonetheless, a substantial proportion work only part time. A staggering 73 per cent of working women from ethnic minority groups are full-time employees, compared to just over half of all white working women. There has been no increase at all in the overall numbers of full-time working women since 1951. Only part-time work has seen a mushrooming of the female labour force, whose earnings rarely constitute a living wage. The majority of these women are mothers, forced to work part time by the lack of affordable childcare and by the prevailing work ethic. In recent years their conditions and pay have been worsened by employment measures exploiting the fact that they have no choice but to work part time.

Service occupations employ 90 per cent of working women. A handful of women have made it into such well-paid male preserves as law, accountancy and medicine; but the majority work in health care and welfare, as teachers, secretaries, cleaners and hairdressers, or in catering and retail, where in 1992 even full-time wages often fell beneath the weekly low-pay threshold of £197. Women from ethnic minority groups tend to be in the lowest status jobs within occupations earning even less money than white women. Non-white nurses are concentrated in work with the elderly and in mental health. Doctors from ethnic minority groups are more likely to have had poorer training opportunities and be in the least desirable specialities and minority ethnic women are much more likely than white women to work in low-paid manual work in hotel and catering. Britain foots most European tables of pay difference: its gross monthly earnings of non-manual women workers average just 54 per cent of men's, as compared to 66 per cent in France and nearly 70 per cent in Germany (Rubery, *The Gender Pay Gap*, 1993).

Among those few women in previously male-only professions, it is true that incomes have risen considerably. But often they still have not attained equal pay. Female solicitors working full time currently receive only 74 per cent of their male colleagues' earnings; women in business and management professions do scarcely better (*Women and Men in Britain 1993*, EOC). The increase of performance-related pay means that many professional women have no way of knowing what their peers are earning. There is also evidence that company perks and bonuses are handed out more liberally to the chaps who, after all, have to provide for families. Clearly the women don't, because it's so goddamned hard to work in any of these jobs if you are a mother. The 1993 National Management Salary Survey found that the difference in earnings between women and men actually gets wider the higher women climb. So much for the notion that discrimination disappears once a woman smashes through a glass ceiling to the heights of success, status and a new lifestyle.

Overall the difference in pay between men and women does appear to be narrowing slightly: women's percentage of male salaries has risen from 73 per cent in 1980 to 78 per cent in 1991. This is due solely, however, to a rise in the number of women earning a more lucrative wage in traditionally male-only professions. There has been no change lower down the scale, where most women work. Women's earnings have hovered at just over half of men's earnings for the best part of two decades. Far from deserting in their droves because they no longer need their men's pay packet, most women are still financially dependent on a man. They have been denied the dignity of a decent wage in payment for jobs which are still considered secondary to the work undertaken by the all-important male breadwinner. The majority of working women are second-class citizens in Britain today, confined to poverty, drudgery and obscurity; and now that the average family can no longer live on one income, most women lack even the option of a return to the old days of complete financial dependency in return for protection within marriage.

All too often, basic biological differences are used to excuse the extraordinary discrepancies in citizenship between the sexes. This argument was typified by a comment from the manager of a large branch of a main high-street bank. The bank has a printed and circulated equal-opportunity policy, yet when asked if it was always the young men who secured career progression, the manager replied, 'Yes, because that's life, isn't it? The woman has got to produce the baby. You can have your fun, but they have to produce the baby. There will never be any equality.' Nowadays both men and women need work, and provided that the workplace adapts, it is possible for women to work and be adequate mothers. Yet for our bank manager and millions like him this is perceived as having your cake and eating it – even though raising children does not take a lifetime and women need work for all the same reasons as men.

No one should belittle the difference between the sexes – it forms the very basis of sexual attraction as the opposite poles of magnets, or yin and yang, pull towards one another and at times repel. But acknowledging such an unlikeness is not to say that either gender should suffer discrimination. Both are essential parts of the most basic human equation. While the circumstances of a milkman and a judge clearly differ, no one would question the right of each to equality as a citizen or before the law. In the same way men and women can only reach true equality through recognition of their substantial difference. A truly civilized society would relish that difference, rather than punish women for their sex.

Women themselves are given confusing and contradictory information about their role in society. Magazines and newspapers profile successful women who 'have it all', suggesting that if they can do it, so can we. In contrast, tiny references to new research findings hint at the reality beneath the gloss. This book attempts to fill that gap with a survey of the discrimination which women still face. General government statistics are frequently not broken down according to gender, so that it is often hard to ascertain whether women are being adversely affected by policies. When it comes to race, general statistics are even more negligent. Where statistics which reveal the position of black women are available, I quote them, but the general thrust of this book covers the wider issues of institutionalized discrimination which adversely affect all women. Obviously different women are going to be affected to a greater or lesser extent according to their circumstances, black women usually more so than white because of their colour as well as their gender. Any reader looking for easy answers will be disappointed: I have no key to unlock the mysteries of presumption and discriminatory attitudes. I only have a desire to present the facts, without which we are vulnerable to myth and rhetoric. I hope that by reading this book, men and women will think twice before believing that we live in a golden age of equal opportunity, one in which the principles of feminism are no longer necessary.

chapter two

divided
kingdom

Men and women rarely work together in Britain. At best they work alongside each other in two separate sectors defined by gender. Nearly two-thirds of workplaces in Britain employ only men in skilled manual work, while half of all workplaces employ only women in clerical and administrative work (Millward, *Targeting Potential Discrimination*, 1995). At worst they have next to no contact in the workplace with members of the opposite sex. No wonder we find it so hard to understand one another. Often we find ourselves divided by location, with women concentrated in schools, hospitals and supermarkets, while men work in commerce and finance. Alternatively, the sexes are separated by hierarchy, with men still dominating the summit of every industry, even those whose majority of employees are women. The consequences of this great divide in the workplace are that women almost invariably earn considerably less than men.

Segregation of this depth and tenacity does not happen by chance. Women are not naturally drawn to cleaning lavatories or taking letters, nor are they better than men at doing these jobs. Men are not necessarily leaders, born to command and incapable of lifting a mop instead of a sword. Jobs are defined by pay as well as by gender, with women almost invariably paid less for any given work. The Equal Pay Act has been extended to include jobs of equal value in order to narrow the pay discrepancies between 'women's' and 'men's' work. Yet the segregation between the sexes at work is being preserved and reinforced by employers and government in order to exploit women as a cheap source of labour and incidentally to perpetuate their dependency on men. In spite of equal-opportunity legislation, women must still opt for the lower-paid work thought pertinent to their sex.

Caroline is one of four high-earning female executives amongst 150 men in a large international bank. 'The secretaries are all women and they're all young and very pretty. But their pay is so low that they cannot afford to eat in the staff canteen.' This banking institution annually makes millions of pounds' worth of profit. Without secretaries it could not function; yet it refuses to pay them a reasonable wage. By only employing women as secretaries, and by insisting on young ones, the bank can pay wages that barely constitute a living. Only 4 per cent of all secretarial and administrative staff earn over £15,000 a year; most earn less than £10,000. Recent research from the EOC has found that establishments employing a predominantly female workforce are three times more likely to employ low-paid staff than a predominantly male workforce (Millward, *Targeting Potential Discrimination*, 1995). Women therefore often get paid less simply because they are working with other women, lowering the market rate for the job. One young man who found himself surrounded by fifty women in a typing pool told the academic writer Teresa Rees that he was unable to support himself on such low wages and would shortly be moving on. Yet the women are expected to manage. The myth of equal opportunity suggests that escape into a better-paid job is likewise available to these women. If they don't seize the opportunity they have only themselves to blame.

In fact two distinct career paths tend to exist, with women

excluded from the fast track by a series of obstacles which have quaintly become known as glass ceilings – though concrete might offer a better comparison. Men climb a staircase up the hierarchy, whereas women must languish in the slow route to nowhere or make an effort akin to scaling a sheer brick wall with suction boots. The common fear of the opposing males is that a preponderance of women will lower the prestige and the salaries of their trade. Some of the exclusionary practices with which they respond can take explicit forms, through sexual harassment or outright hostility; less tangible opposition is based on the assumption that women only want a hubby and kids and that work is just a way of biding time until the right man comes along. The myth lives on that women have jobs, rather than careers they wish to pursue irrespective of their personal lives.

Any claim to appoint an employee on merit fails to acknowledge that, like beauty, ability can lie in the eye of the beholder. Men – who still make most decisions on recruitment and promotion – often judge their own sex on entirely different criteria to those on which they judge women. Male incompatibilities with a job's stated needs are ignored or excused on the grounds that training will resolve the problem. Gender alone may exclude women who fit the brief perfectly well: for example, excellence or assertiveness are simply not liked when displayed by a woman. In the district service centres of the main high-street banks, rows of women are paid to sit at computer screens punching in data. Men are thought to be slower at such work, but rather than not recruit them, the banks quickly excuse them from such hard cheap labour and place them in more responsible positions. Women are likewise thought to be good at dealing with the public; consequently they work at the cash tills of banks and building societies, in dead-end jobs which even the most ambitious find it hard to break out of. In her extensive survey of employment patterns in building societies, conducted in 1989, Lynn Ashburner found 100 per cent recruitment of women as cashiers in regional societies. At branch-manager level, however, men formed 100 per cent of recruitment. 'I could only find evidence of recruitment in management from cashiering grades on two occasions, but neither were viewed as the norm.' One regional building society even specified no minimum educational requirement for manage-ment recruits, while at cashier level there was a stated preference for at least four O levels.

Women left in lower-paid jobs often find it impossible to distinguish themselves. How do you impress your boss when it is mistakes that isolate you from the mass rather than professional excellence, honesty or whizzo ideas? Such talents can actively bar a woman's progress: bank managers value honest cashiers, and bosses want to keep secretaries who can type letters without making mistakes. Lynn Ashburner found that women who did achieve promotion in the national building societies had to work on average twice as long as the men before they could reach the next grade. In the National Health Service it takes male nurses just 8.4 years to reach their first nursing post, while female nurses working without a career break for children take, on average, 14.5 years to reach the same post (*Business ... in the NHS*, 1992). It tends moreover to be those with planning and financial skills – the men – who are most frequently selected for manage-ment rather than those with clinical, administrative, personnel or public health experience.

Within retailing, for example in Sainsbury's, most of the management is recruited from graduate trainees rather than by training and promoting existing staff. 'If I wanted better pay,' said one employee, 'I'd have to go elsewhere. For all they say about promotion prospects, if you're management you get it and if you're staff you don't and if you're on the checkout you've got no chance.' Becoming a buyer is the fastest route up to manage-ment. Most buyers, however, are men, and those women who do begin the long steep haul up to prosperity face overwhelming odds. As Jim, a butcher at a London superstore, points out, 'It is easier for men to progress through the store than for women, particularly in management. The men are very sexist. The women have to prove themselves and be hard and it's not liked. She can't win. Once you are a manager you have to be able to work in all of the departments and it's harder for a woman to get into some of those departments because they know that she won't be able to do some of the heavier work; so usually they get shoved into admin or personnel.' In most supermarkets and large stores, men drive the vans and shift large quantities of produce with forklift trucks at the back while women work as shelf fillers loading kilo after kilo of goods by hand, or at the tills, where they are responsible for considerable quantities of cash. All these jobs are essential, yet the men are consistently paid more than the women.

The world of the arts is equally segregated in spite of its more liberal, cultivated appearance. Stage technicians in the theatre are almost exclusively men, while women work in wardrobe and make up. 'If you talk to the BBC, they will say that there are a lot of women coming through in the industry,' comments Denise O'Donoghue, managing director of the television production company Hat Trick, 'but my experience is that there are still very very few. There are lots of researchers, secretaries and production managers, but at the end of the day the television industry is no different to any other; the higher you go, the fewer women there are.' The jobs which women do occupy in television, such as research and wardrobe, do not provide the essential training required for escalation into management. Women comprise almost half of all employees in advertising; but here too they are concentrated in secretarial and research jobs, rather than in creative or account management work which is not only the most lucrative but also the most interesting (Baxter, *Women in Advertising*, 1990). In the publishing industry, publicity is now considered essential to the success of a new book. Many agents will sell rights in key authors to the publisher who can put forward the best marketing plan as well as the most money. Yet publicists –

who are almost exclusively female – are rarely paid more than £15,000 per annum. The men who staff the sales department earn far more than the women in publicity, on whose efforts they depend.

The work that a woman does is still thought to be worth less than that done by a man. Behind this illusion lurks the idea that she doesn't really need the money, that somewhere in the background is a man willing to take care of her. Well, have a good look around. Such men are a dying breed. While the differences in pay between 'women's work' and 'men's work' are so marked, the barriers of segregation are unlikely to be broken down. Men are understandably reluctant to go for lower-paid 'women's work' and they will also resist devaluing the work that they do by allowing a large-scale entry of women.

As more women do gain qualifications admitting them to professions that were once male enclaves, new patterns of gender segregation are emerging. In occupations such as accountancy, law and policing, increased specialization helps confine women in certain areas. Jackie Malton is a detective chief inspector working in London. 'When I joined the police in Leicestershire in 1970 there was a separate department for women. Women police officers were there purely to deal with searching women, finding missing children, care cases and looking after babies. We were in a different building working seven and a half hours a day, so we never really felt part of the police.' After the Sex Discrimination Act in 1975, they kept the women's section but changed its name to the 'special inquiry unit' in order to comply with the law. 'It suited some women to do that particular kind of work but if, like me, they didn't want to stay there, they would have to be brought out. They never really wanted a woman officer of sergeant level or above to be operational on the streets. When I went into CID as a detective sergeant in plain clothes, women would get all the rubbish, like thefts of prams.'

It's a familiar story, this limiting of women to the lowest-earning sections of their profession. Women managers are concentrated in lower status jobs in the service sector rather than in business or manufacturing, and it is hard to gauge how much they have really gained when the structure of management and job hierarchy has changed with many senior clerical posts relabelled as managerial. Female accountants are concentrated in auditing rather than in industrial management. Women in insurance are more likely to be working in personnel than as actuaries, and women working as managers in retail are in staff rather than store management. Female solicitors are often restricted to low-status desk work such as wills, probate or matrimonial affairs, legal aid and law centre work. As sets of barristers become increasingly specialized and identified with expertise in particular areas, women are becoming concentrated in family rather than in the higher-earning commercial sets. 'There still aren't many women around doing very heavy criminal cases,' says Helena Kennedy QC. 'There is still a feeling that adversarial advocacy is not appropriate for women, that it is not nice to see them fighting a case hard, that it is not very ladylike.' Barristers depend heavily on the clerks of their sets for work: 'He brokes the work, he is the agent taking commission and the clerk system is almost exclusively male,' says barrister Barbara Hewson. 'It can be very difficult for a woman to build up credibility if the set has an all-male culture, and inevitably a woman will suffer.'

While clerks broke the work, it is inevitable that personal prejudices will sway their decision. Men get allocated to high corporate business cases because they will be working for an all-male client base, whereas women get the less prestigious and less well-paid family work. Nearly 50 per cent of heads of chambers report experience of clients expressing a preference for a particular gender of barrister, and that those preferences are accommodated (*Without Prejudice* . . ., 1992). 'My clerk says that he's never encountered direct discrimination,' says barrister Sue Soloman. 'But I'm not sure how many clerks would recognize discrimination if it stared them in the face. The law's a bit like acting; a lot of typecasting goes on.' Once a woman gets typecast as specializing in family cases it is hard for her to break into other specialisms. One or two women in highly competitive and high-earning commercial sets are an asset, pandering to the theory of equal opportunity. But more would threaten the overall status and income of the set as well as individual jobs.

In medicine male principals and partners of practices often confine female GPs to gynaecology, family planning, psychiatry and paediatrics (Bock, *Beyond Equality* . . ., 1992). Only 2 per cent of general surgeons are women, as opposed to 20 per cent of consultants in psychiatry, anaesthetics, paediatrics, pathology and radiology. Women have been allowed to rise in relatively new specialisms which are less glamorous than general surgery. But they are denied access to specialisms such as general surgery and gynaecology, where the men are anxious to retain their status and high income. Only 12.5 per cent of recently appointed consultants in obstetrics and gynaecology have been female. Male gynaecologists are terrified of more women entering their profession in case their all-female client base should desert them in droves. They therefore rely heavily on the old-boy network as a non-biological means of reproducing themselves. Julia is a senior registrar in obstetrics and gynaecology. 'It is still seen that women have NHS work and children while men have NHS work and their private practice. If a woman is a gynaecologist she is doing it for love, for pin money; and by not striving for more money she will bring down the salary and status of the field. They are also terrified of women going to female gynaecologists.' Beverley, a senior registrar in general surgery, feels that women avoid certain areas of medicine because of the demands that are made on them or because they are likely to fail where competition with men is especially great. 'I have seen countless women pick specialisms like anaesthetics and radiology because it is sensible, because you can just about work and have a family and because there are more women already there.' She concedes that once a woman makes it to senior registrar in general surgery, it is perhaps easier at present for her than for a man to become a consultant, 'because people are falling over themselves to appoint a woman surgeon . . . they know that you're a money puller with patients electing to come to you because you're a woman. But that is only possible because having one or two women around is not enough numerically to constitute a threat.'

As a new growth area for jobs, information technology should, according to the laws of equal opportunity, cut equally across the sexes. But Cynthia Cockburn's study in 1986 of men and women working with new technology found that even when women were as well qualified as the men, the men were perceived as the 'technologists', able to take off the outside casing and intervene in the mechanism. Women were the low-paid operators, merely allowed to work the controls. In spite of being a new science, the well-paid profession of computing has quickly become masculine. Girls have less access than boys to computers both at home and at school. Software called 'game boy' is bound to make a game girl feel excluded, and that sense of exclusion has contributed to a fall in the numbers of female students on IT-related courses in higher education, from 26 per cent in 1979 to 14 per cent in 1986 (Rees, *Women and the Labour Market*, 1992).

Men are no longer entering certain professions in the same numbers as before, rejecting vocational careers as doctors and teachers for more lucrative and glamorous work. Consequently, they are vacating certain jobs for women. In 1979, women outnumbered men in education and health by roughly 1.7 to 1. By 1989 the divide had widened to 2.1 women to every man (Labour Force Survey, 1990). Doctors and teachers were once members of highly respected professions. But now that teaching has taken such a battering from government and through media criticism of educational standards, teachers increasingly lack the benefit of status as compensation for low pay. The result is that the profession is becoming progressively more female. Between 1981 and 1990 the number of male teachers dropped from 1 in 3 to 1 in 4 at a time when teachers weekly pay fell by 9 per cent (Millward, *Targeting Potential Discrimination*, 1995). Janice has been a teacher for twenty-two years. 'Amongst parents and users teachers are still valued and respected, but I certainly think that the way teachers are presented in the media actively suggests that there has been a devaluing.' Janet, a secondary-school teacher, feels that, 'It probably does devalue teaching as women are seen to take the easy options. I have my own essay title for the kids – "It is better to be female than male". The sixteen to eighteen-year-olds all perceive women as having far fewer job opportunities and less interesting jobs, so as soon as you have a preponderance of women it seems less important.'

At the top end of the scale in education, however, men are maintaining their hold on headships. The job of head still enjoys status, and relatively good pay now that heads are required to manage substantial trust budgets. Many female teachers have told me that they no longer wish to attempt to become a head now that the job involves more accountancy than teaching. They are unlikely in any case to get such posts while men still want them, for discriminatory attitudes bar them where sheer numbers of men would not. A woman's ability to maintain discipline over the school as well as to manage large budgets will be called into question, even while her ability to manage a classroom or her salary as a teacher is not.

For GPs there are now additional administrative burdens and costs, as a result of the new contract. There is also increased criticism, possibly even litigation, from a public increasingly aware of health issues. Men still outnumber women as doctors. But fewer men than women enter general practice, opting instead for the more competitive, lucrative and glamorous ladder up to consultancy, which is still largely a male stronghold. In 1980 GPs in England numbered just over 4,000 women and 19,500 men. By 1991 the figures revealed the beginnings of a trend, with a rise of 3,500 female GPs to only 800 more men (*Health and Personnel Social Services Statistics for England 1992*, HMSO). 'There has been a lowering of the status of the medical profession, partly financial as doctors don't earn that much any more, but there is also less reverence from patients who question what you do more,' says Dr Lottie Newman, now retired, who has seen considerable changes in medicine. 'The status of doctors is definitely lower in Eastern Europe, but whether that's because there are so many more women doctors there or because the status of doctor was lower is hard to say. Women are much more conscientious as a gender, we don't improvise or bluff that much, we are much more reliable and there is no logical reason why we should lower the status.' When prestigious female-only enclaves open up to men the pattern is different. Men tend to go where the status, money and power is, rarely questioning their right to be there. When for instance, Girton College Cambridge allowed men in as undergraduates, they flooded through the gates, whereas women are still only trickling into the previously male-only colleges (CUWAG, *Forty Years On*, 1988).

One effect of such sexual apartheid is that as certain professions become progressively more female, employers – in particular the state – can keep their labour costs down by preserving gender segregation at work and recruiting a greater proportion of women. In the civil service, women were being actively recruited and promoted at a time when the relative pay of middle and higher grades dropped from 30 per cent to 14 per cent above the average pay for men. This handy but devious way of cutting public expenditure is not beyond any politician's capacity, notwithstanding public commitment to equal opportunity. Our health and education services have been undermined by government and the media at a time when the political imperative to cut public expenditure is urgent. The growing numbers of women employed by these sectors find that reasons of gender alone can keep down their pay. Women are rarely allowed to take a job that would otherwise be occupied by a man. They are enabled, however, to occupy large parts of the service sector simply because men increasingly do not want such work. Thus a vicious circle is drawn: while few men opt for jobs in the women's sector there cannot be greater integration of the sexes. Without that integration men and women have little hope of understanding each other better and seeing their opposites as more than sexual beings.

Prudery versus patronage

A lingering Victorian prudery also divides the workforce: the sexes need to be kept apart. The allegedly irresistible attraction between them is used all too often to exclude women, ostensibly for their own good, when the real beneficiaries are men. Women have to be protected, the myth being that men are unable to control their sexual urges. The emphasis is always on the exclusion of women rather than their right to expect greater courtesy from men. Men and women live and sleep with each other; men watch their wives and girlfriends give birth; and yet a distaste of mixing the sexes lives on at the heart of society.

An official inability to distinguish sex from gender means that though we share the same lavatories and often the same bath at home, in public men and women require separate facilities. Women stand in long queues exercising their pelvic floor muscles outside the ladies at cinemas, theatres and airports while men whip in and out of a urinal with ease, relieving themselves in semi-public behind a swinging door. Public baths are required by law to have separate changing facilities; but all it takes is for one young father to take his three-year-old daughter swimming for her to see more willies than she ever imagined.

Excluding a woman for her own good also excludes her from networking, and from 'important conversations which take place in changing rooms,' says Sophie Anderson, a consultant anaesthetist. 'And in the game of power and politics you want to be where the boys are talking.' When Francesca Brettell was a medical student on attachment to a hospital in Newcastle, she found that there were separate changing rooms for men and women on either side of the theatre, each with a separate coffee room – one for the nurses and one for the doctors. Such an arrangement excluded her from socializing and therefore from networking with her colleagues. It also meant that the men were not put in the position where they had even to listen to the views of the supposedly subordinate women essential to the successful outcome of any operation. 'The nurses determine the whole atmosphere of the theatre because we're there all the time,' says Heather, a senior nurse in charge of an operating theatre. 'We organize the entire procedure, getting the patients and the staff there, while the consultants drop in and out for the actual operation.' She adds that during her ten years in nursing she has noticed a change in the attitudes and authority of the doctors, simply because the nurses have found the heightened self-esteem to challenge them. 'The older women were much more like surgeons' handmaidens. They would bow and scrape and lick arse, but my generation don't have that attitude; we are more on an equal footing. Theoretically we are supposed to be running the theatre. Last Bank Holiday Monday one consultant thought he had booked in an extra two cases with management, but there were no extra staff and I didn't know about it. I said no, I can't open an extra theatre; we don't have the extra staff, and he accepted that. An older generation of women would have phoned round and tried to get people in because he wanted to do those operations, but I'm not prepared to do that.'

Current changes are nonetheless slow. If men and women rarely share more than moments of a working day, with men almost invariably dispensing the orders, then neither learn much about the opposite sex outside their personal relationships. Our prime knowledge and understanding of the opposite sex comes from our private lives, with all that the average relationship offers of complexity, heartache and pain. Worship of the madonna who has just given birth to his first child or anger at the woman who has just dropped him for a better guy inevitably influences a man's relations with colleagues. Flirtation and innuendo enter situations which have nothing to do with sex because men and women have little experience of talking to the opposite sex as equal partners outside the roads to and from the bedroom. 'I think that if you are not prepared to get into a sexual interaction, however unstated, it is very difficult for most men to put you into a category with which they are familiar,' says Denise O'Donoghue of the television production company Hat Trick. 'The net result is that they don't quite know how to manage the situation. It comes down to a question of control; men like to be in control of women and when there isn't that simple hierarchy in a relationship it throws them.'

The ignorance and exclusion cuts both ways. David, a housewife and father, says that when he went to collect or drop off his young son at nursery school he felt open hostility from the mothers. 'I felt subtly excluded from what was going on and could almost hear them wondering – should we allow our child to go to that man's house, will he be safe? A couple of the mothers at the school started flirting with me and then suddenly stopped. They couldn't relate to me as mothers without flirting. They found it awkward but now that there are a couple of other fathers around it's a bit easier.' If more men worked alongside women it would help to highlight similarities between the sexes, as well as their separate needs.

Several professionals are inclined to see a woman as a gendered being rather than as an individual with her own good qualities and weaknesses. Training to become a hospital consultant can take up to fifteen years after qualifying from medical school. It is highly competitive, with doctors moving around the country annually from job to job in order to gain the requisite experience. Success in finding those jobs depends largely on a system of benefactors and sponsors who either give students work or refer them on. 'It's the way that one learns in medicine,' explains a woman consultant. 'Time and again it's the one whose face fits. They appoint not necessarily the best, but the one who is not going to rock the boat. It's such a small world, so enclosed, that you've got to be able to work together.'

There are also times during the long haul to the top, particularly in the jump from registrar to senior registrar, when you need to have undertaken research in a particular specialization. Many of the research jobs available are not open applications. They are often 'soft money' sponsored by drug companies, and depend on the old-boy network. For women this poses particular problems. 'Women may not be on social terms with their consultants in the same way as men because if you are on social terms with a consultant, the first thing that is assumed is that you are having an affair with him,' explains Sophie, consultant anaesthetist. 'When I was a houseman I was invited to the pub along with other members of the team and the next day someone said, "I saw you getting into Doctor so-and-so's car – nudge nudge, wink wink." This just doesn't happen with the junior male doctors. It helps if you're good looking because if they are going to have a woman around they don't want anybody ugly or grossly obese, but if it's a man then it doesn't matter what you look like. Men may decide to become a benefactor to a female junior because they enjoy that reputation or they may consciously avoid it in order not to have those aspersions cast about them; it is easier all round to take a male colleague.'

In Nora Ephron's film *When Harry met Sally*, Harry states categorically that men and women can never be friends without being lovers because the 'sex bit always gets in the way'. He then succeeds in proving his theory when he finds that he is in love with his best female friend. But no one expects colleagues to be either lovers or best friends, merely to work together effectively. If sexual relationships do form – and how else do most people meet when they spend so many hours of the day at work – it is unrealistic to suspect their professional competence. 'I'm terrified of the segregation between the sexes. It's wrong. We have to learn how to live together,' says architect Eva Jiricna. While supervising exams at Oxford Polytechnic Eva noticed that the girls wanted to work with girls and the boys with boys. When she asked the girls why, they said that it was because the boys were difficult to work with. 'But they will have to work with boys every day of their lives; if they don't start now how will they ever learn?'

If men and women are unaccustomed to working with each other, inevitably numbers of men will be unable to distinguish sex from gender in the workplace, particularly when women are mostly their subordinates. A recent survey by the Industrial Society revealed that 54 per cent of women in employment are victims of unwanted attention from men. This ranges from physical abuse through to taunting a woman verbally so that she feels persecuted enough either to leave or just to feel miserable because of her impotence.

Too often when a woman reports harassment to personnel or line managers, the response is to move her away from the harasser for her own good, rather than to reprimand the man. By failing to make the harasser rethink his imbecility, such a policy can exclude the woman and make her feel that her presence alone was to blame, like a rape victim denounced as provocative for wearing a short skirt. A male workforce out to keep women away from 'men's work' isn't slow to learn. Intimidating a woman succeeds in getting her removed: let that teach her for thinking she can be an electrician. For every woman prepared to speak up about being harassed because of her sex, countless others are reluctant to risk their job by talking about it openly, the more so when the prevailing culture at their workplace condones such practices as a harmless bit of fun.

Tracie Simpson came upon bricklaying by chance. At college a teacher asked her class to build a small wall as an exercise. 'Mine was all level and plumb and the teacher was surprised. He asked me if I'd done it before and when I said no, he said, "You're a bricklayer," and I was really thrilled. I thought, I'm not dumb, I can do something after all.' When she went to work for Greenwich Council she found that she was consistently given the secondary work and rarely allowed to build walls. Men would come to stare at her as she worked and jibe her with questions about whether she shaved her pubic hair or did her spirit level fit into her vagina.

The odd joke can be shrugged off and has to be expected. But repeated taunting and antagonism is both humiliating and isolating. Women trained with construction skills tend to work as self-employed builders rather than on sites or with direct labour forces. 'Most of the women who used to work on building sites will tell you about the sexual harassment,' says Tracie. 'But the problem with women is that they don't want to say so at the time. You don't want to do anything which will flare things up and make them worse.'

If a woman does complain and is taken seriously, management will usually move her to another section rather than reprimand male workers for behaviour that they view as understandable. Boys will be boys. In 1990, the Bristol region of British Rail conducted a campaign to recruit more women trackworkers. Because women in mixed teams evidently faced hostility, BR recruited an all-female team of eight workers, rather than challenge such hostility as intolerable. Once again women were given a tiny slice of the action rather than integrated into a whole process.

In Tracie Simpson's view, men working in packs simply do not want women around. Individually her male colleagues behaved quite differently. 'One labourer said to me, "How the hell do you handle it, they just don't leave you alone?" But when he was part of the gang he continued with the jokes and the jibes. Another said he would have thumped them if they had done the same thing to him. They see it, but don't do anything about it because for a man to challenge another man on such an issue threatens his masculinity. But unless you do point it out to them things will never change.'

Tracie is unusual; she recently won £15,000 in damages from her employers as compensation for never being able to work as a bricklayer again. In America, the threat of a sexual harassment case is taken more seriously. Hundreds of thousands of dollars can theoretically be awarded to the victim, while in Britain average damages amount only to two or three thousand pounds. 'Harassment cases have a particularly nasty ring about them,' says Alison Ogden, an independent expert at equal value cases who runs Women's Education in Building, 'because they have associations with telling tales out of school, of being neurotic and somehow unable to cope. The first defence in any harassment case is that it was a joke and why can't you be less sensitive about it. The attitude is that you are the one who is threatening me by being here and the only way that I can deal with it is to make a joke out of it, so why can't you just laugh rather than getting on your soapbox. They are in many ways right, but the emphasis is always on making the woman change in order to make the men feel more comfortable rather than the other way around.'

On a building site it may be normal for a man to shout 'lesbian' at a woman in a tin hat or to wolf whistle at a passer-by in a short skirt. It would be uncouth, however, for a banker or lawyer to behave this way. Their methods of exclusion are more subtle. Kate Parkin is one of many senior women influencing book publishing, at Random House. Her former job was as senior editor at another large publishing house run entirely by men, most of whom were salesmen. Because of her sex, Kate felt active exclusion and hostility. The men would rush into work and come to decisions before meetings over breakfast. Silence fell if a woman entered a room full of them, so that all you could hear was the click clack of her heels as she walked across the floor. At parties a total of two or three women could be made to feel isolated and inadequate by forty heavy-shouldered men making dirty jokes. In one meeting Kate raised a problem she had with the sales department. 'The sales director was furious at having been caught out at having done something badly. He stood up and said, "I'm going to come over there and spank your little bottom." I was outraged. It was a genuine, legitimate problem to raise at the meeting, for someone hadn't supplied the necessary material and the author had had a problem as a result.'

At another meeting a sales manager rushed in to announce that W. H. Smith had just appointed a woman as their new purchasing manager. 'The whole table went Huh! I looked around at the other women but what could you do? Some of these men are freemasons; for them women are wives, secretaries and mistresses. The sales people at Random Century are completely different. Obviously there are unreconstructed men here but there aren't enough of them to inform the culture. Men feel strong in groups where there are next to no women.'

Failing such overt methods of excluding women, other work practices can do it. Of the many outdated assumptions about women, the most tenacious is the myth that for them work is merely a method of earning money until the happy day of dependency on a man. Women still have jobs, not careers, it seems. When a woman marries or becomes a mother she suddenly becomes mysteriously retarded, unable to distinguish boardroom meetings from antenatal classes, or minutes from shopping lists. Her fecundity is interpreted as a divided loyalty, whereas a father who loves his child just as passionately is viewed as entirely dependable now that he has to work to provide for his family. He is likely to be paid more, and more is demanded from him in terms of hours and commitment to his job, dividing his loyalties to both his family and his work.

It doesn't enter the equation that some women choose to have careers as well as families. Others may have no choice in the matter: they're responsible for a mortgage, or they simply feel insecure financially given the increased poverty resulting from a one-in-three rate of divorce. Women are divided into careerists or family women, sometimes blatantly. Clare, an accountant, couldn't ignore the feeling that her boss was not keen on women working. 'I took a collection to him as one of the girls was leaving to have a baby. He said, "I can't wait for the day when they bring yours in." I said, "Thank you very much, do you want to get rid of me?" He said, "Oh, no, no, but I just think that is where women are most fulfilled, at home having a family."'

At other times the management attitude is covert, forced underground by the need for protection from potential litigation or simply to avoid causing offence. Barbara Mills QC, Director of Public Prosecutions, tells of how a senior manager once came to her and said that he had a problem. '"Tell me," I said. "My best candidate for the job is a woman," he replied. At that point he stopped, realizing perhaps only at that moment that he was talking to a seriously successful woman. I said, "But I thought that you had a problem?" It then transpired that this one state-ment was shorthand for a mass of assumptions: she has children and she may have more – what a waste of investment; she has a husband who won't want to move if she is promoted elsewhere; she won't be able to put in the necessary hours; she won't be tough enough – that great male phrase for a male job. These are the assumptions with which we are struggling. They are outdated but still prevalent.'

When Lynn Ashburner undertook her extensive study of building societies she found that women recruits were divided between those perceived as careerists and those who were non-career staff. Unless women could align themselves completely with the male model of supposed unswerving dedication, their opportunities for promotion and better pay were immediately curtailed. '"They are going to leave eventually and have children," said one male cashier. "They say they want a career and they get promotion but they only want a better salary, and they stay in that lower management position and hold everybody else up."'

The excuse for such practices would be nullified if female staff found adjustments made for their biological difference. If they could come back without impunity the management's initial investment would not be lost. Employers want conflicting things from their staff. They demand intelligence and creative drive, competence and get up and go. But they don't want employees to get up and go literally. Instead they say they want stability. However, few men or women now stay with the same employer throughout their working lives. The man who joins the company as a trainee at eighteen and leaves at sixty-five with his clock under his arm belongs to a former generation, not to the competitive labour market of today. Boredom and no prospect of advancement are the primary reasons that both men and women leave their jobs. They move because they can, as does anybody with more intelligence than the average artichoke.

Most women left their employer, according to the Women and Employment Survey (Martin and Roberts, *Women's Employment . . .*, 1980), because they wanted a better job; only 4 per cent had to move elsewhere with their husband. Twenty-five per cent left to get married, because they were pregnant or to look after children. Given the punishing lifestyle of most working mothers and the lack of affordable childcare, that percentage would be likely to drop significantly if the state and employers took a more positive attitude towards working mothers. The myth is that women are more likely to leave their jobs because they have children. Studies show, however, that it is men who are more likely to leave, after on average two years, because they have a clearer career path and are less likely to feel loyalty to their former employer if a better opportunity arises. Often, too, they take their client base with them. A woman may leave to have a baby, but the better the childcare, maternity provision and attitude of her employer, the more likely she is to return to the same job. What employer wants all their staff to stay forever anyway? A reasonable turnover of employees prevents an organization from becoming stagnant.

No factual evidence suggests that mothers are less dedicated or efficient workers, or that parenthood turns a well-tuned female mind to slush. Women are not less ambitious than men, and they consistently show the same potential motivation for success and achievement. The gender gap opens up where the desire for promotion is directly linked to chances of actually being promoted. One survey of a local authority (Maddock, 'Gender Cultures', 1993) found that male managers thought women lacked ambition. Meanwhile the majority of women said that they lacked encouragement from management. Life for a working mother may be more complicated and more tiring, and may force her to place on hold her attempts at promotion or finding a new job, but her mind has not necessarily changed. She still thinks in terms of career, of aspirations for her working life outside of her responsibilities to her children. Women's intellectual capacities long outlive their mothering responsibilities and are frequently enhanced by the experience. There just are different times in a woman's life for doing things in a particular way. Working mothers suffer an immediate disadvantage, when confronted with after-hours meetings and the attitude that the only employee doing his job properly is the one at the office from early in the morning until late at night. Employers who spout their commitment to principles of equal opportunity have done nothing to change the culture which encourages such attitudes. In fact the reverse is happening, as many squeeze more work out of their full-time employees, whose average number of hours per week is rising. Faced with such practices and attitudes, women who also want to be mothers will consistently settle for second best in their careers. Only the toughest, or those best able to afford expensive, high-quality support, will have the option even of trying. The rest juggle, confined by the need for flexibility to low-paying jobs below their capabilities, often as one of the ever-growing numbers in poorly paid, low-status, part-time work.

In areas of work dominated by women, part-time work is accepted and encouraged, as a way of keeping down labour costs. It is rare, however, in any sector dominated by men, where indeed it is considered inappropriate: it simply isn't possible to do a responsible job on a part-time basis, or so the myth goes. Only 3 per cent of women managers worked part time in 1992 according to an Institute of Management survey of its members.

An exception to male part-time work does show itself though in many senior men, who would have us believe that they work all hours. Somehow they combine their highly responsible jobs with seats on the boards of other companies or of public welfare organizations. Such arrangements enhance their status and networking powers considerably. Rarely is it suggested that they distract a man from his paid employment.

Several male MPs combine the responsibility of representing their constituents with law work or lucrative dealing in the City. Many senior men manage to find time for long lunches, nights at the opera that begin at 5 p.m., or for business trips and management training that take them from their desks for days on end. National sex survey statistics suggest too that men of higher occupational status appear to have both the cash and the mobility for affairs. Evidently they can also find the time. It is a truism that the grander the job, the bigger the desk and the less there is on it. The support staff is better too, so that you spend less time doing detailed, lengthy work and more time making decisions based on the efforts of others. However hard men work, and whatever their stresses, they do seem to combine the cut and thrust of management with many other responsibilities which all too often do not include their families. But a woman dares at her peril to suggest that she has to leave work regularly at 5 p.m. and therefore cannot attend that after-hours meeting or fulfil a particular task until the following morning. Too often such an attitude is viewed as lack of commitment.

In rare instances part-time provision is made specifically to help women overcome some of the problems of working motherhood. Even so it may work against them. Beverley is one of the new female part-time registrars in this country, on a scheme designed to help more women up the ladder to consultancy. Part time for her means that she works eight sessions a week instead of ten and is on call one weekend in three, hardly an easy week. Yet when discussing her next training post with a consultant, she was told that he was not prepared to make her an offer because she was part-time and might not be there when he needed her.

Facts fail to back up another myth about the alleged unreliability of working mothers, namely that they are frequently off work tending their children's sicknesses. According to *Social Trends 22* (HMSO, 1992), women are only slightly more likely to take sick leave. In a sample week 5.2 per cent of women aged twenty-five to forty-four had taken a day off as opposed to 3.8 per cent of men. Among twenty- to twenty-four year-olds there was no difference. Given that women consult their GPs more frequently, and that many experience depression and distress as a result of their menstrual cycles and the health and practical problems caused by having children, it is surprising that the figure is not higher. It suggests that women are more reliable than men, and struggle to work in the face of far more difficulties.

Social Trends indicates too that men are slightly more likely than women to die at almost every age. But you never hear that used as an excuse for employing a woman over a man. Admittedly you don't have the costs of maternity leave, but there is the wreath to think of, plus the paid leave that you are going to have to give his colleagues in order to attend the funeral, not to mention the problems of finding an immediate replacement, because death can come more suddenly. At least with pregnancy you have seven or eight months to get used to the fact and reorganize your office accordingly, and if a woman is off work to look after a sick child she does come back. Dead men don't.

While men are given priority over women as the breadwinner, with the most interesting jobs and the highest pay, women will always be seen as men's natural dependants, vulnerable simply because they can and do have children. If men will not move into female sectors of employment – and while the pay is so bad why should they? – there is no room for women in highly paid, competitive and desirable jobs. Many educated, aspirational women currently swotting their guts out will find their dreams dashed as they settle for jobs considerably beneath their skills and their training. Forty-two per cent of men with a degree-level qualification were employed in professional-level jobs in 1988 as opposed to only 15 per cent of similarly qualified women, while in intermediate non-manual occupations 49 per cent of women with degrees or comparable qualifications were employed as opposed to only 22 per cent of similarly qualified men.

It isn't that women lack the skills, qualifications or sheer competitive drive needed to get the jobs that fit their credentials. What excludes them is the labour market's refusal to accommodate their difference to men, particularly when they become mothers. Why are we not also prepared to alter the workplace sufficiently to let these educated women in? Education offers girls ample opportunity, and they are seizing it, doing as well as the boys in exams. But many of them will end up, nonetheless, as part of the growing lump of cheap labour required for the expanding service industries, or working beneath their skills and qualifications.

Women now comprise 50 per cent of students at law and medical school. But while those professions continue to be moulded to male patterns of work, and while men want those jobs, women will consistently find themselves nosed aside. Many are achieving everything expected of them and more. Pass rates for the Medical Research Council general practice exam from May 1988 to May 1991 show that the women candidates gained proportionately twice as many distinctions as their male colleagues (*British Journal of General Practice*, February 1992). Yet they are expected to study at the time when they are most likely to want children. For this reason they face considerable discrimination in a highly competitive recruitment and promotion process, and not surprisingly the drop-out rate is high. Though half of medical students are women, only 38 per cent are at the level of senior house officer and 24 per cent are at registrar level.

Three times as many women solicitors as men have ceased practising ten years after admission to the roll. The same proportion remain assistant solicitors, while men achieve partnership at twice the rate of women (*Report of the Hansard Society ...*, 1990). Drop-out rates at the Bar are high for both sexes, due to the gruelling and largely unpaid research work during pupillage; nonetheless it remains higher for women. A recent survey of the Bar found that women had to make more applications for pupillage and attend more interviews than men and that 70 per cent of women barristers felt under pressure to perform better than their male colleagues.

In British universities between 1975 and 1980 the number of female undergraduates in medicine increased by 30 per cent; but in 1986 women were still only 11 per cent of full-time non-clinical staff and 14 per cent of all tenured staff (*Report of the Hansard Society* . . ., 1990). At Cambridge three-quarters of all academic women are on short-term fixed-post contracts, as opposed to only 39 per cent of the men. In theory the fairly flexible nature of academic life ought to make it easier for staff who are mothers. In fact it is a majority of men who achieve the security of tenure. An Equal Opportunities Commission survey of health authorities in 1990 found the childcare provision of our number-one employer of women to be woefully inadequate – just 3,500 nursery places for the 800,000 women employed by the NHS, with less than 1 per cent of senior house officers in part-time posts. Compare this to the return rate of 70 per cent of mothers at Midland Bank, whose staff have one of the best private-sector nursery provisions (Goss, *Equal Opportunities* . . ., 1991). It costs roughly £250,000 to train a doctor and £40,000 to train a nurse. When only 17 per cent of nurses return to full-time work following the birth of a child the loss of investment is great indeed.

Theoretically, equalizing educational standards of boys and girls should afford equality of income and opportunity at work. But this cannot happen while the labour market is so heavily divided, with the work of the different sexes valued inconsistently. Moreover, huge resources invested in the training of women will be lost forever. Given the political will, it doesn't have to be like this. But government and many employers want a segregated labour market, to keep down their overall labour costs. Such a market allows management to use different systems of pay for different groups of workers, introducing performance-related earnings, which tend to favour men over women, and increasingly favouring the hard core of highly paid male personnel with company cars and private health insurance. Meanwhile the pay of a largely female and increasingly flexible workforce is being forced down. Many of these part-time female workers have no paid holidays, job security or access to training or the company pension scheme.

The result is a divided kingdom, with large numbers of men and a highly select small group of women in the 'have' corner and a growing number of women in the 'make do with less' corner, a pattern which is being exacerbated by changing trends in the labour market. Charles Handy of the London Business School has described in his book *The Age of Reason*, the emergence of the 'shamrock' organization. In this, as one leaf of the shamrock, companies rely increasingly on a highly paid, essential, full-time staff, who happen mainly to be men. The other two leaves of the shamrock, where most of the women are found, comprise staff on retainers with self-employed status working largely from home, and flexible labour brought in as and when required. Theoretically such changes in the nature of work should benefit women, allowing them simultaneously to work and stay at home near their children. The actual result is a reinforcement of the old pattern of female dependency on the more substantial male wage.

A highly segregated labour market also makes much of our equal-pay legislation redundant. For a woman to prove that she is being paid less than the market rate for the job she has to compare her earnings with those of a man similarly employed in the same or an associated industry. But if there are no men working alongside her how can she even begin to bring a case? If large numbers of women working in a given field all receive low pay, then that becomes the market rate for the job. To say that history has determined this state of affairs, that it has 'always been like this', is a feeble excuse in the face of the facts. Sexual segregation and low pay for women are being actively maintained and even encouraged, in order to depress wages.

The government argues that a low-wage economy leads to more jobs. It dismisses accusations that such a policy discriminates against women, by saying that the job market as a whole is open to either sex. While theoretically this is true, it is in fact discrimination and exclusion based on a mass of presumption and prejudice which force women into jobs below their level of skill and education. It is women who have to opt for low-paid flexible work because they cannot find state-funded childcare or afford it through the private sector. Once again women are being subtly exploited because of their sex, a practice which is supposed to be redundant now that we have entered the age of equal opportunity. But the costs are great – wasted resources in training women for jobs that they will never do, and failing to tap their potential contribution to the economy as a whole.

We need men and women working together at every hierarchical level and in all types of jobs if we are to serve the needs of both sexes equally. We need more women doctors, if female health needs are to be understood rather than dismissed as hysterical. We need women gynaecologists, if the uterus is not to be seen merely as a 'box' for growing children, easily dispensed with once a woman's reproductive life is drawing to a close. If women are to have equal access to justice, we need more female judges, barristers, solicitors and police officers to enforce and interpret the law in the best interests of women as well as men. Few women take part in policy-making decisions or in the bills before Parliament which become our new laws. A largely single-sex legislature is unlikely to rise above a limited range of attitudes.

And so it goes on. We need balance, with our children learning from men as well as women if they are to grow up benefiting from what both sexes have to offer. Jenny Abramsky, Controller of Radio 5 Live BBC Radio, says that she is 'no great women's libber'. 'I'm not convinced that there are hundreds of issues out there that are being deliberately ignored, that only women can see. I think that's a lot of crap. I do, however, think that women's experiences are different and we need to make sure that these are fully represented, and that's what gives everything a different dimension. Women are thinking constantly about their kids' education, working out how you cope with it; yet I don't think that education is as prominent on the men's agenda. We spend too much time arguing about the major broad-brush stuff and not enough talking about the nitty-gritty, about what matters to people and particularly to women.'

Nothing is less revolutionary than a proposal to make our society representative. Nothing could make better economic sense than to tap everybody's potential resources. But a vicious circle has to be broken if we are to get the most out of everybody irrespective of their sex. The only way is to raise the pay and equalize the conditions of traditional women's work in line with that of men, so that it becomes more attractive to men. Why is a nurse, a secretary or a teacher paid so much less than a policeman, a sales manager or a solicitor when the work is equally valuable? While the discrepancies in pay are so great it is only natural that men are going to reject women's work and resist attempts by large numbers of women to enter their more lucrative strongholds. The answer must surely lie in eliminating these discrepancies, not in blaming men for refusing to relinquish their privileges.

There is no truth in the argument that we cannot afford the labour costs of equal pay for work of equal value. On the contrary, society cannot afford to forgo the economic and welfare benefits of equality. Why should women bear the brunt of poverty and low pay? Huge rises in the overall costs of labour have been absorbed by the economy over time, but they have been allowed because they were increases in the male wage, while differences in the earnings between women and men have remained constant over decades. The tenacity of this suggests that the pay difference between the sexes has nothing to do with the ebb and flow of the supply and demand of labour, but with premeditated, institutionalized discrimination against a woman earning a decent wage.

Would the costs be that great anyway? Jill Rubery, of the

University of Manchester, estimates in *The Economics of Equal Value* (EOC, 1992) that because women's earnings are so low and they work fewer hours, a 10 per cent rise in women's earnings would mean only a 3.1 per cent increase in the overall wage bill. By comparison the economy absorbed a total rise in wages of 3.8 per cent between 1983 and 1990 when male non-manual earnings went up disproportionately. The benefits of raising pay for traditional women's work include fewer women in poverty and drawing benefits; a greater source of income for women in their old age; and a reduction of labour turnover and training costs, because women would have more incentive to return to work after childbirth and would be more able to afford childcare.

New management practices such as multiskilling can play their part in breaking down the barriers of sex segregation. Economic necessity forced London Zoo to teach its animal handlers how to look after other species. Suddenly the head of small mammals had to learn how to move a lion from one cage into another without getting himself killed. I would have thought that working alongside or even for a woman would be a doddle in comparison. BBC correspondents hired to work for either radio or television must now have bi-media skills and file for both media. They work harder, but with widened skills, simply because management has the will and economic necessity to say so. The obstacles to removing sex segregation are the lack of that will and an economic theory driven mostly by men which decrees that such change is not necessary. If 'women's' work was paid as much as work traditionally done by men, far more men and women would find themselves working side by side, for even male pride dissolves when faced with a job with decent money.

With the right organization and willpower it is possible for any employee, in any job, to work part time. A hospital functions over twenty-four hours, with a myriad of shift systems. It ought to be possible for registrars and consultants as well as nurses or ancillary workers to work part time. If senior executives and management in the city or in major industries can find time for extracurricular activities, then part-time working is possible even at their exalted level. When Jenny Abramsky joined BBC Radio, the newsroom's macho culture made it feared by women and the idea of working part time was completely dismissed. 'We were quite determined to change the culture of this and worked out with the editors a 24-hour shift system which allowed women with young children not to work nights. You have to face it head on and accept that you are going to treat some people differently. Now people in the newsroom accept it. People they like who would have left have come back and it also helped a man who was a carer in the same position.'

If part-time working was available in every walk of life, women would find it easier to marry their career ambitions and domestic responsibilities without sacrifice, and men would be able to spend more time with their families. Meanwhile, the secondary status of part-time workers encourages men to hang on to their full-time jobs for dear life, and women find it easier to put up with their lot rather than risk all by challenging it.

So often we hear that women must no longer think of themselves as victims, that they have to stand proud rather than bleat like sheep. Women are attempting more: they are standing for the jobs they want; they are seeping into every chink or crack in the labour market and lying their way through discriminatory, illegal interview questions about their family commitments. Most women do not think of themselves as victims but many will lay low when faced with some of the hurdles that stand between them and the most interesting and lucrative jobs: the assumptions that a woman's natural place is in the home as wife and mother and that she therefore cannot be completely committed to her job; the assumption that she does not need a living wage because she is being supported by a male wage; outright hostility from the male pack; exclusion from male networking; and the psychological fact that most employers or managers recruit in their own image.

There is not just one glass ceiling, but several, less breakable ones. Only the most persistent women, who are stubborn enough never to take no for an answer, will find ways of getting through them. Others simply put up with their lot, or find it easier to leave in the hope of greater opportunity with another employer. In the words of one young female accountant with an international firm: 'I can't see that they would ever appoint a woman to senior manager, and even to be a senior manager in accountancy is not that good. The only people who earn really good money are the partners, so there's no point in staying in the practice unless you get to be a partner.' The fact that most women are human, and would rather leave or make do, allows employers to blame everybody but themselves for any female lack of success. Women are blamed for being 'their own worst enemy', too emotional, lacking in ambition, or too inflexible; biology or society is blamed for making boys different to girls; and precedent is invoked as a reason for avoiding change. Whatever the partial truth of such conditions, employers and government go to extraordinary lengths to reinforce them.

The new myths about working women suggest that they have only to seize their opportunities, and that it is only a question of time before they work their way up through the hierarchy and are found in equal numbers in all walks of life. But such a future is only possible if the culture of work and the organization of individual workplaces adapt to accommodate women's differences from men. Such a vision can only be realized if men are prepared to stand aside and let women in, and while the alternatives are less well paid there is no reason why they should.

The same myths imply a flourishing of female labour across the spectrum. In fact, patterns of work reflect the age-old British class system. There has been a growth in the number of households where both partners earn a full-time reasonable wage, with many women refusing to relinquish their good jobs when they become mothers. These women may find that more than 50 per cent of their earnings disappear in childcare and that they are permanently tired, but they do have greater economic choice and more independence. They are prepared to make such sacrifices knowing that, in the long run, full-time working motherhood is the only way of preserving their status and sanity. Furthermore, the whole family is better off, with more money for holidays, for toys, for outings, for a nutritious, varied diet and even for private education should they feel that the state provision in their area is inadequate. In turn these families are able to raise the prospects of their children. 'I work because we need the money, to maintain our way of life, to be able to buy my children a good education,' says Kathleen Wheeler, who works at an ambulance training centre and has two children under five. 'If I was at home they'd have nothing.'

These women are the lucky ones. But as the actress Juliet Stevenson says, a lot of them find it easy to forget that many, if not most, women are less well off. 'We have some place now, but we don't have power and the fabric of things has not been significantly shifted, and it remains true that you constantly find men as the initiators of work. It makes me angry when women who have been lucky enough to find their place do not acknowledge that there are many women who have still not found theirs.' For while segregation at work is being encouraged rather than broken down, large numbers of women find that they must settle for second best, for low-paid part-time work which they can fit around their children's needs, and for unsociable hours working when other family members can be relied upon for childcare. Most of these women are dependent on men or the state and their lower income leaves the whole family disadvantaged.

Women are seen as a homogenous group. In fact there are now more divisions than ever among working women. Increasingly, women lead dissimilar lives, with women doctors and lawyers inevitably having more in common with male doctors and lawyers than with a bus conductor who happens to be female. Working women with children often find they have little in common with mothers who are permanently at home. As the designer Jane Priestmann says, 'I find that all of my friends are working women which says something about who we talk to. I'm very suspicious of women who haven't worked. I don't know how to talk to them; there's no common ground except children, and that is false because it changes as they change.'

Women can no longer be lumped together as if they were a minority group. Their experiences, economic circumstances and needs are increasingly diverse. 'The top tier of women are doing well breaking through, but the bottom tier are doing very badly and men use this as a stick to beat us all with,' says Dr Elizabeth Shore, the first female dean of the Postgraduate Medical Federation in London. It is to this small top tier of women, who have succeeded in breaking through the barriers into traditional male jobs and power, that we next turn.

chapter three
life
at
the top

'Glass Ceiling, what glass ceiling?' said a headline in the *Sunday Telegraph* on 7 March 1993. 'The glass ceiling – that invisible barrier to female ascent in business life – is shattering. Women are rising to positions of influence and affluence undreamed of by their sisters 10 years ago.'

They make it sound so easy: centuries of presumption and prejudice wiped out with one sweep of a broom. It is true that a handful of women have become stars, eagerly sought after for interviews and appearances on *Question Time* and the like. Moral pressure does demand the presence of at least one such woman; however, they are a rare and endangered species. Certainly they have economic independence as a result of their earnings, as well as higher self-esteem and more interesting lives. But the price is often high. They still find themselves defined by their gender before their talents, and since they are doing jobs defined by men, they still face problems because of their sex. Meanwhile their speckled presence among the higher echelons of society supports the myth that we have equal opportunity. Thus yet another hurdle is placed in the way of other women struggling up behind them. If these first-comers can reach the top, it is assumed not that they are exceptional but that former obstacles must be disappearing. It follows that all those who fail in their ambitions are not discriminated against so much as lacking in natural talent or drive.

Important appointments are made from the top down. Senior appointments in education, the police and the judiciary, chief executives of core businesses, and other influential positions such as governor of the Bank of England, come from the heart of government. Heads of schools are appointed by boards of governors, who are frequently older people, not representative of society, and likely to hold traditional views of a woman's capabilities and correct responsibilities. The judiciary are chosen secretly by the Lord Chancellor's department, and the Lord Chancellor himself is a political appointment. There is no job description for a good judge, no explanation given for his selection, nor any right of appeal against it. Also the selectors recruit in their own image: most judges are male, old, rich, upper class and deeply estranged from many of the social, economic and psychosexual matters that concern the rest of us.

In a democracy, each vote is seen as one small squeak of an individual which, when added to the millions of other squeaks, reflects the myriad different views within society. It is a crude system in which, in practice, myriad views are refracted to the point of oblivion. This being so, issues concerning women can only be adequately voiced from the top of our political structure. Too often our laws and policy decisions fail women because there are simply not enough women in positions of power. While the institutional fabric of Britain's democracy is still so blind even to women's existence, let alone their needs as citizens, it is hard to see how women will ever make it to the top in equal measure. The Queen is only on the throne because there is no male sibling to do the job. No equal opportunity there. Hereditary titles and seats in the House of Lords, where men outnumber women by roughly seven to one, still pass down from father to eldest son. Life peers are trawled from the senior civil service, retired ambassadors, former members of the military, captains of industry, trade unions and ex-MPs. They are pillars of the establishment and, almost to a man, men. There is an absence of teachers, doctors, charity and community workers, housewives and mothers, the implication being that even in a democracy they have less of value to add to any debate. Only a lack of political will can be blamed for failing to alter the selection of life peers in order to give women a more adequate voice. The small number of women who are in politics or policy making find it hard to act as a critical mass, particularly over anything perceived as a 'women's issue'.

While the occasional woman does make it to the top, others of equal ability find that they reach a plateau and can go no further. Having set out to scale the heights by means ranging from unswerving devotion to downright deviousness, they find either that there is yet another board one stage higher or that in other ways their power is not as absolute as they had been led to believe. Janet Cohen is a director of Charterhouse Bank and writes novels in what must laughingly be called her spare time. She is quite categoric about her position. 'I am not at the top. There are virtually no women on any of the top boards of the merchant banks, only on the subsidiary boards. The top boards are where the real power lies.' Barbara Noakes's opening statement when I interviewed her was, 'Although I am the most senior woman in advertising, I'm still only a deputy.' Even Barbara Mills, unquestionably at the top as the first female Director of Public Prosecutions, feels excluded – on small matters, but excluded nevertheless – because of her sex. 'Although I am a graduate of Oxford University – and also an honorary fellow of my college – I cannot become a full member of the Oxford and Cambridge Club. Why? Because I am a woman. The club issue is a small one but an important one. I don't like feeling excluded.'

The paradox is that we recognize the names of successful women because they are repeatedly used to illustrate the alleged meritability of progress, before which the last bastions of patriarchy are bound to fall. They tend to be seen in two camps: the glamorous – Yve Newbold, Company Secretary at Hanson, Anita Roddick, founder of Body Shop, Gail Rebuck, publisher, and Penny Hughes, the new President of Coca-Cola UK, who prove that it is possible to be both powerful and feminine; and the school ma'ams, allowed into positions of moral authority to practise the acceptable motherly qualities of telling the nation what is right and what is wrong. Betty Boothroyd, the first woman Speaker, was recently described by a political commentator as 'tidying up the House' when she asked the Right Honourable members to go back to their seats. The other most senior women civil servants are Barbara Mills, Stella Rimington at MI5 and Valerie Strachan at Customs and Excise. With the forces of law and order at their disposal, they are seen to exude an extra morality over accusations of corruption or malpractice because of their sex.

The talents of these women are undeniably exceptional given the hurdles of prejudice they have either ignored or surmounted. But for countless others that golden summit inevitably feels unreachable. Jane Drabble, Assistant Managing Director of BBC Network Television, concedes that women are making some progress. 'Many key editorial jobs, including producers of the toughest dramas, are held by women and four editors of science programmes are women; that would have been unheard of just a few years ago.' But she adds, 'The tricky bit is the bit above, the bit where women get squeezed out.' For Diane Oldfield, one of only seven female managers of Sainsbury's 316 stores, the question of where to go now in the company hierarchy is daunting. The next step up is district manager, every one of whom is a man. She has worked for the company since graduating, is now thirty-seven, has no children and feels less enthusiastic about staying in the same job until she retires. 'All of the theory is there, with Sainsbury's a member of Opportunity 2000; but it still feels a bit risky. The next stage is so competitive that the desire to do it is going to have to be absolutely enormous in order to break through that barrier. I suppose eventually I might make it. But it's going to take so long at the rate it's going that I'll be dead. It's the same for so many women: you've made it, but have you really? I've a friend who is an assistant secretary in the civil service but is planning to take early retirement, because she feels that she's reached as far as she is ever likely to go.'

Studies of successful women show that they have many common aspects to their upbringing and education. Attending a girls-only school seems to be the one area where sex segregation helps young women to concentrate and achieve. Yet the numbers of such schools are dwindling fast. Thirty years ago there were more than 2,000 all-girl state schools. Now there are just 240 (*Daily Telegraph*, 7 January 1993), and in many areas they have disappeared altogether. Many parents find they must be able to afford private education in order for their daughters to thrive at school, with a better chance to excel academically. The reduction in girls-only schools is integral to the philosophy of comprehensive coeducation. Meanwhile, the restriction in the number of girls-only places is not matched by an attempt within mixed schools to ensure that girls do not have their confidence squashed by the boys. Attempts to overcome this are an ad hoc affair. Some teachers do monitor the children, and their own teaching methods, to try to prevent boys being given priority. But this is due only to their individual interest in the subject being taught; within our schools there is no concerted attempt to apply principles of equal opportunity.

Outside school, a large proportion of successful women have grown up in a supportive, stable family, where ambition and competitiveness have been encouraged. Their mothers have encouraged them to grow up believing in their own separate identity, rather than seeing them as clones destined to reproduce their parents' life. Fathers are important too. Those who take an active interest in their daughters' development are also likely to encourage confidence in their abilities and, as many do with boys, to play games with them which reinforce drive and competitiveness. 'The unquestioning view of your father that you can do anything fosters singleminded direction in girls. Look at Thatcher. Look at the Longfords,' says Janet Cohen. Janet's father was an industrialist. Because of illness suffered by her mother, she found herself walking around factories with her father when she was just eight years old. As a result, in her job as a director of Charterhouse Bank she feels that she is 'used to talking to men'. 'I've always trained with men, been with men. The civil service is stuffed with them, and I had to adapt quickly in order to learn how to sell to them.'

Even women with less prestigious, but equally important and successful careers can appreciate that their fathers were important. Janet Hutchinson has been a senior secondary school teacher for ten years. 'Our father treated me a bit like the son he didn't have, so I've never felt inferior to men. I feel different, but I've always been able to articulate and stand my own ground . . . I've never felt that women needed special privileges. I believe we're equal but different, and that's the difficult bit.'

Another common trait of successful women is that they are childless or single. An Institute of Management Survey of its members in 1992 found that one third of its women members were unmarried, and only half of them had children. In contrast, 92 per cent of the men were married and 86 per cent had children (Coe, *The Key to the Men's Club*, 1992). A survey of assistant directors of social services in 1990 found that three-quarters of its female subjects were single or divorced, and only 18 per cent had children.

In each case these figures are well below the national average proportion of mothers in the 30-plus age group. It appears that even in health care, an area dominated by women and for which they are supposed to have a natural aptitude, a double standard exists. Many women are having to choose, where men do not, between the nourishment of family life and vigorously pursuing a successful career. It may be that all these women enjoy fulfilling relationships with other women, thus excluding themselves from such surveys. Perhaps their working lives are good enough to banish the very thought of indulging in such old-fashioned nonsense as love, friendship and companionship in a stable relationship. Maybe they do not want to be mothers – but all of them? Or could it be that negotiating the hurdles they face because of their sex, working inordinately long hours in order to prove their commitment, being nice to everybody and developing the sheer strength of will needed to succeed rule out many pleasures that successful men enjoy, namely that of a family? As Barbara Noakes says, 'If a man works fifteen hours a day he gets the support of his family, whereas if a woman works fifteen hours a day she gets divorced.'

Professions such as law and medicine have always been fiercely competitive. Herculean endurance tests such as unpaid pupillage or long hours are excused as essential for separating the wheat from the chaff. They also favour a man's lifestyle over that of a woman. A woman hell-bent on becoming a hospital consultant has to behave entirely like a man. She has to steamroller through fifteen years of hospital training and research, having been five years at medical school. Should she then succeed, she finds suddenly that she is thirty-eight years old. She has just enough time left to have one or two children at the very age which doctors advise is physically least favourable. Her chance of having a Downs syndrome baby are also increased. This is the pattern for most female consultants or senior registrars. Others squeeze a quick one out while they are at the research stage or on annual leave, for to take a career break and slacken the pace would severely reduce their chance of success.

Competition within the medical profession is further increased by the numbers of men fleeing to the sanctity and higher status of consultancy. For a woman training as a doctor to follow the advice of her own medical adviser, she has either to relinquish fantasies of motherhood altogether, or have children and settle for a lower position. As the only female consultant anaesthetist at a London hospital, Sophie Anderson was determined to pursue her career. But she'd had her son just after being appointed to her consultancy. 'I don't know whether I would have become a consultant if I had had Joshie earlier. I was thrilled by the acute side of medicine and coping with emergencies. But to do that job within the structure of medicine as it is, it's either up or out. You either follow the institutional career pattern that is established, or you have to opt out and be a part-time GP or a medical health, or schools, officer.'

Women and men in similar professions tend to form personal relationships with each other. Nearly half of the 640 doctors interviewed by Isabel Allen were married to other doctors. Dentists marry dentists and teachers marry teachers. When both partners are trying to pursue competitive careers and have children, inevitably one career takes precedence. Janet Cohen says that like many women she always accepted that she was unlikely to get to the very top in a conventional structure. 'I accepted automatically that my career was secondary. My husband travels extensively, so I'm left in charge of family life willy nilly, however I'm feeling. I try to get home for supper and I do not travel because my husband does, but you do not get to be chairman of ICI on that basis. I would have had to have been saying to myself in my twenties that I wanted to be chairman of ICI in order to get it. Sheer efficiency and speed has got me where I am now.'

Many prestigious professions such as academia or hospital consultancy demand a willingness to relocate in order to succeed. Helen Mason is a scientist at Cambridge University and an expert on the sun. She graduated with a Ph.D. from the same university and on the very same day as her husband. He is now divisional head at the British Antarctic Survey, earning a great deal more than she does in her job as a part-time research associate. 'One career has been compromised because of the children and lack of mobility,' she says. 'Academic women marry academic men, not the other way round; so getting married is the first hurdle, as there is immediately a problem for both to be able to pursue their careers simultaneously.'

The second hurdle is the children, as Dr Mason points out, because even with childcare someone has to take responsibility. 'I'm not prepared to sacrifice the children and their needs for the sake of my career. Obviously if they were at boarding school, life would be easier; but I want to be a part of their lives, I want to see them growing up. My husband is very supportive, but, even with him helping as much as any spouse can, it's inevitable that one career takes precedence over the other. A woman shouldn't be punished for being non-committed just because she wants to spend time with her children. It should be seen positively, that you are able to take responsibility seriously. I have my career and I have my children; but now that they are older I realize that I have had to choose – a mother puts her children first. I'm not prepared to commute for a better job, and I've made that choice, but I do get angry that there doesn't seem to be any support system or way to accommodate my situation, and I'm not alone in feeling that. Married working women with children find it very hard, and other women are not that supportive; they feel that you have made that choice.' It is hard to understand why women should be forced to make such a cruel decision, like a Brechtian nightmare in which a mother is forced to relinquish her child rather than rip it to bits by tearing it out of the Caucasian chalk circle. Inevitably women will put their children first, and they are punished for it.

Jane Drabble, Assistant Managing Director of BBC Network Television, is in her mid-forties without children. 'It would be hard to do this job with young children,' she acknowledges. She feels that television news is particularly difficult for working mothers. 'It's a soul-selling culture. You work all hours, and that's very damaging to men and their marriages as well. It would be impossible to maintain that level of pressure if news was staffed by women with young children – but the programmes would still go out and be just as good,' she added with a smile. Brenda Dean, the first woman general secretary of the trade union SOGAT, says, of not having children, 'I regret it very much, but I don't feel heartbroken about it, I don't feel bitter; and if you look at women in my age group with careers it's quite common. I know that if I had had a family, I wouldn't have come this far.' Hilary Armstrong, the Labour MP for Durham North West, says, 'It's no coincidence that of the three of us women MPs in the north, none has got kids. The system is simply not geared to women with young children getting into Parliament. The whole party rhetoric about your commitment to the constituency and accountability to the party is making it very much more difficult for women.'

Whether a woman has children or not, it's often difficult to form or maintain a relationship while undergoing any great career change. Jane Priestmann was General Manager of Architecture and Design for the British Airports Authority from 1975 to 1986, and until 1991 Director of Architecture and Design for the British Railways Board. Success, she found, altered the balance in her marriage. 'There were strains as soon as I removed some of my support from the family scene. He was very supportive at first, but then a lot of people said that his attitude changed; and then when I became well known, the balance altered and we got divorced.' Politics and family life also separate like oil and water. Betty Boothroyd, the first female Speaker of the House of Commons, is not married and has no children. 'No man is going to wait until you've got back from escorting that delegation to the Soviet Union or Vietnam, or until you've fought that by-election. They are going to take a big yawn and see who else is on the horizon' (*Sunday Times*, 25 April 1993). As one of a handful of female managers of Sainsbury's stores, Diane Oldfield feels that she has worked so hard that she hasn't had the time to invest in personal relations. 'My energies have always been so channelled into work, that maybe I haven't put enough into my relationships. I've always put work first, so inevitably something has to go on the back burner. I've never been particularly maternal, but now I am coming to the age when you are more reflective about things and I do wonder about the price. It takes so much go to keep going, and at the back of a woman's mind is the balance, what they're giving up; whereas for men that compromise is never there.'

Even when a working woman is not high-powered, the fact that she has a job can be too much for her man. Rebecca began teaching infants when her youngest child started school. Her husband was self-employed and earning less than her, and recently they divorced. 'I was more career-minded, and he was at a loose end and needed a career of his own. He found it threatening and has now found someone with less of a career than himself. Obviously there were other problems and this was just one factor, but when a woman is more high-powered than a man it puts a great strain on the relationship.'

Being in the same profession doesn't necessarily help. When

doctors are married to other doctors, trying to find highly competitive jobs in the same hospital hierarchy is virtually impossible. So too is living a commuter relationship between eighty-hour weeks and on-call commitments. As one doctor says, 'If one of you is doing it, it's bad enough. If two, it's disastrous for a relationship. You cross on the stairs and you're both tired out.' Many choose to keep their relationship over their career, opting, like Elizabeth Heggy, for the less prestigious but less harassed life of a GP near her husband's consultancy job. Elizabeth became a registrar anaesthetist at the age of twenty-eight. 'Being on call is very difficult. I was up all night two or three times a week. I'd just got married and I found it hard to study for my exams on top of all that. Too many marriages split in medicine because it is very difficult for a woman to have a satisfactory life, keep her career going and not feel torn all round.' Others, like Caroline Doig, one of the few female paediatric surgeons in this country, deliberately choose to forsake family life. 'Seventeen per cent of paediatric surgeons being female means about seven women, and about half of these have had children and carried on. In my time I realized that if I was to get married it would have to be much later on. I was trying to prove that I could do it, and therefore had to make more of a choice. I get great affection from the kids I treat. It is possible now to be married and work in surgery, but you have to choose your mate carefully; your home help has to be spot on and reliable. It takes a great deal of organization.'

For those women doctors who do try to be all things to all men, the pressures are immense. There is emerging evidence that stress levels among female junior doctors are even higher than those for their profession as a whole. Primarily this is because the medical career structure poses conflicts of responsibility between their families and their jobs. Generally men are more prone to suicide than women; among doctors, however, women are up to six times more likely to commit suicide than their male equivalents (*British Medical Journal*, 1985, 291). Research by Jenny Firth-Cozens ('Sources of Stress . . .', *BMJ*, 1990) has shown that rates of stress were similar between men and women students, but that the differences emerge when they become junior house doctors. When she examined the reasons, both sexes appeared equally confident and satisfied with their choice of career, with neither reporting a greater level of fatigue. Most stressful for women was the subsequent conflict between career and family life, followed by prejudice, discrimination and a lack of female role models. Some expressed concern at patients' disbelief that the woman standing beside their bed was a doctor; they also found that nurses treated them like nurses, expecting them to fulfil both roles simply because they were women.

When women do manage to juggle successful careers and family life, it seems so extraordinary that we stand back and gasp, 'How did she do it?' A woman is still defined by her gender, by the fact that she succeeds as a woman and a mother, while men are defined completely by their work. 'Why have I been described by the press as "DPP, mother of four"?' asks Barbara Mills. 'Of course it's important that I am a mother of four but it has nothing to do with my work as DPP. Nor was it relevant when I was Director of the Serious Fraud Office, when the same label was attached to me. Interestingly my successor there happens to be a father of four, but he has never been so described by the press.' An interview in December 1992 with John Birt, Director General of the BBC, stressed his mathematical education and his mountain climbing, but failed to mention even once that he has two children. By comparison a profile in the same newspaper of Lis Howell, short-lived Managing Director of GMTV, went into copious detail about her marriage and experience of motherhood. So too did a profile of Yve Newbold, Company Secretary at Hanson, in describing her studies for a law degree as she brought up two children. 'Studying was an antidote to the nappies and sieved prunes. After the children were in bed at seven thirty it was a very quiet time, and I would do four or five hours' reading.' While the efforts of these women are admirable, not to say sickeningly so, such a focus detracts from the importance of their jobs. Double standards in our perception of successful women as distinct from successful men have the effect of diminishing these women, making them freaks of nature rather than talented individuals who deserve their achievements.

If women want to succeed, they also need to be devious. 'The women who rise to the top have to be better at the jobs that they do than the men,' says advertising executive Barbara Noakes. 'The women here are extremely good. I look around at some of the men and I don't know why they're working here. If they were women I'm sure they wouldn't be.' Since they cannot rely on natural talent getting rewarded as a matter of course, successful women adopt a number of strategies to increase their chances. Some find that they have to hold their tongues. Su Maddock, of the Manchester Business School, interviewed female managers in local government around the country. She found that roughly half felt they had not been particularly challenging or outspoken when lower down the ranks and considered that they had been picked because they were seen as soft, tame options. Female gynaecologists cannot admit to feeling premenstrual; they cannot reveal that they miss their own children, nor feel guilt at not being with them as they help another baby into the world. Crying is strictly out of order, because men so rarely do it in public. In the US, some women obstetricians opt to give birth by caesarian section to avoid being seen screaming and sweating in front of their male colleagues. Not trusting what they can do as women, they are reluctant to lay themselves open to the possibility of being seen to fail to deliver their baby naturally.

'It's a man's world; and if you're going to work in it then you have to learn their way of negotiating, because you have to stand up against them or with them, and you don't want to be working all alone,' says Sophie Anderson, the only female consultant anaesthetist at the hospital where she works. Barbara Noakes feels the same. 'I'm more cunning. If I have a sick child at home I ring up and say that these builders are still giving me problems. Some people criticize that heavily and say that you should be pioneering. But if you're talking to children, then you have to get under their skin, you have to reach your target market; you have to talk in terms which they will find acceptable, for it is still the case that if a man leaves early for sports day he's seen as a caring, sharing dad, while a woman who behaves similarly is uncommitted. I think that in the years I have done that, I've done a greater service to women by being deceitful than by being upfront. Women are clever at getting what they want within the family structure, but can be a bit naïve in business. You should adapt your game depending on who you're playing with.'

Because women accept that they are unlikely to reach the very top of their chosen career, they are readier to move sideways. Many choose specialisms or professions where they will be able to do some of the things that interest them rather than risking a head-on collision with their workplace hierarchy. Caroline Doig, a senior lecturer in paediatric surgery in Manchester, was frequently discouraged from going into surgery. 'I wanted to be able to make decisions. The characters of surgeons and physicians are completely different; as a surgeon you have to be decisive, you have to be able to act quickly, you can't stand back and see how things progress as a physician does. I wanted to do something to help.' She knew that she would never make it into general surgery, and moved sideways into paediatric surgery where women were more accepted. There she got her cutting experience, and found that kids were much nicer to deal with than adults. She was also able to apply for a job as a registrar, a position never previously held in that area by a woman. 'There was a lot of umming and ahing about appointing me, but after I left they had no qualms about appointing another woman. Women are much better at finding their way around brick walls, while men will keep on battering up against it, hanging on for years without taking your advice, at which point they really do have to vanish because you told them years ago that they weren't good enough.'

Many women are quick to admit that they occupy their present job only because a man gave it to them. Given a segregated hierarchy it is hard to see how else they could get there. Jenny Abramsky applied for the job of editor of PM, two grades above the one that she occupied, simply for the experience of applying for and sitting through boards within the BBC. Although she was appointed, she says, 'I don't believe that I would ever have got the job if it had not been for one man who wanted to bring in new people. The rest of the board was against my appointment, but he believed in me. I wouldn't have been given this job if it had not been for John Birt, who appointed me without a board. It still depends on individual people.' Similarly Gail Rebuck, Chief Executive of Random House, never dreamed of such heights. 'I never thought that I would do this job, it was not something that I aspired to. To me the glass ceiling was absolutely unbreakable and I was happy at the level that I was. I thought I ought to accept the job when I was offered it because it would be weak not to, but I was worried about whether or not I could do it. And then I grew into the job and it was less terrifying.'

However she gets there, a woman can be uncomfortably visible once she is seen to have succeeded. Some, such as barristers, feel that high visibility among a sea of suits helps their career. Some sets need to be seen to recruit at least the odd woman, and there's also pressure to appoint more women as QCs. Anne

McAllister, a barrister of ten years' call, says, 'In many ways it's easier and better for a woman, because there is a will to appoint women as silks. But there is still a sense that women have to do twice as well to get that high in the first place; women cannot afford to be seen to be at all sloppy.' Such visibility can be intimidating. In the Civil Service, Barbara Mills has worked all her life with more men than women, 'which has the disadvantage that you stand out and you're conscious that you're being watched. It's suspicion, rather than outright hostility; you're unusual. When a person who is different comes along, it does slightly change the ecology of the group; and I have found that I've been treated like porcelain or slightly patronized. I've also found that when I speak bluntly, men don't like it; they think that it's an attack on them personally.' Men too, it seems, commit the crime of being overemotional, in their inability to separate personal slight from professional criticism.

Sometimes sexual difference helps. As General Manager for Architecture and Design at the British Airports Authority, Jane Priestmann was responsible for the coordinated design of seven airports plus the Underground link to Heathrow, and in charge of a workforce of men. She found that it was 'easier for them to accept me as a woman in that role than to have a threatening man around. It was very much a male world and, while they were not openly hostile, it was difficult because they were so engineering-based, with very particular attitudes to design; and they were very territorial in their approach. In many ways being a woman made the difference, it helped them accept great change. It didn't help me very much, but it did mean that I was less of a threat to them.'

In contrast, Diane Oldfield, manager of a Sainsbury's store, feels that many men are apprehensive and don't know how to treat her. 'They can't take it naturally to save their life; they find it awkward and aren't sure how to react.' As a consultant anaesthetist, Sophie Anderson finds it works against her that she is also known to be a mother. 'I don't hide the fact that I am a mother, so they tease me: "Ah, so you're here today," they say, as if I wasn't there on all of the other days, when they haven't seen me simply because we weren't working the same shifts. If they don't see me they think that I'm not working. Whatever I do I'm noticed more as a personality, and what I do gets commented on.'

In medicine as in other professions networking is crucial to progression. Sophie found, however, that when she joined an informal group with other women consultant anaesthetists for support, it was immediately viewed with suspicion. When she had to change her on-call arrangements so that she could attend one of its meetings she had to explain why to her boss. 'It spread round the building; they were all horrified and felt threatened. What is this group, people asked, and why do you go? Suddenly it became an issue. There are certain groups that they belong to that I have never been invited to because I stand out so much as being different socially; and why should David want to come and mix with all their wives? Yet my casual socializing with a group of women at an informal meeting with no agenda posed a threat.'

Double standards are common for men and women doing the same job. Sarah, now the editor of a Sunday colour supplement on a leading national newspaper, was appointed as deputy managing editor of arts when she was two months pregnant. When the man appointed as editor of arts withdrew, Sarah went to her boss and said she would like the job. Her employers gave it to her, but felt that, unlike her male predecessor, she could do the job without a deputy, evidently for reasons of gender. She also encountered immense hostility and felt suddenly isolated in a highly responsible job. In vain she asked the outgoing editor if she could shadow him for a while. The deputy books editor was so exasperated at hearing he was to work for her that to her face he spluttered, 'This is a farce!' 'Why, because I'm a woman and younger than you?' she asked. 'No, it's just a farce,' he replied as he stormed out of her office.

To the tabloid newspapers, Julia Somerville has always been a favourite target as ITN's newscaster on *News at Ten* and the only female anchor on election night in 1992. But she found herself depicted as a tempestuous prima donna after demanding equal billing with her two male colleagues over reading the headlines. 'I wasn't prepared to be the adoring female that backs up the grizzled male, although I now feel like the grizzled female. This was interpreted by the press as Julia the Prima Donna, when all I really wanted was to be equal.'

Since she's more visible than her male equivalents, a successful woman's conduct is interpreted differently, as typical or atypical of her sex, rather than relevant or irrelevant to the job. 'If you're a woman and you do a good job, people will notice you; men will remember that you did it and you will stand out amongst a sea of businessmen,' says Oonagh Harper. As a principal executive in a top-grossing firm of solicitors in the City, she works for an organization with 250 staff and fifty-three partners, of whom only five are women. 'But if you are bad they will remember you too and that can lead to entrenched prejudice where the whole gender is blamed.' It can be immensely isolating and often lonely.

Jane Drabble, in her job as assistant managing director at BBC Network Television, feels that she was successful as someone with a good record in programme-making and the valuable experience of having contributed in policy-making circles. 'When you are making programmes, you work together as a team to create something greater than the individuals involved. This stops as you get nearer the top. It becomes a hierarchy with great rigidity, lack of consultation, and secrecy, with decisions made before and after rather than during meetings with winners and losers. Men are used to working with other men and inevitably that creates a certain atmosphere. I did feel lonely at the beginning, not because of the lack of women around me but because I didn't seek the support of other women. Women are nervous about being a woman with other women. We have been so indoctrinated against feminists as killjoys.'

With men in a majority at the top of every hierarchy, it is hard for the women there to constitute an effective lobby. Lacking enough members of their sex to make them feel comfortable as women, they have no alternative but to adopt male models of behaviour in order to survive. Caroline, one of only four senior women among 150 men at a major international bank, once found herself being publicly shouted at by a male colleague in sentences ripe with expletives. 'What I wanted to say was, "How dare you talk to me like that, how dare you talk to anybody like that?" But if I had said that people would have thought me uppity and weak. So what I did was point my finger back at him and say, "And fuck you too," which is not in my nature – most women don't want to stand around shouting and swearing at other people – but it probably did me a great deal more good.'

Having attempted to fit in with the prevailing culture, women are then likely to find themselves either blamed for being 'men in skirts', more male than men, or dismissed as bossy, bustling females, guilty of behaviour which in men is praised as evidence of natural leadership. Within the House of Commons, fifty-nine women MPs cannot possibly sway the culture or the content of debate when they are surrounded by 651 men. As women, their small number means that they find themselves swamped with representations; yet they must also juggle their personal views with political pragmatism and the policies of their party. Angela Knight, Conservative MP for Erewash, says, 'I don't believe you can join an institution and then immediately set about changing it. It needs to evolve gradually so it works in the way the rest of the world works.' Whether or not she wants to change Parliament, she cannot do so effectively while women lack representation or an adequate voice. On certain topics, too, the voice they have is notably mute. Between May and November 1992, during debates on the future of Europe, there were 110 speeches from men and only six from women (*Independent*, 6 April 1993). In discussion of 'hard issues' such as economics and war, the men do the talking.

Looking for Cultural Change

We look to the few women who do hold positions of influence as guiding lights. We expect them to change the culture they find themselves in, to kick down centuries of discriminatory practice and to feel automatic empathy for other women's secondary status, simply because of their gender. We accuse them of being 'queen bees', content to sit surrounded by adoring males and doing little to advance other women. Men spend much of their working lives politicking or stabbing each other in the back to secure their own progression; and yet we expect integrity from the women competing with them. An ambitious woman has to have a halo around her head and espouse basic feminism, in principle and practice alike, if she is not to be labelled a 'token woman' or an 'executive tart'. We expect too much. To succeed, these women have sacrificed much in their personal lives, or juggled their diverse responsibilities to the point of personal exhaustion. Why do we also expect them to be a latter-day Joan of Arc, carrying the flag of feminism into a world of men on whom no such ideological demands are made? How can they possibly find the time?

Yet when a woman is the solitary token on committees or boards she often finds herself expected at every turn to raise the flag for her sex, that being one of the reasons why she was appointed. If she does have the audacity to speak up for the 'minority' interest she was appointed to represent, she is then labelled a 'troublemaker'. All she usually wants is the luxury of approaching issues in their entirety, rather than from a gendered perspective. Dr Lottie Newman was recently appointed as the only woman non-executive director of the health care insurance company PPP. 'They wanted me because I was respectable, but also because I was the only GP and because I was a woman, so they got two for the price of one. Had I been lesbian, disabled and black they would have got five for the price of one. The other PPP members are now beginning to get used to the idea that I might have contributions to make other than on the subject of women, because it does get a bit boring always having to be the one to say the same old things and stick up for the female perspective.'

Women in positions of influence can sometimes become catalysts of change simply by their presence. 'I've always taken the view that it is better to be a token woman than to have an organization with no women at all,' says Barbara Mills, who feels that there have been times when she was taken on as just that. 'If you get in as the token woman, don't be sour about it; you can turn it into something else where you are treated as a proper member of the organization, and they won't look at women as tokens in the future.' Barbara Noakes goes a little further by saying, 'All women in business have a responsibility to behave in a way that makes men more receptive to employing women or at least less disinclined. They're already slightly less disinclined and it may be getting better, but women are still the exception rather than the rule and viewed with fear and trembling.' Subtly but surely these individual women in positions of power are changing things for the better. Their numbers are increasing, if slowly, and once there they prove it is possible for a woman to do their job; they also provide a role model for younger women struggling in their wake. With one foot in the door women are, as Jane Drabble says, 'Agents of change irrespective of who they are, for they have no vested interest in keeping the system as it is.' Whether or not they carry the flag of feminism, they do change things for the better, if only by subtly altering practices in a way that few men notice.

Among women tough enough to make it to the summit of their trade, those with families become exceptionally talented at juggling several responsibilities at once, an essential requirement for effective management. 'The women I've seen at the top work in a slightly different way,' says Barbara Mills. 'Those with families become pretty good at allocating their time and making priorities. There's no time for personal slights; you just get on with the job and pick what really matters. I'd never run anything until 1990, except juggle demands of working and family life; and then the skills that I'd hoped I'd acquired came into their own – spotting the problems before they hit you, managing the priorities, making sure people get on with each other, time-tabling and targets.' Oonagh Harper, principal executive of a top-grossing firm of City solicitors, says, 'Good management is enabling; it is not about commanding but about allowing others to shine, and women are instinctively good at this.' New theories of management are indeed mushrooming, with executives of both sexes tearing off to country hotels for lessons in 'total quality management': how to get the most out of their team by introducing a kindlier, more attentive management.

Morale and the overall welfare of any organization is bound to benefit if decisions affecting employees' daily lives are reached after consultation. Yet too often, men in positions of authority see this as a sign of weakness, a 'female' softening of approach they feel to be irrelevant to the workplace. Many fail to see that leadership with generosity of spirit is far more likely to produce the required results. Jane Drabble feels, 'You can either say, it's a man's world and a man's game, so play it their way. Or you don't have to do that; you can play it your own way, but it's tough. When I was first made editor of programmes I only had a male role model, that of a decisive boss who didn't allow for deviations. Then I discovered that you don't always have to know what you want. I experienced the shedding of a stereotype, that it could be different, that the way to manage effectively was to involve others in the decision-making process, and people didn't dismiss me because of it. Sometimes a decision is obvious, but sometimes it isn't and it takes time and thought to reach a good or a better solution, and I found that other people were distinctly relieved at this sort of approach. That experience encouraged me to think that there was a better way to come to a conclusion; but that's hard when the system doesn't work like that.'

For a woman surrounded by men, negotiating can be tricky. Brenda Dean says, 'I probably did have quite a stern, tough image, which was necessary in negotiating, otherwise people would have said that because I was a woman, I was being a bit more soft than a man would be in that position. I didn't let that get at me, but it was always at the back of my mind; so I had to set my negotiating parameters, because all of the men's parameters were set out for them. They knew that a good way was to thump the table; but I couldn't do that because I would have been a "neurotic woman", whereas if Bill, my predecessor, did it, he was regarded as strong.'

'If women were negotiating with each other we would say exactly what we meant and get to deals very quickly,' says Janet Cohen, who has been successful during her banking career in negotiating many mega-million-pound deals. Men hold money back, assuming automatically that the vendor is asking for more than the object is actually worth. 'My negotiating is a different style; I go for the deal,' she says. 'When I was buying Unipart there was a heartrending meeting when I laid briskly on the table what we were prepared to pay, keeping nothing in hand. Men are so used to holding a bit back that there was a fight about this after the meeting with my clients and I went home wondering whether perhaps they were right. As I walked up the street one of the children was hanging out of the window, shouting, "Mummy, there's someone called Graham Day on the telephone." Graham was then chairman of British Leyland and he asked if that was my best offer and then said, "Well, you always tell the truth, then you've won." '

But such honesty can work against women, particularly self-employed professionals whose time is money. Elinor Parker is very successful as one of the few women dentists with her own practice. She knew nothing about managing money or running a business and feels indebted to the group Women in Dentistry. 'I could ring someone up and ask questions like, "What's the difference between an invoice and a statement?" without feeling silly, while all the men talk about is how much they are grossing. In six years on the executive of Women in Dentistry I have never heard anybody tell me how much their house is worth. It's very supportive and good fun, because we discuss the actual problems behind practice organization and not how much you are earning.' But faced with an open-mouthed and vulnerable patient in the chair, it's not easy to be hardnosed about business. The NHS will pay for only six and a half minutes per appointment of a dentist's highly skilled time; and private patients who are happy to spend fortunes on their car will resent paying for their teeth. Throughout every branch of the profession, women dentists earn less than men. In stratified salary scales this is because men are the chief dental officers; but in private practice it's because women spend more time on each patient and therefore their turnover is less. 'I'm not a high grosser and it can put you in a terrible dilemma,' says Elinor Parker, 'because you can spend hours doing something to get it right but you won't get paid for it.' Inevitably a woman dentist feels she has to toughen up in the face of stiff competition from a majority comprising males. By earning less than her male partners in the practice, she would only reinforce the myth that the presence of a woman lowers the profession's status. None of which benefits the consumer, that poor victim pinned to the chair by a quivering drill, who should be entitled to know he or she is getting the best job possible, *and* value for money.

The supremacy of greed and profit can also challenge barristers, who are likewise self-employed. A case that goes to court will earn more than one that doesn't but women barristers are more concerned to act common-sensically rather than resort to aggression and role-playing. 'Women see the case as a whole and want to try and resolve it without litigation,' says barrister Anne McAllister. 'They are more interested in solutions, rather than winning cases. Court is the least efficient method of getting to the truth that you can devise.' But rather than settle as many cases as possible out of court, both the health and wealth of the nation are regularly betrayed by the cost to the taxpayer of administering justice in this way.

Many women have grown up allowed to express their fears and anxieties, whereas boys are more often conditioned to suppress any expression of doubt or emotion. It can be hard for women to remain tough in highly masculinized environments, at times when they really want to collapse in tears. Losing an important court case or experiencing a maternal death can be immensely stressful. But the boys do not buckle publicly, however devastated, so the girls too must deal with it as part of the job. 'The stress is in the very public nature of failure,' says Anne McAllister. 'It's an anxious-making job and you have to disguise your anxiety. It's like doing an exam all of the time, because you have to memorize everything in order to be on top of the facts, and if you fail it's like a jumbo going down. It is good to be anxious, rather than confident about winning a case, because that means you are not complacent; but it takes a toll on your nerves nevertheless.' As senior registrar in obstetrics and gynaecology at a London hospital, Julia was unlucky enough to experience a maternal death. 'You can drown in it by churning over and over in your mind what you could have done, or you can say that it had nothing to do with me; but it's very hard for women to say the latter and not blame themselves, when things go wrong.'

A female perspective sometimes makes an immediate difference. Jane Priestmann feels that by her presence in charge of architecture and design at both British Rail and the British Airports Authority she helped to soften the look of our stations and airports. 'Women are nesting people; they know that making spaces into places is quite important. People really are quite stressed about travelling, particularly with flying where they worry about missing their flight, and if you have a nicer atmosphere that helps to make it easier. We had a restaurant in Terminal One which I wanted to make look less like a canteen and more like a place where people would like to spend time. We introduced an apple tree with false blossom-in-spring. The engineers found this very hard to understand; it wasn't what they were used to, and it was hard to get some fun into it in those early days. Having a woman there helped that softening; we introduced some cheerful carpets and nicer loos. All of those attitudes come from women.'

Such changes in management style all help to shift our culture closer towards the needs and views of women in practical terms. But are they so revolutionary? Patriarchy and prejudice still rule over a national workplace that is inflexibly arranged, and where most women are meanly rewarded in a highly segregated labour market. How else can it be, while there are so few women at the top to influence the culture? However talented and tenacious such people may be, we demand from them the efforts of super-women by presuming that they can change more than their own individual lives. Meanwhile adherents of the old order can exploit the presence of one or two women in senior positions to perpetuate the illusion that we have equal opportunity; for if some can make it, those who do not are merely lacking in talent.

With just a handful of women at the top, reaping benefits that men once enjoyed exclusively, male work practices and traditional assumptions about women can continue largely unchallenged. The longer the process of equalizing power between the sexes, the greater the danger that each woman will be moulded to the prevailing male culture rather than being true to herself and her sex. 'I really don't think that we shall have arrived,' says Barbara Mills, 'until a woman gets into a top job and it's not noticed that she is a woman; that it's what you are rather than what sex you are that matters. Then I think we shall have made it; but I don't think I'll ever see that in my lifetime.' For Gail Rebuck it will take a great deal longer. 'My children won't see an end to it, nor will theirs; but maybe after that . . .'

chapter four

punishing
motherhood

Resting between contractions as she went into labour with her second child, the economist Heather Joshi found herself wondering just how much two children cost a woman, in terms of lost income. Her subsequent research revealed that it came to a great deal. Against the lifetime earnings of a woman who works full time and doesn't break to have children, she compared those of one who goes out to work full time at seventeen, takes eight years out to have two children, and then works part time while her children are at school. The earnings of the latter were 57 per cent lower (Joshi, 'Changing roles . . .' 1990). But women lose more than just income, and therefore the means to economic independence, when they become mothers. They lose status, and their health can be diminished; often too their marriages suffer, through conflicting demands on their time as they try to provide for their children. It is no longer possible for most families to live on one income. Yet working motherhood is still seen as a luxury rather than a necessity. Because employers and the state have both refused to accommodate their needs, all too often women are punished for what nature compels them to do, namely seeking to provide and care for their children.

We afflict mothers from conception onwards: with stringent

maternity provisions, and hostility from employers and colleagues; with dismissal for pregnancy; with inadequate childcare; and with poverty. As a result, working motherhood is bound to be punishing. 'If we had a culture where women felt comfortable about working with children, then we would see a revolution,' says Gail Rebuck. 'I've seen young editors who are bright and want a career, and then have children and are infused with this guilt that they are going to be less than perfect mothers if they work. That's the backlash fuelled by the popular press.' Women are capable of more than one role at a time; of being mothers, workers and lovers. They could indeed 'have it all' – were it not for the very fabric of our society, the age-old myths that resist the possibility by saying, 'Why should they?'

Motherhood changes a woman's life and can cost her a great deal; yet she is still not allowed complete control over her fertility. Contraception may remain available on the National Health Service but it is harder to get now that family-planning clinics are closing, leaving the local doctor as its only source. It is also not one hundred per cent reliable. A recent report by the Royal College of Obstetricians and Gynaecologists estimated that one in three pregnancies was unplanned, even though in 70 per cent of these cases contraception had been used. Financial restraints have meant that a pregnancy-testing service is not always freely available from local general practices; instead, many young women now have no choice but to pay for expensive home pregnancy testing kits. Without abortion on request up to the twelfth week of pregnancy, women who might not have wanted to go full term have little choice but motherhood and potential poverty. In the event of a pregnant woman's decision not to become a mother and risk dismissal, along with financial hardship, she must still go grovelling not to one doctor but two in order to be certified, like some sort of lunatic dog, as psychologically or physically unable to continue with the pregnancy.

In Britain the right to abortion seems to be under repeated attack, from right-wing pressure groups and private members' bills attempting to limit the numbers of weeks during which a termination can be carried out. Other European countries allow a proper choice, so that abortion up to twelve weeks is available on request in France, Italy, Greece, Denmark, Belgium, Sweden and Austria. While the overall number of abortions in those countries has not increased, the number of late abortions has dropped dramatically. A woman really does know her own mind. When she says yes to an abortion, she means yes and she wants it as quickly as possible. Delaying tactics will not necessarily make her change her mind, only cause her more grief. True equality of opportunity begins here. Over 90 per cent of women have at least one child, and they are made even more vulnerable in parenthood by our refusal to trust them with control over the timing of their reproduction.

The number of working women with a child under five has risen markedly from 24 per cent in 1984 to 47 per cent in 1992. But there has been no corresponding rise in childcare provision. Society's message is clear: it will only tolerate women working if they pay for doing so. Taking maternity leave or pay, and combining paid work with motherhood, is still not seen as a basic right even though many families now depend on a mother's income to keep them out of poverty. In 1991 women in Britain contributed approximately one third of the average weekly household income of £282.71 (*Family Expenditure Survey*, HMSO, 1991), a considerable rise on the 1989 figure of 17.3 per cent. Yet society neither helps a mother work, nor makes her feel she has a right to do so. Regardless of the evidence of research, a deep, almost subliminal idea is encouraged to needle away at her conscience – a child needs its mother all the time. The guilt can go with her everywhere, exacerbated by the notion that all women have a natural proclivity towards motherhood.

At work she feels guilt about not being a good enough mother, and not spending more time with her children; because she has children she also suffers guilt at not working hard enough in her job. In both quarters working women feel compromised and inadequate. Where roles were once clearly divided and respected, they are confused by new myths and half-truths, so that whichever road they choose, women can no longer do the right thing. Mothers who don't give up work are viewed as irresponsible and selfish for wanting to have it all. On the other hand, full-time mothers are viewed as foolish or self-sacrificing by those who believe that, regardless of the difficulties of early motherhood, a woman must maintain her career and independence.

Young women now work. Most have earned their own money for most of their adult lives, and enjoyed independence and access to the material goods of this world. If as a society we fail to let them continue working when they become mothers, we punish them and their children at the very time when they need more money. The longer her absence from the labour market, the more likely a woman is to return to part-time work with fewer opportunities for training and promotion, and less pay. Over one quarter of the women in the 1980 Women and Employment Survey (Martin and Roberts, *Women's Employment*, 1980) who returned to work on a part-time basis within a year of the birth of their first child went back to a job at a lower level. Among mothers taking a break of one to five years, this figure rose to 44 per cent. Many women must face the necessity of returning to full-time work immediately after the birth if they are to maintain their status and their income.

The link is clear between the extent of part-time working, the amount of income lost through motherhood, and the availability of childcare. Heather Joshi's comparative European research (Dale and Joshi, *Economic and Social Status* . . ., 1992) reveals that while an average British mother loses 57 per cent of her gross earnings, the equivalent proportion in Germany is 47 per cent, in Sweden 15 per cent, and in France only 1 per cent. As many as 38 per cent of French mothers with a child under four are in full-time work, with only 14 per cent returning to work part time. In contrast with Britain, there is state nursery provision for every three-year-old, and 20 per cent of under-threes – over ten times the British number – are in publicly funded daycare. A woman's ability to earn a living wage once she becomes a mother is directly related to the availability of childcare. In Britain that means largely using private care, so that only mothers able to afford the high fees of approximately £100 per week per child can even begin to maintain their hold on a full-time job and the career ladder. The rest have no alternative but to take one of the growing number of low-paid, 'flexible' part-time jobs.

Pregnancy and motherhood are viewed so negatively by the majority of employers that many women feel they have to hide their motherhood tendencies, whatever form these take. An impending birth is welcomed when the child is your own. But when it's your secretary or some other indispensable member of staff who becomes pregnant, the assumed disruption in your working life makes the expected baby an irritating, expensive bore. Expressions of maternal instinct are tantamount in many workplaces to declaring a lack of commitment that could get one passed over for promotion and blight a promising career; even before conception itself, motherhood can make you feel guilty. Having avoided pregnancy through their twenties, career women who find themselves pregnant 'by accident' at the age of thirty-four feel they have to apologize. Such is the fear of their employers' hostile reception, however positively the news may be received by family and friends.

The new Trade Union Reform and Employment Rights Bill

of 1993 gives all women the right to maternity leave for fourteen weeks regardless of how long they have been employed. This does at least improve on the previous unfair statutory provision. A separate bill is to deal with the issue of whether or not a pregnant employee is to be paid during her absence, and if so, how much. At the moment only one in five women qualifies for statutory maternity pay; the rest are either self-employed or have not paid enough national insurance contributions. Only one in five firms improves on the statutory terms for maternity leave by topping up rates of pay or allowing a longer period of leave, and many women only get to keep this extra maternity pay if they return to their former employer for a minimum of three months.

For a new mother to spend as much as three months off with her baby she usually has to work right up to the birth. If her physical condition forces her to take maternity leave before the birth, she has even less time at home to recover afterwards. The British limit of fourteen weeks is the very minimum to be found in the European Community. In France women have six weeks off before the birth and ten weeks after on 84 per cent of their earnings, with the opportunity for unpaid parental leave until the child is three, at which point he or she can enter one of France's full-time nurseries. Italian women have two months off before the birth and three months after on 80 per cent of their pay, with the opportunity of six extra months' parental leave on 30 per cent of earnings (Holtermann, *Investing...*, 1992).

In Britain we still have no statutory provision even for unpaid parental leave or for any paternity leave, both of which are left to individual employers. Nine out of ten fathers are now present at the birth of their babies; but if they have no paternity leave from their employers, they have to take the time off as sick leave or holiday. Over three-quarters of working fathers take an average of eight days' leave at the time of a birth; 54 per cent take it from their holiday allowance, reducing the time they can spend with their families at other parts of the year. It is interesting that researchers find little variation by social class in these figures (Holtermann *et al*, *Parents* . . ., 1993). Meanwhile the law withholds any acknowledgement that men want to be with their partners during the birth of their children, and that they also prefer to be together as a family during those first few precious days. It would be an investment in the family unit from the very beginning if we encouraged the increasing numbers of men who want to be with their babies during the early moments and days of life and who want to support the mother, cook her meals and deal with the outside world while she is bedridden and breastfeeding. Surely true commitment to equal opportunity begins here.

Most women want to spend as much time as possible with their new baby, and recovering from the ordeal of giving birth. This means that many feel forced to lie about their due date in order to be able to work up to the very last minute. They are then likely to feel guilty about the possible effects of this additional stress on their baby's welfare in the womb. Jenny Abramsky had just been appointed as the first woman editor of the *PM* programme on Radio 4 when she found herself pregnant with her second child. 'I hid it for five months and lied about when it was due so that I could have time off with the baby, and left work nine days before Maya was due.' But the best-laid plans can backfire. Jenny had to find a new presenter for the programme, and came back to work for one half day a week only ten days after her daughter was born. 'I regret that now; I was foolish. But I was under tremendous pressure. I was still the only woman editor; the personnel officer didn't know what you did in this situation; and the controller of Radio 4 said, "Well, it's fine with one child, but I don't think you'll be able to cope with two." So I felt that the onus was on me to prove that it was possible.'

Many find working while pregnant a generally positive

experience. But a substantial minority encounter hostility or discriminatory attitudes for the first time in their lives. Questions such as 'Are you coming back to work?' begin to make them wonder whether they should. Male and female colleagues who do not have their own children cannot know the emotional and physical turmoil of pregnancy and childbirth. Often they view the right to maternity leave as some sort of skive or holiday, and resent allowing pregnant women lighter workloads. A woman is often made to feel that she is creating insurmountable difficulties through the need to provide cover while she is away. If her responsibilities are divided among existing staff, great strain can be placed on her relationship with her colleagues, who may resent the extra workload caused by her pregnancy. They are also likely to be unforgiving if they have to pick up her responsibilities at short notice should she encounter difficulties with pregnancy, such as bleeding and threatened premature labour, or simply exhaustion. It's hard to imagine a man, or a woman, being treated in the same way if they had been involved in a serious car crash. An accident which could seriously disable, nay, destroy your life, is viewed sympathetically; but pregnancy and birth are seen as a wilful self-indulgence for which you must pay heavily.

Dismissal is the punishment for pregnancy given to substantial numbers of women. The Policy Studies Institute estimates that approximately 4,000 women each year lose their jobs in this way, and a further 8,500 have to leave because their working conditions are not suitable for pregnancy. Complaints to the Equal Opportunities Commission of dismissal for pregnancy rose by 50 per cent in 1991. The National Association of Citizens' Advice Bureaux also reports a marked increase in such complaints. Pregnancy dismissal is against the law, but it is often very hard to prove. Sometimes the dismissal is blatant – an accountant in Devon complained to a Citizens' Advice Bureau that her employer had expressed his 'moral outrage' at her unmarried state and announced that he was reducing her salary by 40 per cent because 'she was not doing her job satisfactorily'. A young woman in the north-east was dismissed by the proprietor of the home she was working in with the words, 'It isn't very nice having someone with a big belly working here.' According to evidence collected from Citizens' Advice Bureaux around the country, other employers make a vague attempt at masking their disgust at pregnant women working – a woman in Manchester was sent a letter by her employer stating that she had been sacked due to body odour. An accountant in Sussex took a week's annual leave just after she had told her employer that she was pregnant. On her return she was told that she could leave immediately as the girl who had done her job while she was on holiday had coped well and they didn't like her attitude.

Such hostility to working during pregnancy is bound to make women secretive and guilt-ridden about relaxing and enjoying or simply adapting to the momentous rite of passage of pregnancy. A woman may experience pregnancy and birth only once or twice in her life; yet she will feel torn between two immense responsibilities which are seen as contradictory as soon as her pregnancy becomes public knowledge. What does this level of stress do to the baby growing inside her? What sort of foundations do such attitudes and pressures lay for a pregnant woman's lifelong career as a mother? What has happened to the respect we once had for the stress of pregnancy and the all-important work that women do when they bring children into the world? What do we say as a society when we place such little value on our mothers- and children-to-be?

If a pregnant woman avoids feeling compromised or confused about her changing identity at work, she cannot escape the ton of guilt dropped on her by increasing health fascism. She must not smoke or drink alcohol or coffee. For fear of listeria, she should avoid soft cheese, eggs and ready-made salad in a bag. She must wash all fruit and vegetables, and avoid gardening where cats may have left their faeces in case she contracts toxaemia. Both infections could kill her baby. If she comes into contact with German measles, blind panic ensues. The pressure is on to produce a perfect baby. She must eat a truly balanced diet boosted by multivitamins and iron, preferably for at least three months before conception in order to boost the IQ and constitution of her foetus. A process which was once left entirely to chance has now to be moulded to increase the possibility of producing a perfect baby. Massive advances in antenatal care and obstetrics have increased the chances of producing a healthy baby tenfold, but they have also helped to ladle on the guilt.

Given the knowledge and technology available to us, a perfect baby is what we now expect. Mothers are more likely to blame themselves if something does go wrong, where once it was one of nature's decrees. Every puff on a cigarette or glass of wine is stolen furtively rather than enjoyed. As the birth approaches, the conscientious mother cannot even relax in the knowledge that medical advances have reduced the pain to be endured and the likelihood of death, because the natural birth movement urges her to prove her womanhood by giving birth without drugs and so defeating the control of technology. It's natural, they say, so you can do it without pain relief; but so is having a heart attack. The moment arrives; it's bloody painful; the first-time mother doesn't feel in control, having no actual experience of birth, and somehow the theory of antenatal classes and the endless reading of how-to books doesn't match this reality. She begs for pain relief. She produces her darling, perfect baby who bonds bloodily with her breasts moments after birth. She cries with relief and joy and then she feels guilty. She didn't have the perfect, orgasmic, joyful birth that birth gurus write about; the one that she has been dreaming of for the past nine months. She gave in to drugs, she had to be helped, she couldn't do it all by herself. She feels cheated, as if she has failed.

Developments in antenatal technology, increased use of

Caesarean delivery and the ongoing row over the ethics of abortion focus attention on the welfare of the foetus. Often a pregnant mother feels that she is no more than a suitcase and that interest in her welfare ceases as soon as she has delivered her all-important contents. We take great care of our women while they are pregnant and in labour; but when the baby is a week old, the health visitor stops coming, and brand-new mothers are left to cope on their own. Where there is interest in health and welfare, the emphasis is on postnatal depression rather than on general health. Childbirth can seriously impair the well-being of a woman for years. Almost half the 12,000 women who gave birth at Birmingham Maternity Hospital between 1979 and 1985 reported health problems that had developed for the first time in the subsequent three months. These ranged from backaches after epidurals, to headaches, bladder problems and limb pains. But according to a study by the hospital, only 34 per cent of the women reported these symptoms to their doctors. Sixty-eight per cent developed stress or incontinence, but did not consult their GPs because they did not consider it serious enough, or because they dismissed their symptoms as a 'woman's problem' (*Nursing Times*, 8 Jan 1992).

Every woman feels that a small part of her dies with the birth of each child, when so much of her life force has gone into its creation. But we tend to sweep the after-effects aside, through ignorance or through determination to prove our personal strength and independence. Childbirth is a natural process, and tribal women may well go off into the jungle, have their babies in the company of a few female friends, swaddle them on to their backs and go back to work. But they can take their small babies with them wherever they go, protected by customs and rituals which afford respect to the new mother. By contrast, we are in danger of losing any maternal respect completely by kidding ourselves that we can split our bodies in two, push the little darlings out and then go back to work unchanged. If pregnancy and labour are natural, so too are diseases; but while employers and employees may accept absence through sickness because it can happen to everybody, sickness through pregnancy and childbirth may befall only half the population and is accordingly less acceptable.

'We know nothing of the severity of the impact on women's lives of childbirth,' says Christine MacArthur, from the research team at Birmingham Maternity Hospital. 'Our enquiries have revealed an enormous and previously unrecognized problem, a level of morbidity and impaired health far beyond anything which might have been expected.' By refusing to acknowledge women's difference from men, and the particular needs that result from reproduction, we force them to pretend that these needs do not exist. This, they feel, is the price of being able to 'eat their cake and have it': to continue with their working lives and have their children too. Only fourteen weeks of maternity leave is allowed before they have to conform once again to a model of work shaped by men. Many women are so keen to get back to work after childbirth, in order not to lose their status or income, that they are in danger of damaging their health in the long term.

The new mother, in a former life a lawyer, teacher or bank clerk, is barely home and used to hormonal chaos, breastfeeding and broken sleep before she has to decide whether or not to return to her former life. The pressure of returning to work and proving that nothing has changed can be enormous. Often it spoils those precious early months of motherhood. For some, like Elizabeth Heggy, a doctor, the pressure is too much and the choice of full-time motherhood is easy. 'I want to bring her up; I simply couldn't or wouldn't want to hand her over to a nanny. I don't see myself back in full-time medical work, with on-call commitments. I'm not prepared to do that ever again – it's so stressful. I feel content for the first time in my life; it's just wonderful – I can sit and watch her for hours on end.' For other mothers, like Briony Ackroyd, a senior registrar in general surgery and a single mother, the choice of returning to work was easy: 'I love what I do and the thought of not doing it is simply mindboggling. The stress of the working mother is a myth. I know that I wouldn't have as much to give my daughter if I didn't work; plus she wouldn't have the role model of a working doctor mother.'

But for most women the decision can never be so clear cut, so black and white. It is a world confused by the conflict of intellect and emotion as well as that between work and home. Beverley Doyle is a successful businesswoman running her own recruitment agency: 'I find it very hard. Some women are hard-nosed and can divorce the two; but I miss him and I feel that I'm not being a proper mother – I'm not doing all that I want to do for him. Part of me feels that giving up work would be like giving in. I'd be happy in the short term, but in the long term I would surely miss work. At the end of the day children grow up and lead independent lives and you can never be completely happy.' For most, economic necessity requires them to go back to work. Hilary Scott, a single mother who has worked for Sainsbury's for the past fourteen years, felt that she had no choice. 'At first I wasn't happy about leaving him: it's like leaving half of you behind. But I need the money; I have to provide for him.'

When women have done nothing but work, the rules and routines of paid employment are so familiar that they can provide a reassuring refuge to a young mother. Mothering has to be learnt, while other work by now comes naturally. It can be isolating and frightening having to cope with a tiny screaming baby whose needs you don't understand and whom you haven't yet got to know. For one ward sister, getting back to work offered relief from severe postnatal depression. 'Work was exactly what I needed to restore my identity and self-esteem. My first day back was so enjoyable – everything seemed to come back to me. I felt that I was a "real" person again, with a brain that worked.'

But if employers and colleagues are even faintly hostile to mothers working, then going back to work after maternity leave can be extremely difficult. Most mothers have mixed feelings at first: pleasure at being back at work, but unease from missing their babies. The guilt at leaving their child when so young and helpless can be exacerbated by such questions as 'Who's looking after the baby?', however innocently motivated. If a woman is welcomed back to work she is more likely to feel that her return is in the baby's interests. But if she finds that in her absence her desk has disappeared and her responsibilities have been taken on by somebody else, effectively demoting her, then indeed she may question whether as a parent she is doing the right thing. Why stay where you are not wanted? One woman who had worked for fourteen years as a staff supervisor at Woolworth found that on her return to work her job had virtually disappeared. 'My office was locked and cleared out; a trainee manager completes all my previous duties, and I felt like a spare part.' An information systems group manager for a local authority which boasts of being an Equal Opportunities employer found that: 'The department had been reorganized in my absence and those who had been my peers were now my bosses and those who had been my subordinates were now my peers – one of them occupying my old desk. They were all men and had got on very well without me. Junior staff assumed that I had requested a downgrading and was working part time.'

Many employers' very keenness on the principle of equality of treatment makes them refuse to acknowledge the difference between a young mother and the other staff, in case they are seen to be giving the mothers an easier time. A sagging abdomen and breasts aching with milk bear witness in vain to the difference. In Portugal, Spain, Greece and Germany women are allowed time away from the workplace to breastfeed their babies (Collinson *et al*, *Managing to Discriminate*, 1990). Italian employers have to allow a woman two one-hour rest periods every day, until her child is a year old, to enable her to breastfeed. In Britain women sneak off to the quietest loo in order to express milk into a bottle for their baby, or simply to maintain their milk supply and relieve the agony of bursting breasts.

Hostile attitudes to mothers working, and an absence of any recognition of their specific needs, make women feel that they must hide their responsibilities to their children. They feel guilty merely at having to leave work at a set time in order to pick up their children from the minder. Often women are grateful to have a job at all. Rather than being outspoken, or 'whingeing' about their difficulties, they absorb them in silence and almost disappear in a process of self-annihilation as they attempt to prove themselves no less efficient as workers because they are mothers.

Many women feel the need to be completely with their children whenever they are not working. After the day at the office is done, they overcompensate by doing another day's work at home. Former interests get swamped in playdough, cutting and sticking, nights in front of the video and weekends socializing only with those friends who have children in order to maximize available 'quality time'. Sophie Anderson's young son is looked after full time by his father while she works as an anaesthetist. 'When I come home, I take over. So we have less family life because I'm aware that David has looked after Josh all day and that he must be free to do whatever he wants to do. My sacrifice is there, as I don't really like to go out unless I know that Josh can come with me. I don't go shopping with girlfriends or go to the theatre, but I am happy to make that sacrifice. Another woman consultant once told me that this has happened to her, and I was shocked; I thought, how awful. But now that my time is so precious with Josh, I've sacrificed adult company.'

For those who love their job, it is work and its benefits in income and social networking, rather than private self-indulgence, that is the main prize. 'There is no time for me, but then that's my decision,' says publisher Gail Rebuck. 'I could easily have decided to work part time, but I happen to enjoy what I'm doing. The biggest change was when I took over as chief executive. It became more difficult to keep a rigid time-frame, more pressurized; and therefore I'm more tired.' Barbara Noakes says that in all her time in advertising she never felt great guilt about not being with her children, and was just grateful that they could learn to put one foot in front of another. 'I was not jealous of a nanny seeing it first.' But when she attended a meeting of high-powered women in advertising at which the birth guru Michel Odent was giving a talk, she was struck by the amount of guilt in the room. 'The atmosphere was riddled with it. It was only when Michel Odent said, well, if you feel that guilty, bring them into bed with you – drag their bed into your room; they're much more vulnerable at night – that you could almost hear the sighs of relief as an "official" person said that it was OK.'

It is not surprising that working women should feel such guilt, given the obstacles they have to surmount if they want to pursue their career, combined with the tenacity of the myths surrounding motherhood. But working women have not yet persuaded society to accept that women are capable of both if their needs are accommodated; nor have they insisted that their children are not damaged as a result. Instead, new-fangled concepts such as 'quality time' have sprung out of nowhere. 'Quality time' allows a woman to appease her guilt, provided that she gives every spare moment and every ounce of spare energy to her children, thoroughly overstimulating them so that they remember who their mother is. Most children, particularly those at nurseries, have had their interest more than adequately engaged throughout the day, and long for nothing more than the solace of bed. Their wailing is for peace at last now that mother is home. But a guilty mother interprets this as anguish over her absence, a crime for which she feels she has to overcompensate.

If women cannot afford private childcare, often they must opt for part-time, evening or weekend work so that they can rely on other family members, and often on husbands or partners, to look after the children. It is frequently in the poorest families that the fathers appear to be doing most for their children. Large numbers of women with children have part-time jobs with unsocial hours: 78 per cent of those working in the evenings have children under sixteen; 38 per cent have a pre-school-age child. In order to find unpaid care, approximately half of all part-time working women rely on their partners (Dex, *Women's Attitudes* ..., 1988). These men have no option but to take responsibility for their children if the family is to benefit from the mother's income.

Adapting can take time, however, and be fraught with difficulties. Barbara works for the Co-op in Exeter as a part-time shelf-filler four nights a week, from 8 to 11 p.m. She took the job when her two smallest children were two and three. 'When I first started it was a bit of a social shock for him because he had to stay in and couldn't go to the pub, plus he'd get a lot of flack from his mates. It did cause problems at first, but I had to really stick to my guns. After a while he realized that he had to do it because we needed the money, plus he's now much closer to the kids. But it did take nearly a year for him to come round. It's a big cultural shock.' If a man has been raised by a mother who never worked, and feels his masculinity threatened by not earning the entire family income, then the reversal of traditional roles is indeed hard to take. But in order to keep the family together, many men do prove capable of change. 'To begin with the house was in a state when I got back and I had to put my foot down. But after six or seven months I noticed that he's begun to tidy up; plus the money I earn is no longer pin money. He's in the construction industry, and when he was laid off for a while last Christmas, my money was our only income.' After a while Barbara's husband found that he was beginning to gain far more from his children than he had ever lost, particularly now that several of his friends were also looking after children in the evenings. 'When I was ill once, I said to the children that I would do the bedtime stories. But they were adamant that daddy should do it. "He reads them much better than you do," they said. You should have seen the smile of pride on his face.'

There has been a revolution in the way men and women organize their family lives. While surveys do show that women are still taking on the majority of domestic tasks and responsibilities, men are changing, and sharing more of these. Partners of full-time working women take on more childcare and domestic chores than partners of women working part time; many wives employed full time say that they couldn't possibly combine both responsibilities without a supportive spouse. In a comprehensive survey by the Institute of Manpower Studies in 1992 of women managers and professionals who had returned to work after having a baby, evidence of the evolution of 'new man' can be found. Of the women who replied, two-thirds relied on their partners occasionally, 15 per cent regularly and 18 per cent every day. Those with school-age children relied most on the fathers to take at least some responsibility for their family's welfare.

By refusing to relinquish either their career or motherhood, women have provoked a phenomenal cultural change. They have forced many men to accept that they have to be involved with their children and cannot simply come home and read the newspaper if they want to continue enjoying the nourishment of family life. As Gail Rebuck says, 'No partnership where both work, with children, could survive without cooperation and flexibility.' This is an advance on previous generations of fathers, many of whom rarely touched their children or expressed affection, let alone pushed the buggy to the park or shovelled mashed banana into the mouths of offspring. It is also an irreversible change, in that more fathers do now want a real relationship with their children.

But while it is women who earn the lower wage in most families, it will always be women who are forced to compromise in order to support the man's earning power and so lessen the impact on the overall family income. Though many men want to spend more time with their children, often they find that the terms of their job restrict them. Too few feel able to challenge their work culture by saying that they cannot attend that important after-hours meeting because it is their turn to pick up little Sammy Jo from the childminder. Women still take the overwhelming responsibility for looking after their children, whether or not in their company, and it is this, twenty-four hours a day, which is the most exhausting aspect of parenthood. When they become fathers, many men have an urge to provide, and put in even more hours at the office than the weekly average of forty-six that now seems to be required of the British worker. They feel a need either to make up for the sudden loss or lowering of the mother's income at a time when the family may desperately need more money, or simply to escape to the comparative peace and quiet of work.

In the rare instance when the woman is the parent capable of earning the most money, the results can be refreshing. Charlotte is a barrister of ten years' call, married to an academic in Cambridge, with two school-age children. She lives in Cambridge and commutes to the Bar, leaving at 7.45 in the morning and getting home at 8 p.m. Her husband cares for the children after school, and cooks dinner while Charlotte puts them to bed. They eat together and he then works for an hour or two while she slumps in front of *Newsnight*. Living on an academic's salary is out of the question, and her larger income is viewed as a blessing rather than a threat to male pride. She and her husband have devised a practical and flexible partnership which enables both of them to work and pursue their career interests as well as be adequate parents.

The idea that any of us can be more than adequate is a fiction. But because Charlotte shares a caring relationship with a husband who welcomes her career rather than resents it, she does not feel that she squeezes out every last ounce of energy juggling a demanding career with motherhood. Rather, she feels content and able to cope. 'I don't get to take them to the dentist or go to PTA meetings. But is that so important for my identity as a mother, when I know that their father is doing it?' Her relationship softens the blow inevitably dealt by the competitive and often gruelling nature of her work. 'People say that it must be difficult; but the fact is that I chose it and I share the responsibilities. I have a friend in Cambridge who leads a similar life, but has a far less supportive husband. Consequently she does feel under greater pressure and is far more aware of discrimination at the Bar than I am, perhaps as a direct result of her domestic situation.'

It is rare for the traditional roles to be completely reversed: only in 3 per cent of families does the father take primary responsibility for the children. Unemployment often forces a man to do more to help around the house, but it rarely results in him assuming full-time care. Men rarely earn so little that it is worth their while to give up employment completely in order to look after the children, rather than pay someone else to do the work. When they do, it can cause additional problems where the woman is reluctant to relinquish her motherhood function entirely. Instead of roles being swapped, she becomes confused by assumptions about what 'proper mothers' should do.

David looks after his four-year-old son full time while his wife, Sophie, is the principal breadwinner, having found that his acting career had come to a standstill. Both parents were reluctant to hand over their precious son to a nanny after years spent bringing him into the world through fertility treatment. In spite of long experience of mothering, David feels that women have a natural aptitude for the job. 'Nature prepares them psychologically, emotionally and hormonally to do this job that much more easily, which isn't to say that men can't or shouldn't do it. It's that much easier for a man to do a woman's job, or for a woman to do a woman's job, because of the technology [washing-machine, hoover, etc]. But if you pretend that there isn't a difference, then you're running into trouble.' David's feelings of inadequacy as a 'mother' make the isolation, loneliness and lack of status of his caring role that much more difficult to cope with. But they are exacerbated by Sophie's reluctance to relinquish complete control as the child's mother. 'She is the patriarch who says, we'll have blue wallpaper in here, won't we. Whatever the decision, she will insist on being a part of it; so every aspect of my territory is invaded by her, and she brings her professional personality into the home. We've had two or three big arguments about Josh's bedtime, because I know how tired he is, or what he's eaten, or that he's been pulling a particular trick all day like throwing things around. And then she comes in, he throws some things, I tell him off, and she says it doesn't matter; and I'll say, it does matter, I've been working on this all day. Don't undermine me. Men are more willing to accept that women rule the roost. When they come home, they want to play with their children, but accept it if the mother says that it's bedtime.'

Young men and women expect and want greater equality in their relationships. While romance never dies, many of them have ditched the more ludicrous expectations of the past and have high hopes of finding a partner who will be an equal. Tom, a 23-year-old baker at Sainsbury's, says, 'I wouldn't want a wife sitting at home all day; it would drive me mad. I think a woman needs to lead her own life, for what do you have to talk about if she doesn't? I know a lot of young women these days who are just not prepared to stop at home all day long with the kids.'

More and more young women no longer see themselves as unpaid servants in a relationship where they earn housekeeping money rather than their own wage. They want more from young men than just their pay packets; they want them to be good fathers to their future children, and they have more sense than to see marriage as a form of escape. 'I'm not looking for a partner as a financial crutch,' says 28-year-old Margo, a tennis coach. 'I'm looking for an equal partner, a relationship where we can mutually support each other.' Sylvie, a cashier from Sainsbury's, longs for escape. 'But the way out is to get a better job, not marriage. I see marriage as a partnership between two people having children and getting more out of life.'

Analysis in the *British Social Attitudes* survey (Jowell *et al*, 1992) shows that, in seeing their partner ideally as an equal, women are only a few percentage points ahead of men. Forty-seven per cent of women, as opposed to 41 per cent of men, disagree with the statement that 'a husband's job is to earn the money and the wife's job is to look after the home and family'. But that percentage swings to a substantial majority of 18- to 34-year-olds when the sample is broken down by age. Sixty-eight per cent of women and sixty-five per cent of men disagreed with any alleged need for the traditional family structure; yet these are the very people who will find themselves pushed back into the nuclear family model, round pegs in a square hole, as soon as they have children. Our work culture, employment legislation and childcare have not adapted to support men and women as parents; nor do they enable them to build enriched and more stable relationships. Society has instead sought more subtle means of excluding mothers from the workforce to preserve an outdated and dying notion of the happy nuclear family.

Men who live with the mother of their children, and witness their family's difficulties, are usually well able to understand them. When Beulagh Bewley was teaching postgraduate medical students, the majority of whom were women, one pupil felt that she had temporarily to give up studying. Her child was showing signs of developmental problems, and evidence of abuse from the nanny had just come to light. Beulagh encouraged her to go, 'Because she might never forgive herself if she did not devote herself wholeheartedly to her child at that particular moment,' and because she felt that as an intelligent woman her student could always find a way back into medicine. 'It was quite sweet, really, in that it was the men on the course who went for me and wanted to know why we hadn't done more for her.' When the GPO was building a new sorting office in Glasgow, the plans for the building included a fitness centre and a snooker hall. It was the men who raised the issue of a workplace nursery as being more essential. With wives who work, men know how difficult it is to find affordable childcare and how much their family income suffers as a result. In the case of Glasgow, they didn't succeed, but at least they tried.

Contrary to one pernicious new myth, many men actually *like* living with women who work, finding that it enhances the relationship rather than ruining their machismo. Janet, who has two children, is forty-two and for the past six years has driven one of London's black taxi cabs. 'When we first got together he was very traditional and thought that mothers shouldn't work. But now he says that were we ever to split up, he'd have to have another relationship with a working woman. He likes not having to work so hard to support someone else. He likes the fact that I'm strong and independent and that I buy a round in a pub.' Men with full-time working partners are far more likely, according to *British Social Attitudes* (Jowell *et al*), to reject a traditional set-up, and to do their fair share of the domestic chores. It may be that men who want a wife at home find one who is prepared to stay there. But it may also be true that only after living with a working woman do men discover that the benefits are far better than they ever imagined. Thereafter, they are unlikely to want a return to complete responsibility for the financial welfare of several other people, even were this an option. Increasingly men see their home as a sanctuary and want to be involved in the running of it. They want to spend more time with their children and their women, without regarding such pleasures as emasculating.

In families trying to cope with both parents working, the price nevertheless is often high. Couples rarely have time to be alone together if the woman is leaving for work the moment the man sets foot in the door. Where both parents work full time in professions which demand long hours of commitment, children rarely see them during the week. It is not necessarily the fault of either partner when relationships suffer and marriages break up, for without adequate time together how can they talk and build up trust? However hard individual men and women try to maintain stability, their families get next to no help from the state, which still sees children as private commodities that parents have to provide for rather than as citizens with a public right to education and protection.

The childcare calamity

So limited is the amount of daycare in Britain for young children that it is not even coordinated in a database. There is no list of childcare options available at a national level; nor is there a register of minders and nurseries, even though the Children's Act of 1989 states that there should be. The provision of daycare is patchy, with most workplace nurseries (and there are only a few hundred in the whole country) concentrated in the south-east; some local authorities have no pre-school nursery education at all. First-time mothers have to rely on informal networking and rumour to find out their options. This can be particularly fraught for a new mother who is, inevitably, a little emotional, with mixed feelings about whether she should go back to work at all. Vivette Ferguson, a single mother, went back to work for financial reasons when her daughter was nine weeks old. 'However, I couldn't find a childminder. A neighbour looked after her for a while, but she suddenly gave up doing it at half term and I had only a week to find someone else. I got very depressed, so much so that I wondered what was the point of living. Another neighbour, who was very supportive, had a nanny and I sent Naomi to her for a while, but it was expensive. Bernie wasn't contributing anything towards the children or the rent or the bills. I put Naomi's name down for the council nursery, but they told me that I did not qualify, because although I was a single parent, I was in work. So, in desperation, I took her along one morning and left her there. I said that if they didn't like it they could call the police. She was given a place after that. I was so relieved, because otherwise I would have to resign my job.'

For many parents, expensive childcare and nursery provision may be just about possible with one child. It is far beyond the scope of the average female income when the costs are doubled, with two children, even allowing for the complications that arise from children of different ages having different needs. Karen is a technical officer in the mechanized letter department for the Post Office in Glasgow. She has had the same employer for eleven years and earns a good salary of £18,000. After deductions she takes home £220 per week, of which she spends £20 getting to work and back. If she were to put both her children in the one private nursery in her area she would have to pay £140, leaving her with £60 per week. 'It's very difficult finding adequate childcare that's acceptable,' she says. 'I'm on the waiting lists for the state nurseries, but they say that because I'm in a stable relationship there's not much hope. Most of the minders are older women who just watch over them and don't teach them anything. You've got to pay to get decent childcare, and in the end it's just not worth your while working.'

Karen's sister-in-law has just been made redundant and has a small baby, so she will 'watch over' the children when Karen goes back to full-time work after maternity leave. But Karen is hesitant about trusting the arrangement until she knows that it will work. Her employers have shown no interest in setting up a workplace nursery. 'Their attitude is that it's your choice if you don't come back, and they do nothing to encourage you ... I like working and we need the money. You spend years building up a career, your position and your skills, and then you become a mother and almost everything is taken away from you. The technology has changed so much just in the last six months while I've been off having a baby that I couldn't possibly go back after five years without starting again.'

Survey after survey of parents with young children has shown that parents want more childcare. Susan McRae found in her study *Maternity Rights* (1991) that half the women who had worked during their pregnancy wanted more childcare facilities, one in five women wanted flexible working hours, and nearly half wanted the fathers of their babies to have time off work at or after birth. The sole concession that successive Conservative governments have made to millions of working mothers is to exempt from tax the costs of their children attending a workplace nursery. Big deal, with only 425 workplace nurseries in the whole of Britain. I suppose it's a start.

The term 'workplace nursery' is now bandied about so often that one could be forgiven for thinking it describes a commonplace aspect of employment provision. Those that do exist provide full-time places for only 12,000 under-fives, over half of them in London and the south-east (*Equal Opportunities Review* 42, 1992). The mother lucky enough to benefit from tax concessions through sending her child to a workplace nursery is a rare bird, and in severe danger of becoming extinct. In a recession, nurseries are the first thing to go; for example, the

BBC's exemplary workplace nursery at Television Centre is soon to be privatized. Midland Bank has also changed its policy, having developed the largest programme of workplace nurseries of any private-sector employer, with 850 places in 115 nurseries (*Incomes Data Services 521*, 1993). It is interesting that the effect on the Midland's staff retention had been considerable: in 1988 only 30 per cent of women returned after maternity leave, but by 1992 this figure had risen to 75 per cent. The bank originally indicated that approximately 325 workplace nurseries were to be set up. This was amid public enthusiasm for equal opportunities in response to the implications of the 'demographic time bomb', the sudden drop in school leavers available for work. Now that the labour market has proved to be static, and banks are shedding staff rather than coaxing mothers to return after maternity leave, Midland believes that they have sufficient nursery capacity to meet their current business needs. They also have a new owner, the Hong Kong Bank, under whom outspoken management commitment to equal opportunities has disappeared. In 1991, thirty-four private employers were followed up who had taken part two years before in a Working for Childcare survey (*Equal Opportunities Review*, 31). Twenty-two companies had said that they were considering a workplace nursery; but by 1991 half had rejected the idea, and a further five had ruled it out for the near future, due to the 'high' costs involved and the recession.

A common excuse from companies is that a survey of employees has found workplace nurseries to be unpopular. If it means dragging children through the rush hour, many mothers would understandably prefer to find local care rather than risk their child's welfare in the commuter crush. It is also true that, childcare being so precious, workplace nurseries can tie people to their jobs. But most mothers, if made to choose between a workplace nursery or nothing, would gladly opt for the former as the price of being able to work at all. Lacking the incentive of legislation, employers provide workplace nurseries not because they believe that mothers have a right to their former jobs, but because it suits them from a business point of view.

Some workplace nurseries can fall short of their purpose. Sainsbury's is a member of Opportunity 2000, a Business in the Community initiative, and, as at Midland, the majority of its employees, some two-thirds, are women. The chain has three workplace nurseries, one at head office and two at branches near their accounts office. Priority is given to management staff whom the company wishes to retain, and costs to the staff range from £50 per week for the lowest earners to £100 for those on salaries over £27,000. Most of Sainsbury's female employees are on low pay and are unlikely to be able to afford the nursery fees even if they were to obtain a place. In October 1991 there were only eighty-seven female deputy store managers, seven managers and eleven senior managers, many of whom in any case had no children. It should come as no surprise to Sainsbury's senior management that they are not deluged with applications for places at their workplace nurseries. Meanwhile increasing numbers of their women employees can only opt for tedious part-time flexible working from which there can be next to no escape through training and promotion.

According to Sainsbury's annual report for 1992, the company opened twenty-one new supermarkets in 1991, when their profits zoomed upwards by 25 per cent to £632.2 million. This, the highest real increase in four years, made David Sainsbury the richest man in Britain. I asked a senior member of personnel whether the potential for a workplace nursery was costed into new sites. That, she said, depended on the size of the site and whether there was a need in that area to retain management staff. No more nurseries were planned, because they were too costly, and Sainsbury's would rather put money directly into people's hands through childcare vouchers, although that proposal too was on hold until the recession eased. Vouchers are in any case no good if you can't find the childcare. Car parks, cafés, public lavatories and even petrol stations are indispensable aspects of customer service, but it seems a workplace nursery cannot be justified even though two-thirds of the staff are female. So much for family-friendly policies.

But why should it be the sole responsibility of the employer to provide childcare – a service in which a company will have next to no expertise and little vested interest? Why does the state abdicate any responsibility for a coherent and equitable approach to children, when so many women clearly need it? It's no good hiding behind the idea that women should stay at home and look after their children, because they clearly aren't doing this any more. They are too busy earning money so that by spending it they can lift the country out of recession, and there is every indication of numbers of working mothers increasing in the years to come. The government's own figures predict that one and a quarter million more women are likely to enter the workforce by 2001. If so many women are working, and are likely to continue working when they become mothers, the question of whether or not you provide daycare should be secondary to the quality of the care provided. The state could provide daycare for children which is in many cases better than that offered by their mothers.

Government policy on childcare pretends to be neutral. It states that children are the prime responsibility of their parents, and that childcare provision should be left to market forces. But by giving official encouragement to deregulated labour, and without a state system pledged to support working women through the provision of childcare, our entire political and economic infrastructure favours men over women. There are also anomalies in the policy and provision of childcare. If workplace nurseries are exempt from tax, why aren't all private nurseries? Petrol, even clothes, are frequently tax exempt but a man or woman could walk naked to work and still do his or her job. I doubt whether even Virginia Bottomley could function as a government minister with a three-year-old at her side.

If the government is keen for the market to provide child-care, why does it not make conditions more favourable for this by encouraging local authorities to make suitable property available, removing nurseries from the uniform business rate, and viewing nurseries as educational institutions rather than businesses? Allowances of up to £50 per week for childcare costs are available for some participants on the government training programme. So you can train to get a better job, but what happens then? You're skilled, and potentially more employable. But you can't go out to work, because you still can't find or afford the childcare. To qualify for unemployment benefit, female claimants with dependent children have to be able to say that they could make immediate arrangements for the care of their children should they be offered a job. But it is clear from the statistics that they can't. This requirement directly discriminates against women for it does not apply to fathers claiming unemployment benefit. One result, according to the Unemployment Unit, is that the numbers of women eligible for unemployment benefit are severely restricted.

Our ad hoc, cheapskate approach to childcare is per-petuating divided opportunities for women; it is also con-tributing to the polarization of resources and capabilities of the next generation. The majority of women who remain in full-time work with the same employer after the birth of their baby are less likely to find themselves demoted than those who leave and then attempt to re-enter the labour market when their child is older. They are also more likely to have access to company occupational schemes, and sick and holiday pay. Those who leave for part-time work because there is no childcare, or because they want to spend more time with their children, almost invariably move into secondary sectors of the labour market where they lose out on pay, job security and benefits.

In turn the wages of those working in the childcare sector are generally low. For this reason, and because childcare has not been integrated into our economic base but is seen as a cost unworthy of tax deduction for the self-employed, a huge black economy services the ever-growing number of women who refuse to relinquish their jobs on entering motherhood. Large numbers of young girls are employed as au pairs/nannies on a cash basis, without the requisite stamps or tax being paid, because we refuse as a society to recognize their worth. These are yet more women to add to the growing list of the invisible poor who lack the benefits of our national insurance system. Friends and neighbours and even family members are paid cash for their services. As professional incomes rise faster than earnings in childcare or in manual and semi-skilled jobs, more mothers rather than fewer are able to afford the services of less fortunate women. Between 1980 and 1991 there was a 259 per cent increase in private nursery provision and a 137 per cent increase in places with childminders (*National Commission on Education . . .*, 1992).

Meanwhile day nurseries are being closed as local authorities look first for cuts to their non-statutory provisions, and find it cheaper to place children 'in need' with minders. There are now signs that in certain boroughs even nursery education may be closed to make the books balance. If local authorities are not obliged by law to provide a service for children under five, they can cease their subsidy with impunity. This means that the available childcare services the wealthy, who can afford to pay for it, along with the very poorest, most disadvantaged families who come under the category of having children 'in need' and are heavily subsidized by the state. There is very little care accessible to the huge number of families who fall between these extremes. Childcare is as essential to the economic infrastructure of our country, and to true equality of opportunity, as public transport and the telephone. Without it being recognized as such, and brought into the real economy, there will open up an even greater divide in the educational standards and prospects of the next generation.

By punishing mothers for working we also punish the children. We know from research that the mind of an under-five is ripe for stimulus and knowledge. A child who can read before it is five and attending full-time education by law has an advantage for life over a child of that age who cannot read. Children learn fastest during their first three years; never again will they be able to gain so much knowledge so quickly. By five a child's basic attitudes towards education, and its strategies for learning, have long been fixed, perhaps negatively. Nursery education is more important than university education and yet it is severely under-resourced. Education does not begin with school at five, but at birth. All research into the effects of daycare has shown that children with nursery education have better developed language and better cognitive and social skills. If they habitually listen and relate to several adults, they are exposed to a greater use of language and more varied stimuli. From an early age they understand more of what it is to be part of a social group, and of society, as well as belonging to a family. If the quality of daycare is high, with good ratios of staff to children and a positive atmosphere, children can excel. They benefit in particular if they come from homes lacking in stimuli such as books and educational toys.

In America the Ypsilanti Study (Hennessy *et al*, *Children and Daycare*, 1992) found that children with pre-school education were more likely to complete their schooling and go on to further education. Girls were less likely to become teenage mothers and more likely to have jobs, and boys were less likely to be arrested by the age of nineteen, than those with no pre-school education (Cohen, *Childcare in a Modern . . .*, 1991).

Other US research backs up these findings: Berrueta-Clement and his colleagues studied 126 children from impoverished families, with half attending a high-quality nursery, and followed their progress through to young adulthood. He found that the children with nursery schooling were more likely to have jobs and to have completed their education and training, and less likely to be sent to special classes. Those children without nursery education were more likely to be detained and arrested by the police and the girls were more likely to become pregnant as teenagers (Hennessy *et al, Children and Daycare*, 1992).

The word 'quality' has to be stressed when discussing childcare. In London, the Thomas Coram Research Unit (Hennessy *et al, Children and Daycare*, 1992) has found no difference in the level of problem behaviour between children in or out of daycare. But there was evidence that poor-quality daycare may be associated with problem behaviour. The Unit followed a group of 250 first-borns between 1982 and 1991, in what was the only large-scale cohort study on the effects of daycare at a time when the numbers of working mothers, private nurseries and childminders were rocketing. They found that children from a disadvantaged background were likely to do better than they otherwise would in an environment that provided the toys, space and educational investment often lacking in their homes. Overall, children who had been in stable daycare, whether at nursery or with a childminder, had a more advanced vocabulary, and better language and social skills.

Good nursery teachers are trained to understand the needs of children at different stages of their development. They know how to stimulate them in a way that many mothers do not. Yet only a quarter of our children attend a half-day nursery attached to an infants' school. And we wonder why so many of our children cannot read at seven or why many leave school at sixteen for nothing but crime? Meanwhile, polarization enters into the very substance of the next generation. Those who have shall allow their children to have even more in future through private nursery education, and the children of those who have less will be even less likely to improve their lives through better education. Little official account is taken of the fact that improved education leads to improved skills, so that in the end the whole society benefits.

The only evidence found in disfavour of daycare for young children has yet to be proved. Researchers in America have found that children under one can form insecure attachments to their parents if they are in daycare for more than twenty-four hours a week. But children who have been permanently looked after by their mothers throughout the first year of life can also form insecure attachments to their parents, and many of these dreadful relationships last for life. How do you judge attachment anyway? A young child who does not leap into his mother's arms as she picks him up from the nursery may be a contented and secure child who has had such a busy and stimulating day that he has not had the time to miss his mother, rather than a child suffering from early insecurity. If the need for full-time maternal care were ever proved conclusively, there would be positive solutions available such as extended parental leave, or shorter working hours, until the child is a year old.

Working motherhood does not damage children when the benefits are increased family income, a happier, more fulfilled mother, and a more positive role model for the men and women of the future. Bad-quality daycare, however, can damage children's welfare, and it is towards establishing a high-quality national provision for all our children that we should direct our efforts, rather than pursuing policies which conspire to keep women at home with their children. There is a misguided arrogance in the mother who assumes she is always the best person for round-the-clock childcare. 'It is good for babies to be with professional carers,' says Nicky Padfield, an academic lawyer and mother of three. 'Professional mums are not necessarily as good. To be stuck at home with Mum all day can be the least stimulating thing, particularly if it's me and I'm reading the newspaper.' And yet the myth that children need their mothers every minute of the day has a tight hold over working mothers.

Other, poorer countries such as Spain and Portugal, who openly value and cherish their children, are rapidly expanding education provision for their under-fives. But Britain is reducing ratios of staff to children where it cannot cut nursery education completely, just because there is no political commitment to educate our very youngest people. Spain has recently reformed its education system to meet the different needs of two distinct phases – from birth to six, and from six to twelve. Portugal opened 470 new nurseries in 1992. We need to say as a nation that education is important, that it matters from birth, and that it has to be evenly distributed throughout the country. If young children need more adult input and smaller classes, it may even be that the ratio of teachers to pupils should be altered radically to correspond to their age: thus three-year-olds would be in classes of six; five-year-olds in classes of ten; ten-year-olds in classes of twenty, and twenty-year-olds in classes of forty.

In some rural authorities, playgroups are the only form of under-fives provision. Playgroups were first set up in the early 1960s by a number of mothers who recognized the importance to children of learning social interaction through playing with one another, and who were fed up with the poor statutory alternative available. Half a million children attend playgroups, but often for no more than ten hours a week. Roughly 13,000 of these children have their fees paid by the state, but it is mostly parents who finance the playgroup network, providing some £100 million per annum at approximately £5 per week. The government gives only £7 million. Two generations have passed since Lloyd George said that play was nature's training for life.

Play teaches a young child much of how the world works before language can effectively convey information. Within an orderly, safe but spacious environment, play shows children a great deal about their own bodies and how to relate to each other. Playgroups are more important now than ever: in many areas it is no longer possible to join neighbouring children safely out on the streets, and as families become smaller there are fewer children to play with at home.

Yet playgroups, being non-statutory, are all too often the first local authority service to be cut. Many are finding it particularly hard to cope in the current economic climate, given that their budgets are so low. In 1989 one third of the members of the Pre-School Playgroups Association received yearly grants averaging £328, while the average expenditure was £3,686. Wages for playgroup staff are low, averaging less than £2 per hour. This can mean a high turnover of staff and less stability for the children; sometimes, too, dramatic increases in local authority rents force playgroups to the point of closure. Fees to parents have risen to an average of £1.51 per session, which is way beyond the means of many low-income families. Here is yet another gross anomaly in our childcare policy, or lack of it. Since state nursery education is available, if only for roughly a quarter of our under-fives, why is it not also free for children who attend playgroups, often the only stop-gap between isolation at home and full-time education from five?

Childcare problems do not disappear when a child goes to school since full-time education does not follow the same hours or holiday arrangements as full-time work. For many women, finding care for children aged five to eleven can be harder because the hours it must fill are bitty and irregular. Some 2.5 million five to ten-year-old children have working mothers, and the Kids Club Network estimates that about 20 per cent of all primary school children – nearly 1 million – are left at home on their own. Not only is this illegal, no one knows the hidden costs in terms of accidents or crime. The Kids Club Network is yet another remarkable organization set up by mothers attempting to cater for their children where the state does not. Around the country it has approximately five hundred projects, run on a shoestring. Tess Woodcraft of the Kids Club Network emphasizes that the children it serves need not just care but an opportunity to play in a safe, structured environment where they can be in control. 'Most of the school day is taken up with structured learning, and they can't play in the streets. Play is crucial for a child's development. It helps them to grow and cope with change, and equips children for a fast-changing world.' In 1993 the state pledged £45 million to after-school care, the first time any government has acknowledged such responsibility.

Meanwhile women are still blamed for turning their offspring into latchkey children while they go to work in order to provide for them and preserve their own careers and self-esteem. The guilt many mothers feel at being absent as their children's needs change and become more sophisticated can be great indeed. For most, their children are a part of them and when separated for too long it can feel as if limbs have been severed. It really hurts to be apart. Jenny Abramsky's children are old enough now to be left alone, but it hurts her more not to be with them than when they were small. 'My son is doing GCSE, and I'm not there, when he comes home, to help him. My daughter is embarking on puberty, and there are things that she wants to talk about. I am constantly torn between my responsibilities as a mother and my responsibilities here, particularly as this job has got bigger and bigger. It's very easy to influence a child under ten, but very difficult when they're in their teens. If it's difficult and you are not around, do you start failing to influence them? I haven't worked it out. A friend of mine gave up work when her children were twelve and sixteen. I thought it extraordinary at the time: she's gone through all that and *now* she wants to give it up? Now that my children are virtually the same age I understand her.'

But if Jenny Abramsky or any of the other working mothers that I interviewed for this book had given up work, would they have been any happier? Smaller families and a disturbing decay in community spirit make mothers of young children more isolated and vulnerable than ever, while the devaluing of motherhood has lowered women's self-esteem, particularly when that is all that they do. Decia was seventeen when she had her first baby. 'The actual birth was all right and the pregnancy was all right; but being isolated because of having the child, not having anyone around, was terrible. That's when my weight problem started, because all I'd do was eat. I felt so bad that I didn't want to get dressed in the morning. I was in a desperate state; and then my sister-in-law told me about the playgroup, and that brought me out of myself.' For Karen Lawson, if an arrangement with her sister-in-law breaks down, there's the choice of losing almost all her earnings by placing her two small children in a private nursery, or giving up her career and opting for isolation just outside Glasgow. 'Young women with kids here have nowhere to go. They're isolated and get depressed; it doesn't help if you're stuck in the house. I like working, and I'm not happy in the house all day long. The thought of going back to work after maternity leave is like a light at the end of the tunnel.'

Full-time motherhood is one of the most exhausting and demanding jobs on earth. It can be the most fulfilling; it can also be the most boring. There are moments of sublime joy in being a parent, when your child is happy, funny and sheer bliss to be with. But there are times, often daily, when children throw tantrums, scream and kick; when they demand that bit too much because they know you are tired; when a mother wishes she was on the other side of the earth; when rage takes over from exhaustion. Attending to young children's physical needs, coupled with the emotional demands of making them feel cherished and stimulated, can leave a full-time mother utterly drained. Disciplining a small child is tiring beyond belief, and saying 'don't do that' or 'be careful' hundreds of times a day can make a mother feel that she is nothing but a barrier to the dangers and horrors of the world rather than a means to discovering the good. Full-time motherhood means round-the-clock responsibility, without a day off or a change of routine. If you are ill and there is no one to help you, you cannot ring in sick and stay in bed. Full-time mothers do not have a nanny or a childminder to rely on for part of the day; they carry on regardless because they have to. You just have to hear the weary tone of the parent in the supermarket queue, repeating firmly for the tenth time 'put that back', to know that the fatigue and relentless tedium of motherhood can be just too much. Yet these are the very women whom the myth of motherhood holds up as duty bound to be exemplary.

'The family is the natural and fundamental group unit of society and is entitled to protection by society and the state.' So spoke the International Covenant on Civil and Political Rights in 1966. Society is founded on nothing but families, most of whom have children who will make up the society of the future. They are our most important asset and yet we underinvest in them by expecting mothers to raise them to be balanced, healthy, socially integrated and responsible human beings without pay, assistance or a day off. Our negligent childcare policy fails the growing number of women who expect and want to work and it fails our families by refusing to invest in educating our youngest minds when they most need it. The worlds of work and home are kept entirely separate; children are rarely seen in offices or on city streets, while they are commonplace in a shopping precinct. Grudgingly, women have been allowed to enter the workplace, but only if they leave their children behind in the other world inhabited only by young families and their carers. The House of Commons has no crèche but it does have a restaurant, a bank and a post office. Trinity College, Cambridge, one of the richest landowners in the country, spends, I am told, more on wine than it does on books, and budgets next to nothing on childcare. We cannot continue pretending as a society that our children only exist hidden within places that are not our concern. We have to integrate the world of infancy with the one beyond, so that our children learn more about adult work. To quote a leader in the *Independent* (5 September 1991): 'Working mothers put fewer burdens on the state than non-working mothers. More broadly, the mental and physical health of mothers and children represents an investment in the future which it is shortsighted to neglect.'

The socially valuable work that families do in raising children needs support from the state. Instead, a new moralism attempts to force women back into dependency, as inaccurate claims spread despondency at the collapse of the family as we once knew it. 'Across the political, moral, intellectual and religious spectrum, almost everyone agrees that small, warm, caring families are the single best hope that children do not end up as criminals. Unfortunately they are a dying breed. The abnormal family seems now to have become the norm,' said the *Sunday Times* (7 March 1993) in the panic surrounding the tragic murder of two-year-old James Bulger. Politicians and journalists point to a doubling in the number of lone-parent families since 1971, and declare this to be evidence that the very fabric of the British family is under threat, as the new, emancipated woman kicks out her useless man with relish. But closer inspection of the General Household Survey reveals that approximately 83 per cent of Britain's children are living within two-parent households. While there has been a substantial rise in the number of households where people live alone, when it comes to having children, men and women are behaving responsibly and it is after all the children we should be primarily concerned about.

Though the family may be changing largely through women wanting and needing to work, it is certainly not facing extinction. Men and women still seek and form lasting and nourishing relationships with each other, and most of them go on to have children. The one in three divorce rate is a statistic thrown out so frequently that it now conveys a message, suggesting that humankind is no longer equal to making marriages that last. Less is said of our culture's tardy acceptance that people need not be trapped for life by their mistakes. The rise in the divorce rate should surprise no one given other current changes in society, such as lack of faith in religion, and the success rate of the pill. Most importantly there has been a tacit but fundamental reappraisal of what marriage means. Do you need to marry somebody whom you love and want to share each day with, when you can just as happily live with them outside wedlock? When people can survive well into their eighties, and change considerably during the course of a lifetime, should marriage necessarily last until death? Undoubtedly these influences have changed the form of family life, but they have not persuaded people to abandon it entirely in favour of a communal existence of solitude.

Headlines focus nonetheless on their own prime suspect for the increase in disrupted families. 'Divorce rate linked to women working,' announced the *Independent* (22 June 1993). 'Researchers believe that the high British divorce rate – one for every 2.3 marriages – is because the nation has the highest proportion of working women in Europe, so wives have more financial independence.' This baffling statement describes a country with one of the lowest European proportions of women working full time. Britain also has one of the highest rates of women in part-time jobs, with wages that rarely guarantee financial independence. The shifting sands of family life are largely incidental to the fact that women now work as well as mother a family. There is no evidence that the career woman is forsaking family values for the sake of a fast car – rather she is sacrificing many of her own needs in order to combine paid work with motherhood and so provide more for her family. 'Divorcees drink and smoke their way to an early death,' shouted a headline from The Times (12 November 1991), as if an unhappy marriage was somehow better for your health. Countless research shows that children of divorced parents suffer, but their experiences are compared with children of stable relationships rather than with those of unhappy marriages. Rarely is poverty through divorce touched upon, or the financial hardships resulting from the woman's economic dependency. The nature of women's employment has not changed so radically as to suggest that it is female 'emancipation' through paid employment alone that is contributing to the divorce and birth trends. Most women still enter lengthy, often life-long partnerships with a man and bear him two children, and it is still death which kills off most marriages, not divorce.

When marriages or other longstanding relationships break down irretrievably, usually the men and women concerned go on to form other long-term alliances. That, after all, is what most people want in their heart of hearts; when we are lonely we all dream of companionship. Lone or single mothers are rarely so for all time. They go on to form relationships – hopefully better – with other men and women. Of children born in the early 1970s, 83 per cent of children initially with lone mothers were living in two-parent families by the age of sixteen (Lawson et al, The Politics of Pregnancy, 1993). Children can suffer as a result of acquiring a stepfather or stepmother. Others find, however, that this gives them greater stability, and their numbers are bound to increase as living with a step-parent becomes more acceptable and men and women learn more about fulfilling such a role.

Alarmists point to the rise in the number of lone mothers as evidence of impending anarchy, its embodiment the household formed without a man. In truth very few women indeed actively choose to become single parents. Most mothers raising their children alone are victims of family breakdown, and they are particularly vulnerable to isolation and poverty. Only 17 per cent of lone mothers in 1991 had incomes exceeding £237 per week compared with 51 per cent of lone fathers and 81 per cent of married couples (Holtermann *et al, Parents* . . ., 1993). Over two-thirds of lone parents live on less than £100 per week. Single mothers have half the employment rates of married mothers; of those who are not working, 95 per cent are on income support. Fewer lone mothers now work, despite a general increase of women in paid employment. In the decade to 1988 the proportion of single working mothers had dropped from 47 per cent to 22 per cent, with a comparable loss of full-time jobs (Lister, *Women's Economic Dependency*, 1992).

With fewer mothers able to work, more children are growing up impoverished. One in four babies in Britain is born into a family on means-tested benefits. The Child Poverty Action Group estimates that over 3 million children are living in households with under 50 per cent of the average income. Society does not consider itself to have a problem with mothers being dependent, provided that they rely on men rather than the state. Now, however, there are fewer men able to support these women. The response of government to the poverty trap holding so many mothers has been such Draconian measures as the Child Support Act, and a proposal to prevent access to housing for young single mothers, in an attempt to push these women back into invisible dependency on the family. In addition to other deprivations, our social security system penalizes a woman for working by refusing to deduct her childcare costs.

Without a husband or partner to rely on, all family costs including childcare usually have to be borne by one income.

There is likely to be no one else in the home to call on for casual care, and if the absence of a father follows an acrimonious split, this can mean his parents or other family members are also not available for unpaid childcare. There is nobody with whom to share the day-to-day responsibilities any more than the joyful moments or the worries when a child is ill or in trouble. As Sindhu Hope, a single mother, says, 'There is no one to be there for them when they hate you – no one else to be the monster for a while. There is no one supporting me in dealing with it. This is the isolation of being on your own. I feel that it's not that I particularly need a partner, so much as access to, and inter-action with, other adults. It's difficult to get out often, and I'm exhausted. I begin to get caught in a spiral of feeling down and wanting company, at the same time as not wanting company because I'm feeling down. Being the sole adult is a lot of effort – consistent, insistent effort.' It's no help that although many women bring supreme dedication and success to the difficult job of raising children alone, as single mothers they still bear a social stigma. Even now they are blamed for their predicament, and lumped together into one big basket labelled 'problem'.

An alleged rise in teenage pregnancies has also set off sounds of alarm. Over the 1980s such pregnancies have increased slightly, from 58.7 per 1000 to 69 per 1000 in 1990 in the fifteen to nineteen age group, and from 7.2 per 1000 to 10.1 per 1000 in girls aged thirteen to fifteen (Office of Population and Census Studies, *Birth Statistics*, 1991). This is not such a drama-tic rise as to suggest that our nation's youth has been corrupted to the very core by sexual promiscuity, and by 'children having children'. Two-thirds of all teenage births are to eighteen- and nineteen-year-olds, who are considered adults by law and there-fore able to make their own decisions. Compared to the 1960s, women's changed expectations, more effective contraception, and easier access to abortion has made motherhood far less common among the under-20s.

Given that teenage motherhood has always existed, the revolution we are seeing is an increase in the mothers from this age group who are unmarried. There is less pressure on men to 'do the right thing'; and less pressure on young women to give up their babies for adoption. Roughly three-quarters of all teenage mothers, approximately 250,000 women, are single, and the state responds with panic to the question of who will support them. The fact is that approximately half these women are cohabiting with the child's father, and of the remaining fathers most see their children on a regular basis, providing what they can in the way of cash.

At every age a small percentage of mothers will regret parenthood, casualties of an experience that no one can be sure of coping with or liking until they actually try it. For most single mothers, having a child is entirely welcomed. Ironically, from a physiological point of view the teens are the best time to give birth. Yet the 'problem' is presented negatively by journalists keen to fill space with discussion of a trend, albeit a tenuous one, and by a government intent upon reducing the numbers of single mothers on welfare. Virginia Bottomley, herself a teenage mother, has pledged in a white paper entitled 'The Health of the Nation' to halve the number of teenage pregnancies by the year 2000.

There is, however, a misunderstanding as to why many single young women have babies. It is assumed that these children are unwanted, as so often in the days when young mothers genuinely did have less choice. Dropping out of school, unemployment, lack of hope for the future, low self-esteem, isolation and poverty are usually seen as the inevitable tragic results of teenage pregnancy. But there is increasing evidence to suggest that the pre-existence of these factors may actually prompt young women to have a baby, given their lack of other worthwhile occupations. Often it is not irresponsible adolescent sexuality that leads to motherhood so much as active choice. If,

119

before conception, these women had had the chance of training and acquiring skills, they would perhaps be seen as making a more positive contribution to a society which didn't then have to support them, rather than being hopeless victims of man's insatiable lust.

With affordable childcare, many single mothers would be able to come off welfare and contribute to the economy by paying tax. Women all over the country want and need a support system of trained workers to help them in the extraordinarily difficult task of raising a family. Government hides, meanwhile, behind outdated attitudes, intimidated by the costs. It cannot interfere with the family, its argument runs: families themselves must provide for their children's welfare. Yet the government seems well able to interfere when this suits it. In place of childcare, what women get is the Child Support Act of 1991, which meddles without compromise in family life, in return for savings on the welfare state which are bound to be small. The nanny state intervenes in family life to suit its own doctrine of cuts in social security spending, but it sidesteps any initiative that would enable families to take better care of themselves, raise the educational welfare of their children, and support lonely single mothers by helping them get back to work.

A more constructive attitude towards providing childcare would ensure savings on welfare state payments for single mothers that were far greater than any sums raised by pursuing absent fathers. Sally Holtermann and Karen Clarke have analysed the costs of childcare based on a tripartite arrangement between parents, employers and the state, a system common to many European countries. Parents would meet one third of the cost overall, with families on low incomes being charged nothing and those on high incomes paying 100 per cent. The state would pay two-thirds, taking a mandatory contribution from employers. Consequent savings on benefits and the flowback to the exchequer in tax and national insurance contributions are estimated at £1,080 million a year. This sum can well bear comparison with the £922 million proposed for improvements in childcare to release parents into paid employment. Clarke and Holtermann estimate that, to meet demand, Britain would have to increase current childcare provision fourfold, with children of school age rather than under-fives having the greatest need. Since at least a million more women are likely to enter the workforce by the end of the century – half the intake of law and medical schools for example is now female – that demand for childcare will continue to increase.

Its potential benefits include not only short-term savings but an investment in society's future through its human capital. Early education and stimulus could give our children a better start in life and further spare the state expense by reducing the numbers of young offenders. It costs approximately £60,000 per year to look after a child who has been excluded from school for behavioural problems, many of which show themselves as early as three or four. Children are not regarded as a potential national asset, but as a private indulgence. Yet they are our future, and investing in them is as important as putting money into roads, railways or the motor industry. Only in this way could John Major be taken seriously when he said, 'The government is determined that every child in this country should have the very best start in life.'

More equal access to childcare, and therefore to jobs for women, would help our children towards equality of opportunity, not just between the sexes, but between the rich and the poor, between those able to provide for themselves and educate their children and those who cannot. By returning more women to work, society would lose less of its earlier investment in their education and training. All working parents, but particularly mothers, would suffer less stress in combining the heavy responsibilities of a job and a family. The benefits – better mental and physical health, greater family stability and personal satisfaction – ought to be integral to our quality of life.

But childcare which simply liberates a woman to work like a man is not sufficient. There has to be a fundamental change in our approach to the work ethic so that men too are allowed to be effective parents. Fathers who want to go home at a reasonable hour and see their children should say so and should realize that other men feel the same way. Elizabeth Heggy's husband is a consultant anaesthetist. 'He puts in a great deal to our daughter, but wants to be able to put in more. He recently had an argument with the surgeon at the hospital about the length of the theatre list. He said that it was simply not acceptable, and of course it was 10 p.m. before they got through the list and visited everybody. But he also feels that he's under pressure, that he's not doing more, as there are others who work even harder than he does. There's this tradition in medicine that unless you're absolutely exhausted and there until midnight, you're not committed.' If the culture of the workplace would accommodate women's need to be parents as well as employees, it would establish a precedent enabling men, too, to spend more time with their children. It must only be a question of time before a man invokes the Sex Discrimination Act to challenge those few privileges on offer to women in a limited number of companies, such as career breaks or job sharing. Any man in crisis over his lost identity as sole breadwinner need only look to his children for a new role; children after all need their fathers to be as willingly available as their mothers. It cannot be healthy for the offspring of large numbers of hardworking professional couples to see so little of their parents. The answer is to adapt the hours and conditions of work for both sexes, rather than to force capable, qualified women back to full-time motherhood.

Women are paying for their wish to be mothers, as well as for the need to work. The danger is that the river of guilt through which so many working mothers swim will burst its banks on to the next generation. If you put yourself in the wrong, the child will pick up on that weakness, so that a woman who feels herself to be a dreadful mother may thereby become just that. This destructive model for family life doesn't spare the mother who is permanently at home, if she feels isolated and lacking in identity. Gina has two children and a wealthy husband. She doesn't need to work for money and has help with the children. She nonetheless craves a career and a sense of identity now that we live in a society where motherhood is not enough. 'As a mother I always feel behind in knowing what I believe in and what I want to pass on; and I feel sad that I haven't got something more concrete to give them. I haven't taken a path that I want to be able to hand to them. You project your own ideas, your own ignorance, your own confusion. If I'm dissatisfied with myself, I know that my children will receive that as knowledge.'

For themselves, women want more than their mothers had, and they want more for their families than they had as children. The vast numbers of women who cannot find affordable childcare and adjust their hours accordingly will work for almost any wage if it means providing that extra something for their children. As Carol Peggie, who has a job as a nursery teacher, says, 'Women want the material things that their mothers didn't have. They want to improve their own life, and the kids want more as a result of watching television – and why shouldn't they?' Publisher Kate Parkin feels that she is a better mother for working at something she enjoys, and which makes her fulfilled. 'We just have to look back at our own mothers to see the difference – mine worked part time, but would have been infinitely happier working full time. She bore the brunt of all of the organization, and I remember her being cross most of the time; a cross and frustrated woman, who grew into someone who was great fun to be with when we grew up and she started working. However tired I am, I don't get cross with Susannah. I could have had the worst day in the world, and I go home and there she is, cutting out and painting – so different to everything I do at work.'

Excruciating tiredness is the main symptom of working motherhood. Most women resent this mainly because it means that they cannot do more for their children, not that they cannot do more for themselves. Though it's a tough way to live, the majority of working mothers wouldn't have it any other way, believing that they have just as warm and secure a relationship with their children as those women have who do not work. But the price is high. 'There's another day's work ahead of me when I get in at night,' says Kathleen Wheeler. 'You show me a man who does what a working mother does. He never says, I'm so tired I'm going to have to go to bed early; but he does say frequently that he thinks there must be something wrong with me, and that I ought to go to the doctor because I have to go to bed early.'

For some women exhaustion is too high a price, and work has to go. As the middle-class North London daughter of a feminist, Heti had done everything required of her. Having got her O and A levels and graduated from university, she set up her own successful business. Making and selling hats, she had an identity. But the father of her small child is in film and often works long hours or is away from home for weeks at a time. 'It was ridiculous when I was working full time and he was working full time. We never saw each other, not that we see that much of each other now; but when I did see him there was this frightful fight for the time on your own, for that extra half hour in bed, and not to have to get up in the middle of the night.' When Heti discovered that she was sick of the sight of hats and that customers weren't paying her for them anyway, she gave up work, and doesn't regret it. 'I'm quite happy not working, but my family finds that hard to accept. I went for a walk this morning with my stepfather and he kept saying, "Well, what about you, what are you doing?" I say, "I'm just minding the baby, I've learnt that that is quite a valuable thing to do." But where I come from that's hard, because that's not what I'm meant to do, I'm meant to be set in this career.'

Teaching is supposed to be one job whose hours and holidays allow women to combine the work with having children. Yet many female teachers find themselves oppressed by old-fashioned attitudes and, given that their earnings are not princely, the high cost of childcare. Elizabeth Monroe, a teacher of children with special needs, and a single mother, moved back to Edinburgh from Surrey to be nearer her family. 'I found it difficult in Surrey; people didn't know me, and life was a constant juggling act. I'm always guilty either about not being at school enough or not being at home enough.' Her son has found it difficult settling into a new school, but Elizabeth is rarely able to visit him there. 'I'm so cut off; I don't know who his friends are. Even if you have the ideal job for a mother, in teaching, childcare is still a problem. It depends on the head's understanding of the need to balance work with family, and most of them are men.' Angela Oxley, another single mother and a teacher of English to secondary-school children, feels that stereotypical attitudes towards working mothers are the hardest thing to deal with. She was head of English when she became pregnant, and encountered antagonism from male members of staff who thought 'that I wanted it both ways. They felt that I should either be at work and fully involved with after-school drinking, or fully at home and on benefit.'

For those single mothers, in work and with a career, giving up their job is not an option. It would mean exchanging career, identity and precious income for an outdated notion of family life and an empty existence of poverty on benefits. For women living in two-parent households, giving up work is still not an option. Their families depend on their income for essential items; also most women know how hard it would be for them to get back on to a comparable part of the labour market when their children are older. They are realistic enough to know, too, that marriage no longer necessarily lasts a lifetime. If only for this reason, it would be foolish to close off any route to earning a living, particularly if they have had an education, and acquired skills they do not want to lose. Why should these women still be asked to sacrifice so much in order to raise their children unpaid, where men are not?

Until we get the good-quality childcare we need, women are relying on their age-old ingenuity and sheer strength of will to find a means of living. Kirsty is a primary-school teacher with two small children, who found life so stressful that she had to seek therapy. 'I wanted to maintain my individuality as well as have children. I wasn't going to be the sole carer, with Mid bringing home the money. In the end we introduced a third person, my neighbour upstairs, who looked after them as well. But I got extremely stressed – it happens to so many working mothers now. I went back to work too quickly; I wanted to prove that I could do both, and I wasn't ready for it. I began having problems with Mid; and I ended up needing counselling when Harry was fourteen months old, because it all became too much.' Now things are better, 'I'm learning to take a little time for myself after teaching, before I go into the mother role, and I actually do both things much better that way. You have to look after yourself. If all you're doing is giving out, you end up not doing anything very well. My kids come first, but I have to make sure that I have that time and don't feel guilty about it. At the end of the day everybody benefits. I think it's easier than before for women to make the decision to go out to work. But if you have children, you have to be in a profession that gives you enough money for help. I think it's a very confused period for women; it will be interesting to see what happens in the next decade. In the end it's about choice. If you want to go out to work, there should be provision for you to do so, with your children looked after in a safe, stimulating environment and not feeling like you've palmed them off. If you don't want to work, then you should be able to do that as well and not be living on the poverty line . . . that would be the ideal world.'

chapter five

in
poverty
and
obscurity

One half of all full-time working women earned below two thirds of the average weekly male wage in 1992, principally because they were lacking in skills, educational qualifications or experience, or because they were working in service industries (Dex, *Women and Low Pay*, EOC, 1995). The scant statistics available appear to show that women from ethnic minority groups get paid approximately three quarters of white women's hourly pay. Of the 11 million women in employment, 4.5 million work part time, of whom 3.5 million are mothers. Though most young women work, as soon as they become mothers they are immediately divided by income. A stark absence of affordable childcare means that those who cannot maintain their income through professional full-time work can opt only for 'flexible' low-paid employment. Maternity halves the number of women in full-time work, but considerably increases those officially employed part time. Many women do actively seek part-time work; others have no choice. In either case they find that the mere status of part-timer guarantees them a lower income, no employment protection, and few of the benefits available to employees with full-time status. Part-time work is the only sector of the labour market which is expanding rapidly. The majority of its workers are women, exploited as cheap labour because they are mothers, because of their sex.

Approximately one third of all mothers who return to full-time work after the birth of their first child later switch to part-time work, according to the 1980 Women and Employment Survey (Martin and Roberts, *Women's Employment*, 1980), because of the strain of maintaining both responsibilities. Flexibility is sold to them as the main perk, and as an advantage which somehow mitigates the drawbacks of low pay, low status, little employment protection, next to no training and limited prospects for promotion. An investigation on pay and gender in Britain by the Industrial Relations Services found that there was, according to most of the personnel staff interviewed, no need to make special benefits or retention payments to part-time staff, because part-time working was itself sufficient inducement. One bank in the study employed part-timers on a twilight shift for clerical work, and paid them on a flat rate rather than on the same basis as the rest of the clerical staff. The women on this shift were mothers, with the same skills acquired through working for the same employer prior to parenthood. But not only were they paid less as the price of fecundity, they also lacked the pay progression available to the rest of the clerical structure, and had no opportunity for promotion. Some of these women even worked for part of the day alongside full-timers who were paid a higher hourly rate. Questioned about this, the employer said that the reward for part-timers was 'greater job satisfaction and access to the mortgage subsidy scheme'. By greater job satisfaction one must assume he means being able to work through the night because there is nobody to look after your children during the day.

During the late 1970s and early 1980s some building societies faced the considerable cost of introducing new technology. They were able to offset this by employing greater numbers of part-time workers, in the form of women returning to work after becoming mothers. Almost all cashiers now are women. In 1970 only 4 per cent of building-society staff were part time; by 1985 that figure had risen to 23 per cent. The majority of these women had once worked full time for a building society and so were more than adequately qualified. Nonetheless Lynn Ashburner's extensive study of building societies found that 'regardless of the years of service, experience or qualifications a woman had, a move to part-time work meant a total loss of employment advantages. It also meant a considerable reduction in pay and being limited to only the most routine and mundane work with no opportunity for promotion.'

Paying part-timers less pro rata, and not paying for breaks or holidays, is now common amongst retailers, and a growing practice in other sectors. A study of twenty-nine establishments covering all sections in five regions of Britain (Howell *et al*, *Employers' Working Time*, 1992) found that full-time employees of both sexes were much more likely than part-time staff to receive paid premiums for night work, weekend work and overtime. Simply by being categorized as part time, employees assume secondary status irrespective of the work they do, this being the price of so-called flexibility.

'Flexible' would only describe a genuine perk if women part-timers were able to decide when they wanted to work. One of the main functions of the personnel department at individual branches of supermarkets is to ring round its flexible staff to see if they can fill in at short notice when people ring in sick or simply do not show up for their shift. Banks also employ people for this purpose, on special 'on-call contracts', which deny pro rata pay or benefits. Some part-time staff in building societies are expected to work full time over busy periods such as Christmas, most of which are periods when their children are on holiday and when they would rather spend time with them. 'It is the flexibility that part-time work offers that women like, not the type of work or lack of opportunities,' says Lynn Ashburner. 'Over half of the part-time women in this study expressed dissatisfaction with the type of work they were doing as well as their pay and conditions. All but two would have preferred full-time work had they been offered it and had they adequate childcare.' For low-paid women with children to support, it must be hard to say no when offered paid work at short notice; it's equally hard to find someone to look after the children. When you have children you are less rather than more flexible, and this can seriously discriminate against women. In provincial theatres, for instance, there is a pecking order for those 'on call'. Changeovers from one production to another have to be done quickly, sometimes overnight; consequently this is very well-paid work. If you are available when called, you get the work; but if not, you drop to the bottom of the list. Employers who boast of their flexible working arrangements are claiming thereby to run a family-friendly workplace; most of them, however, do little else for mothers. Neither the banks nor the major retailers have even improved on statutory maternity pay; nor do they offer subsidized childcare for their lower-paid staff.

The real reason for employing women on a part-time basis is that it is considerably cheaper. An Institute of Personnel Management report cites a department store which calculates the real hourly cost of a part-timer at approximately 12 per cent less than that of an equivalent full-time worker. This is contrived through savings on the occupational pension scheme and national insurance contributions, and on paid morning and afternoon tea breaks, for which part-timers are not eligible (Hewitt, *About Time*, 1993). With similar economies in mind, finance personnel at one hospital estimated that employing a worker for forty hours per week costs approximately £300 more each year than hiring two people for the same overall time. A further advantage seen in hiring part-timers is that if they are brought in to do a job specifically when they are needed, they are less likely to stand around chatting, idling away those hours when there is less to do.

Consequently opportunities for part-time work are mushrooming. In its officially acknowledged forms it constitutes one-fifth of all work in Britain, and is expected to rise to a quarter by the end of the century. The increased use of flexible labour, with lower pay and almost negligible conditions, can be found in every area of employment where there are women in substantial numbers – in nursing and teaching, in the leisure industry, for example cinemas and bingo halls, in retailing, in banking and in building societies. While the EOC finally succeeded in March 1994 in persuading the House of Lords that part-time workers (that means women) should not have to work an extra 3 years before qualifying for the same redundancy rights as full-time workers, we have yet to see government rushing forward with enthusiasm to alter the law. Individual women still have to prove that they have been unlawfully dismissed. All the EOC have won, against overwhelming odds, is the right of individual women to have their case heard in the first place.

The limit of £54 per week below which no national insurance contributions are due encourages employers to pay less than that figure. This denies increasing numbers of female employees the right to accrued benefits such as maternity pay, unemployment benefit and state pension. Because these women tend not to appear on any database, it is hard to know exactly how many are earning low rates of pay. Anecdotal evidence suggests that their numbers are high, and rising fast. In a written answer to Hansard on 11 January 1993, Patrick McLoughlin estimated that 2.75 million people were below the PAYE threshold of £66 per week, and 2.25 million people earned less than the lower earnings limit for National Insurance contributions. Almost half of Britain's 4.5 million part-time workers, 83 per cent of whom were women, worked less than sixteen hours per week, according to the 1980 Women and Employment Survey (Martin and Roberts, *Women's Employment*, 1980), who also found that one in five had no paid holidays as opposed to one in twenty full-time workers, and that one third of all part-timers received no sick pay.

It is now estimated that half of all working women in Britain – more than twice the number of men – are employed on atypical contracts describing them as part-time, temporary or self-employed. There is another hidden bonus to this trend, for the Public Sector Borrowing Requirement. Without the benefits of sick and maternity pay, unemployment benefit or a full state pension, these women will draw less on the welfare state, being forced back on to a male earner for their support. Traditional male sectors of employment, by contrast, are not increasing their use of a part-time casual labour force. In most heavy manufacturing, shift work with paid overtime is more common. Likewise, though many consultants, doctors, MPs and chief executives work what could be part-time hours, in order to accommodate private practices and other concerns, their pay and conditions are not docked accordingly.

Sheila is a mother of three who has been employed for the past ten years filling shelves overnight for Tesco in Llanelli. She works four nights a week from 9.30 p.m. to 6 a.m. Approximately forty-four other people are on the night shift, 80 per cent of whom are women with children. Only four of these forty-four staff qualify for full-time status by working thirty-six hours a week; they also get full membership of the company pension scheme, where their contribution is matched by that of their employer. Part-timers no longer get paid breaks. A premium is paid for Saturday work, but to qualify you have to be full time. Women who work from 3 p.m. to 10 p.m. are not eligible for the night premium, even though they work for part of their shift alongside full-time women who do receive the premium. All the cleaners are employed part time, on £2.50 an hour, which is likely to leave them under the lower earnings limit and therefore with their stamps unpaid. They have to work two full years before they qualify for any paid holiday. Most staff in Sheila's store are part time, but a decade ago 'it was the other way around, with most people working full time'. Her hours on the night shift fall just two hours short of full-time status, disqualifying her from a pension contribution paid by her employer and from paid breaks or bank holidays on a pro rata basis. When she gets home from her shift she gets the children out of bed and off to school before going to bed herself. 'I can only sleep between ten and two. You get terribly tired, but you get used to it; and it's the only job where you can earn and look after the kids.' In spite of the exhaustion, Sheila insists that she wouldn't want a day job. 'My youngest is a diabetic, and I want to be there for him in case anything should happen. It means I could take them shopping or to the beach. If I had a better education and could get a better job, then maybe it would be different.'

The one advantage to working night shifts is that Sheila can earn an hourly premium of £4.99 instead of the basic £3.73. But even this added cost is a thorn in Tesco's side. 'They regard the night shift as a necessary evil,' says Sheila, 'because it costs them more than it would if they were to put us on a twilight shift between 5 p.m. and 12 p.m., with a very heavy crew and without the premium. But you can't fill shelves as fast that way if you are also open and selling. They've never ever liked nights, and they've always tried to get rid of it. There are rumours going around that they're going to try and cut down on the numbers working nights.'

In spite of the tiredness, the repetitive nature of the work and the low pay, Sheila feels that working has given her distinct advantages. 'I think that if I hadn't gone out to work, I would have accepted life differently. But work opens up different things; it has broadened my outlook, and I've made good friends and met interesting people, particularly through my work with the union. You're a vegetable if you don't go out to work. Work has showed me that I have the capacity to do more. It has changed me, and now I tell my kids, "Go and get your education, you can always use it." I'm always pushing them on to do more, because education offers choice. If I had more choices available to me, what could I be doing now?'

Because shelf fillers are in the shop only when it is closed, some workers feel they are not treated so well. 'We're forgotten about, and it's really rare that you see the manager,' says Barbara, who has four children and works at the Co-op in Exeter. 'Shelf filling is the hardest work, but on the lowest grade and the worst paid. It's heavy work, lifting all of that produce, and you have to put out so much per hour. The intensity of it is very tiring, and it can be dangerous if things fail.' Barbara is paid £3.24 an hour, while staff working on the delicatessen get £3.40. It is hard to see how managers can justify such a discrepancy, when both jobs are essential. But it is the distinction between full- and part-time workers that Barbara really resents. Ninety per cent of staff are employed for less than thirty hours a week; all of them are women, many with children. Only those few full-timers included on the nightshift get an extra £4 for working unsocial hours. The part-timers' former shift has been cut from four hours to three, and their fifteen-minute break has been cancelled. This means that in order to take home the same money, part-time women have to work an extra night.

'We do exactly the same work; it's just that they want more out of part-timers. They squeeze you, and the legislation allows them to take advantage.' When Barbara went to the manager and said they wanted the same unsocial-hours premium as the full-timers, he said no, because 'we were women and had children and it was the only time we could work, so how could we say that it was unsocial?' Daytime work is impossible because the costs of childcare are so prohibitive that 'it would cost me more than I earn'. Her manager, like countless others, knows that women in Barbara's position have no choice but to accept his conditions; many also subscribe to the myth that their wages are just pin money and therefore they can work for less. 'There is such a bad attitude to part-time work,' says Barbara. 'But with more and more people doing it, it becomes the norm. The manager simply said, "Take it or leave it; there are loads of people waiting for this sort of work. We'd be able to replace you, no trouble." '

It's particularly in retail that the use of part-time flexible contracts is increasing. Once, a firm would merely replace one leaving full-timer with a part-timer. Now, whole policies have swept into place under which some food retailers employ nobody for more than fifteen hours a week. One store in Leicester only hires people for a maximum of seven hours per week. This means that every one of their employees, bar the management, has no national insurance contributions paid. In January 1993, the Burton group announced that it was cutting 2,000 full-time jobs; the company hoped, however, that most of the staff thus made redundant would apply for the 3,000 new posts it planned to create – for part-time workers.

Many shops now keep extended opening hours, and most large supermarkets never completely close down even when not open to the public. If there are people working in a supermarket twenty-four hours a day, seven days a week, a multitude of different shift and payment systems can be disguised, with employees on shorter shifts and women attracted to night and twilight work. Some supermarkets have as many as a hundred different systems, with numerous low-paid women working less than sixteen hours a week. Staff are brought in when they are needed, for example so that every check-out till is occupied between 5.30 p.m. and 8 p.m. and over the weekends.

In order to cut their hourly pay, many Sainsbury's staff who appear full-time to the casual outsider are in fact categorized as part-timers. One, 'a section manager store instructor' who has been employed by the company for fourteen years, works from ten to six, five days a week. Most would consider this a full-time job. But because she works less than the full-time period of 39 hours a week (her breaks are not paid for), she is paid on a part-time hourly rate which, she estimates, costs her about £100 per month. Unpaid overtime is expected, as an established aspect of the work ethic. 'People try to keep to their hours,' says one staff member. 'But if you're five minutes late you get told off, and then at the end of the day you are expected to stay behind. They bollock you if you're late, but if you want to leave on time they won't let you. They give you so much responsibility in this company and then pay you shit. I work a more than fifty-hour week, rather than thirty-nine.'

Several staff agreed that roughly ten hours unpaid overtime per week was the norm. These included a baker who had recently allowed himself to be demoted because he resented working long hours for so little extra pay. Failure to comply can put your job in jeopardy, or compromise your ascent up a steep slope to management where for an extra £50 per week you can don the bovver boots and kick arse yourself. An older woman, who had worked at W. H. Smith for fifteen years, sums it up. 'I'm not well paid enough to do all this unpaid overtime. In my twenties they would have put it down to lack of motivation; but now that I'm older I feel that it's my choice as to what I do. But that pressure is very stressful for the younger ones, as the attitude from management is that if they're not prepared to put in the groundwork then why should we bother?'

In return for such treatment, every member of staff I interviewed from the rank and file – dominated by women to the point of exclusivity – seemed to take home about £130 per week. Many are young and still living at home because £130 is not enough to support you, particularly in London. The work is mind-numbingly dull and repetitive, and many of these women are capable of contributing a great deal more. The problem is that nobody wants them to. Supermarkets want lump labour to fill shelves and pass produce over electronic tills as fast as possible. Where that's all they require, the escape routes of lower-paid workers are severely limited.

When I interviewed staff at a London store, two intelligent, articulate and funny 23-year-olds sat before me, one a man, the other a woman. The man had become a manager in the bakery, working long hours for £850 per month. 'I gave it up because you just don't have any other life as you're tired, the work is so physically draining.' Having worked five years for Sainsbury's he plans to leave and do a degree in computer sciences. 'If you stay here, you're here for the rest of your life. The younger ones really want to get out, and everybody would jump at another job for more money. The trouble is, there aren't that many out there to go for.' But for his friend sitting next to him, the prospects were less rosy. She had already earned her degree in a less vocational subject and saw little prospect of either escape or promotion. 'For all they say about promotion prospects, if you're management you get it; but if you're staff you don't.'

In their access to training, according to national data (Payne, *Women Training . . .*, 1991), young women experience considerable discrimination, with opportunities reduced by one third or more in comparison with young men. They are only half as likely to get training specific to the job that they are actually doing, as many trapped in low-paid repetitive jobs know all too well. Women from ethnic minority groups are far more likely than white women to go on to higher education, but far less likely to get a job at the end of it. Black Caribbean and Indian women are twice as likely as white women to be unemployed and are therefore twice as likely as white women to be on government training schemes. The discrepancies are even wider for women working part time with only half as much access to training as those in full-time employment. Large enterprises are more likely than small ones to offer staff training. This is particularly bad news for women employed part time since they tend to be concentrated in small workplaces: 51 per cent of all such women work for firms employing fewer than twenty-four people (Clarke, *Women and Training . . .*, 1991). The *Labour Force Survey* of 1989 shows that twice as many men as women, working part time, received job-related training, even though their numbers are negligible. Such a discrepancy suggests that few men are allowed to languish in dead-end jobs for long, while the women are expected to make do.

Women dominate the service industries, which employ 88 per cent of all part-time workers – overwhelmingly in female, subordinate areas. Sixty-two per cent of health authorities restrict part-time working to lower grades; over half of NHS ancillary part-timers work under sixteen hours a week (*Equal Opportunities Review 45*, 1992). A third of all nurses work part time, 52 per cent of whom have dependent children as opposed to only 16 per cent of full-time nurses. The majority of part-time nurses are on lower grades with a half of all unqualified staff, whereas only one fifth of senior nursing grades work part time (Seccombe, *Motivation . . .*, 1992).

Anecdotal evidence suggests that part-time nurses, many with years of experience, are rarely left in charge of wards, which is a recognized way of scoring up points for promotion; they are also likely to get the routine, less interesting tasks. The number of part-time nurses is steadily increasing, as are bank nurses – temporary staff used to cover for shortages or recruitment difficulties within a particular hospital. Bank nurses have no continuity of service; so they are not covered by employment protection legislation, and they get no sick or maternity pay, nor any pension or annual leave. They are paid hourly, and although the rates vary, staff tend not to be paid in keeping with the grade of work for which they are qualified.

Most bank nurses are highly experienced, and work either to supplement their low pay, or because they are lone mothers or they find childcare costs prohibitive on a nurse's low salary. Three-quarters of them have dependent children. Bank nurses are employed directly by the NHS, 98 per cent of them part time. Agency nurses work for private concerns, and include fewer mothers and more overseas nurses wanting to earn extended stays; most are employed full time. Between 1990 and 1991 there was a 31 per cent rise in the number of bank nurses, while agency nurses decreased by approximately 40 per cent.

The price of continuing free health care may well be an increase in part-time nursing. So at least says Professor Roger Dyson of the NHS Management Executive, in his paper *Changing Labour Utilisation in the NHS Trusts* (1992). Professor Dyson maintains that with the creation of the internal market, the use of labour has to be more efficient. He makes little of casualized employment of men, but considerable reference to the increased use of contract as opposed to core labour among women. 'It offers an employee the opportunity to opt out of a standard contract based on the concept of a working week or a working month, the original of which lies in the needs of male manual workers in the nineteenth century ... If a woman with a young baby wishes to practise and maintain her professional competence at times in the day when there is family support for the child, why should that not be possible? If a mother with young school-age children wishes to work only Monday to Friday, 9.30 to 3.30, with all school holidays as leave and no commitment to out-of-hours work, why should this not be possible?'

It sounds wonderful, but what Professor Dyson merely mentions in passing is the cost of that choice – lower pay, minimal prospects or training, and diluted terms and conditions. He foresees a future where patients would be able to attend out-patient clinics and use diagnostic services outside of normal working hours. However, he acknowledges that the Whitley Council terms and conditions currently governing all health staff 'would be wholly inappropriate ... The distinction between core staff and contract staff enables the trust to work towards a flexibility that allows staffing and labour costs to vary more in proportion to patient/client flow.' The distinction between employed and bank nurses could be extended to other areas of work, with staff given 'the additional benefit of a gross fee for those who would be prepared to consider self-employed status'. While this flexibility is tenuously extended to all, women would be the principal 'beneficiaries', as the people assuming most childcare responsibilities. What Professor Dyson does not take into account is that extending this flexibility to other areas of health care would increase job segregation between the sexes, as yet more men desert satisfying vocational professions for better-paid work with more security in order to provide for their families.

What a nurse actually does on duty is also being questioned, with trendy American practices such as 'patient-focus care' being introduced to reduce the time nurses spend 'ready for action' rather than actually working. Patient-focus care seeks to make nurses more multiskilled and therefore more cost effective. It enables them to do X-rays, by bringing the equipment to the patient's bedside rather than waiting for a porter to wheel the patient off elsewhere, or, after a six-week physiotherapy course, to massage a patient rather than sitting around chatting until a trained physiotherapist arrives. All very well; but will nurses be paid more for these skills? Does it mean that if a nurse is shown how to use a scalpel she becomes a trainee surgeon? In each ward a small core of highly trained staff would have health care assistants, who would not be qualified nurses, who would change dressings and stroke brows. This would substantially reduce costs, but would it also reduce the quality of patient care, when changing dressings and stroking brows can be essential to monitoring a patient's condition?

Nurses carry on caring for patients irrespective of management restructuring, and despite theories claiming to devise new systems for the work they already do. As always, it is because so many nurses derive great pleasure from the value of their work that their commitment can be exploited. 'You can't not do your job,' says Heather Hutchinson, a sister with thirteen years' experience, in charge of an operating theatre. 'An awful lot of nurses are really committed, and they will take tons of bullshit

142

and yet still do the job. I've been through loads of management changes, but the job you actually do, saving people's lives if you like, never changes.' She feels that tighter budgets and fewer staff have made it ever harder for nurses to do a good job. 'It's real front-line stuff now, and airy-fairy notions about nursing, like patient-focus care, just don't help matters. In an operating theatre, all you have is a body on a slab. I never see an awake patient, so what use is continuity of care? We try – of course we try – we look after every patient as if they were our own mother.'

Rates of £2.50 an hour, on daily shifts of two or three hours, mean that to pay for their needs many women must work long hours, often combining several part-time jobs. Low pay makes every week a struggle, squeezing out the pennies to cover rent, bills, food, and fares to and from various workplaces. It means that women can easily get into debt, and are permanently exhausted working both day and night shifts to make ends meet. It may mean doing an early-morning cleaning job before going home to get the children off to school, and then on to a dinner-lady job, working in a shop on a low hourly rate, followed by bar work at night, when other members of the family can be relied on for childcare. Carol works 32½ hours a week for four different employers in Birmingham, none of whom pays a national insurance contribution on her behalf. Overall, she takes home £76.98: for working as a part-time cook in two pubs, as a sales assistant in a greengrocer's shop and as a cleaner. Two pounds an hour rewards efforts which are necessary, valuable even, to her various employers. Yet her labour is considered by the state to be unworthy of any registration, monitoring or accountability. In both pubs she cooks, serves the customers and washes up. At the greengrocer's, 'For five and a half hours I serve, restock and clean with just a half-hour break for lunch. I wonder what the hell I've done to deserve this lot. I am totally exhausted, but I still have to run a home and care for a husband and two children.'

Carol is one of the millions of invisible working women in

this country whose efforts help to turn the wheels of industry and commerce. But the state does not consider her important enough to qualify for employment protection nor for entry into our contributory benefits system. Such exploitation, of Dickensian proportions, flies in the face of all pretence that women now enjoy equal opportunity with men. Out of approximately 17 million women of working age in Britain, nearly 3 million earn such low wages that they disappear from the national statistical database. Imagine nearly 20 per cent of Britain's available working men unaccounted for by our tax system. Questions would be raised in the house about tax evasion, about poverty, about altering our tax and benefits system. It would become a matter of urgency to know more about actual standards of living, rather than encouraging people to live as scavengers.

Poor women, poor children

Most of Britain's poor are women. When they are also mothers, their children too are poor. The number of women living in poverty – defined as income below 50 per cent of the mean after housing costs – has risen, according to government figures, from 2.2 million in 1979 to 5.8 million in 1988 (*Independent*, 24 June 1992). This is due in part to the rapid increase of women in low-paid work, while average pay differentials between men and women have barely shifted. The Child Poverty Action Group estimated in 1987 that roughly 4.5 million women and 3.2 million men were living on or below supplementary benefit levels. Meanwhile, the top 10 per cent enjoyed a real rise in income of 46 per cent between 1979 and 1989 (Written Answers, 26 Oct 1992).

Taking their family responsibilities seriously can also push women towards poverty. In a low-income family if it is the woman who manages the budget she is readily tempted to put her own needs last. If casual, unaccountable and low-paid work is easily available, the prospect of a few hours here or there for extra pounds to buy food or children's clothes can be irresistible. But the growth in such methods of working has widened the gap between the rich, with households living on two reasonable salaries plus perks, and the poor, where a couple live on one low male salary or unemployment benefit, plus whatever casual work the woman can squeeze into her day. This in turn has contributed to spatial as well as individual poverty in Britain. Those who can afford it move out of run-down areas, leaving the poor to sink irretrievably on decaying estates in areas of low employment. Mothers like Decia, a playgroup worker whose husband is unemployed, long to move out in order to give their children a better future. 'Home itself is ideal, because it feels cosy; but it needs to be in another area. I'm not happy with what's happening outside; I get worried about my eldest son, because there are so many drugs around, and I'd rather he didn't have to see it so often. I'd like money to be a little easier, but I am managing because I organize. In January I start getting drinks in for Christmas; by June I've sorted out who's having what for Christmas, and then by October I've only got three presents to get, so I can manage it. But moving is only possible if we were to get a transfer, and I don't hold out much hope of that.' If low-paid women are not trapped on estates, they are likely to be stranded in the country, where facilities are poorest. Only one third of Britain's driving licences are held by women. Consequently they rely more on public transport services, which have been substantially cut in many rural areas. A Rural Development Commission Survey found that the ten counties where female incomes are lowest comprise rural districts in which women are likely to be single, elderly and living on the state pension.

Such poverty also leads to an inadequate diet and bad overall health. The average increase in the incidence of TB between 1987 and 1991 was 10 per cent, but over just the first two of those years it increased among young women by 15 per cent. TB is particularly prevalent in the poorest inner-city areas such as, in London, Hackney and Tower Hamlets. In addition to poverty, stress has an effect on the general health of women. Trying to be all things to everyone, suffering the medical complications and exhaustion of motherhood, or caring for a sick or aged relative all lead to illness and depression on an enormous scale. In the sixteen to forty-four age group women consult their GPs nearly twice as often as men do (*General Household Survey 1991*, HMSO, 1993), frequently as a last resort, having dismissed every symptom as merely a 'women's problem' in order to carry on regardless. Women accordingly depend upon the health service more than men, and are worse affected by any cuts that it suffers.

Yet it is society's refusal to reward women adequately for the work they do that helps whittle away their self-esteem and provokes ill-health. Women who repeatedly consult a doctor are more apt than men to be regarded as hypochondriac, rather than as having a condition which has not been correctly diagnosed. They are twice as likely as men to be diagnosed as suffering from clinical depression, and more readily admitted to a psychiatric hospital. Two-thirds of all psychotropic drugs are prescribed to women, largely on the assumption that little can be done to improve the patient's lot other than make the symptoms more bearable. Men are more likely to be referred on for therapy, implying the possibility of cure.

Pursuing a career on male terms has inevitably imposed on women a number of 'male' stress-related ailments such as heart disease. But female heart patients, even when more disabled than men, are less likely to be offered open-heart surgery (*British Medical Journal*, 30 April 1993). Growing hospital waiting-lists affect women in any case more than men, given their longer expectation of life. Meanwhile the specialisms of heart- or neurosurgery have shorter waiting times than those for unglamorous operations such as the removal of cataracts or hip replacement.

Yet all discussion of delayed referrals ignores the predominant sufferings of elderly women.

Within much of the benefits system, women are also 'invisible', falling through the net designed to prevent the worst forms of poverty. They form the majority of those claiming non-contributory social security and means-tested benefits, which are of lower value than contributory benefits. Our social security system assumes that work means paid work, and that the family unit is based on a male breadwinner and a female dependant. As a result, women, like men, must work without any break in their national insurance contributions in order to qualify for unemployment benefit or even, in some cases, a state pension. Women were only 32 per cent of those claiming unemployment benefit in 1990, and 63 per cent of those on income support. In 1991, 3.2 million women – but only 2 million men – depended on means-tested income support and lower value benefits (Lister, *Women's Economic Dependency . . .*, 1992). No more than 15 per cent of female old-age pensioners were entitled in that year to a full pension. One third got nothing at all, mainly because they'd been unable to maintain a full contributions record while raising children. There is a substantial rise in the numbers of women paid less than the lower earnings limit for national insurance contributions, and hence with even greater poverty to look forward to in their old age. It is impossible to justify such institutionalized discrimination with the fiction that men can or do entirely support their women and children. Among women of working age, over 70 per cent are in paid employment and more than a million households are lone-parent families headed by women. An image persists of women as secondary earners, who can somehow make do with less money because they need less food, don't like going to the pub and are marvellous at turning a piece of old cloth into a ballgown. The implication is that all women get access to an adequate income through their partners, being almost certainly lucky enough to have found one worth having.

147

Why should women be poorer in old age as the reward of raising children for no pay? Two and a quarter million women currently earn too little to contribute towards their state pension. With a one in three divorce rate, what will they live on when they retire? Their husband's income? As yet divorce is not a common experience among pensioners; but it's likely to become so with a projected figure by 2025 of a 13 per cent divorce rate (Joshi, *Pension Consequences . . .*, 1990). Ex-wives may well be awarded half of the value of the family home, but they have only just won the right to half of their husband's occupational pension scheme for the period when they were married. The pension companies have resisted this change by arguing that it will cost them that much more to administer. The ethical question of what these women should live on in their half a house, when they have no pension scheme of their own because they have raised the man's children rather than working, doesn't seem to enter the equation. In any event, there will be no recompense for the thousands of ex-wives who have already lost out financially because the decision to split the man's pension on divorce will not be retrospective.

Personal pension schemes are of limited value to women, when they can be on low incomes for long periods, or out of the labour market completely, caring for children or the old. Occupational pension schemes favour men because they have higher earnings, fewer gaps in employment and are more likely to work for an employer who provides a good pension scheme. In 1991, 61 per cent of men belonged to their company's occupational pension scheme, as opposed to only 55 per cent of full-time working women and only 17 per cent of part-time female employees (*General Household Survey*, 1987). In 1988, 46 per cent of single women and only 15 per cent of married women pensioners were receiving occupational pensions, and the amounts they were receiving were significantly lower than those received by men. If a male pensioner on an occupational pension becomes a widower, his income remains the same. But if he dies first, most schemes reduce the widow's payments by roughly a third. She can make do with less to live on now that he is dead, whereas he, when alone, would it seems have needed the original full amount.

Until the recent EC ruling on equalizing access to company pension schemes, most official part-timers were excluded from company pension schemes, even though fairness dictates that they should be allowed entry with their contributions matched by their employers on a pro rata basis. The days of people joining a company for life are over. Men as well as women now work for a variety of employers, and breaks in employment, or a variety of flexible contracts, are increasingly commonplace. It is essential that we adapt our welfare state and our employment practices accordingly to make them fairer and to prevent increased polarization by gender of pension resources, especially given an ageing population. Many of these women will be those currently earning poor wages, with next to no private pension insurance and erratic national insurance contributions. Conversely the majority of these older men will be protected by occupational schemes.

Only two small groups of women escape the present pension trap: childless women with similar employment patterns to men, and mothers who return to work full time soon after the birth of their children. Once again a crucial aspect of Britain's infrastructure refuses to take account of differences between the lives of men and women. Wilful blindness on the part of our social security system to the needs of women is condemning millions of women to poverty in their old age while significantly larger numbers of men can look forward to retirement in relative affluence. Once again the assumption is that enough men moved by gentlemanly honour will make themselves available to look after the poorer sex. This assumes too much. More perniciously, these discriminatory policies allow men the power to decide whom they provide for, whereas women are prevented from determining their future on an equal footing with men. While reluctant to give women credit where credit is due, the social security system leaps at any opportunity that can afford savings. With elimination of the one female privilege of early retirement at sixty, women will now have to wait an extra five years for their pension. The estimated savings are considerable – approximately £4 billion per year (*Independent*, 13 April 1993). Being able to draw their pension earlier had compensated women to some extent for its being lower. But rather than equalizing the retirement age at sixty-three, the government has taken advantage of a lack of resistance to rip women off. 'Women are aware that opposing the change, after demanding equality in other spheres of life, would leave them open to accusations of hypocrisy,' said an *Independent* leader in April 1993. 'The Government has spotted the weakness and according to inspired leaks is poised to exploit it.'

Because it is women who primarily take responsibility for the young, the assumption is that they can also be prevailed upon to look after the sick and the old. There are approximately 6 million carers in Britain. Of these, the one million caring for someone else full time tend to be on small incomes, since they cannot work, and are living on savings and benefits. They also have costs such as extra heating and laundry bills, as well as one-off expenses in adapting their homes to cater for their dependant's disability. Three-quarters of these carers are women; the men are mostly pensioners looking after their wives. If the men are younger, higher average male salaries allow them more choice in buying in extra help. There's usually the wife, too, who might be prevailed upon to look after his family as well as her own.

People often choose to care full time because they want to be there for their relatives when they are needed; they wish to cherish a loved one who is terminally ill, or they seek to provide loving care and company for an older parent who once looked after them. They often sacrifice their careers, quickly becoming de-skilled; they suffer extreme exhaustion, sometimes to the detriment of their own health; and though they get little in return they save the state a fortune in institutional care. It has been estimated that carers save the state between fifteen and twenty-four billion pounds each year in community care costs (*Family Policy . . . Bulletin No 6*, 1989). That figure is likely to rise considerably once the government's 'Care in the Community' policy takes hold, and as more parents live on into their eighties. The double burden of juggling work and motherhood could extend well after our children are adults, for just as offspring are old enough to leave home, our parents are sufficiently aged to fall ill and become dependent. If, as predicted, there will be fewer resources to care for our ageing population, it is the family who will have to take increasing responsibility for its old, and that means women. By pursuing policies which encourage part-time work among women, the government can argue that these 'flexible' workers can just as well turn from raising their young to looking after their old. Only women with full-time professional careers and higher salaries will be better able to buy in help.

In spite of the savings they represent to the welfare state, and the gruelling, incessant nature of their work, carers are entitled only to the invalid care allowance, which is considerably lower than unemployment benefit or the state pension. In 1988 the rules were changed. National insurance credits paid with the invalid care allowance were no longer to count on their own towards unemployment benefit. This means that former full-time workers who have been unable to earn cannot claim unemployment benefit when they finish caring. Invalid care allowance ceases immediately, even though the person they were caring for may well have died. There is no period of grace for grief or adjustment. If the welfare state can no longer support all its dependants, these hardships dictate that adequate support should be given to carers in the community: for the most part, women.

The silence of the state in this respect speaks volumes. Meanwhile the benefits system's blindness to women's specific needs and difference will persist while women are absent from public decision-making, and for as long as the typical family is seen as having a male breadwinner. Little good would come of changing unemployment benefit to a private insurance system along the occupational pension model. Without allowance for interrupted work patterns, women would still lose out, for the same reasons that they currently fail to benefit from a private pension. Women trapped on benefits because they have young children should be allowed to earn a decent wage without losing the bulk of their income on childcare. So long as women form the majority of the low paid and the poor, government and policymakers have a duty to address their needs as distinct from the needs of men; and until an effort is made to do so, the welfare of women is likely to be overlooked.

While it is true that many women actively seek part-time work to be on hand for their families, it is also the case that recent legislation has deliberately encouraged the growth of this flexible, low-paid and poorly protected work in traditionally female sectors of employment.

Professional carers have seen their pay and conditions substantially reduced as a direct result of the National Health Service and Community Care Act of 1990. Under these regulations, local authorities must provide much of their community care services through contracts with voluntary and private-sector organizations. To win these contracts, pay and, in particular, conditions of employment are being forced down, a pressure made easier by the fact that once again most of these organizations employ women. Citizens' Advice Bureaux around the country cite worrying evidence of this trend. A woman with twenty-one years' experience as a part-time home help for a local authority in Kent was called for interview and required to sign a new contract. This made considerable changes to her hours, changed her place of work, and put more emphasis on nursing care. An employee of a private nursing home in South Wales had her contract changed when the home was taken over by new owners. They increased her hours and reduced her entitlement to holiday pay. A woman in a private residential-care home with no written contract found herself working anything from six to seventeen and a half hours a day, wearing different hats depending on her employers' needs, from assistant matron to cook.

Subcontracting, and the 'Redundant' Wages Councils

The policy of subcontracting as many public services as possible to the private sector, where market forces are allowed to reign supreme, has a direct effect primarily on women's pay and conditions. Local authorities and businesses all over the country are trying to reduce their costs by contracting out all functions outside their principal business activities. Avoiding overheads such as pensions and national insurance contributions amounts effectively to reductions in the rate of pay. While these should theoretically cut equally across both sectors, in reality earnings have declined according to gender. Companies need high-quality financial planning in order to make more money, and talent in this field is highly sought after and well paid. Cleaning, catering or typing needs the minimum of training; payment for them can be forced down, and standards sacrificed. You can water down the detergent or give schoolchildren a cheaper cut of chip, but the fundamental cost of these services is labour, female labour.

Private contractors accordingly seek to squeeze down pay by employing large numbers of women on flexible contracts.

Employment practices which might be considered unseemly if used by a reputable company or a local authority can be hidden behind the huge swamp theory of market forces. If services are subcontracted, the ultimate employers can wash their hands of all responsibility for most of the staff and simply pay the bill. MGM/Cannon cinemas made all the cleaners in their 130 cinemas redundant in January 1993 so that a contract cleaning company could do the job more cheaply. Head office at the Inland Revenue have contracted out all their typing and secretarial services to the private firm Blue Arrow. The latter's main area of expansion is negotiating contracts for the management of whole sectors of employment, rather than just providing individual staff. Three-quarters of Blue Arrow workers are women, mostly on temporary contracts without benefits such as sick or holiday pay.

When many local authorities put out their cleaning and catering to compulsory competitive tendering, the lowest bid receives the job irrespective of the service provided. For this reason labour costs have had to be reduced in order to propose attractive bids. This has been done either through direct reduction in wages, or by employing fewer people to do the same amount of work. Often such contracts are won by the existing cleaning or catering workers within a local authority or health service. This does not necessarily mean that the conditions of the women they employ are any better. The use of part-time and casual labour, with deteriorating pay and conditions, has increased irrespective of whether the contract has been won 'in house' (Citizens' Advice Bureaux, *Job Insecurity*, 1993), as shown by evidence from Citizens' Advice Bureaux around the country. A woman who had worked for six years in a school canteen in Kent was informed by her new employers when the contract was put out to tender that all employees would have to accept new, 'less generous' contractual terms. When domestic services at a hospital in Greater Manchester were likewise tendered, employees had to reapply, to the successful company, for their jobs. Those who were accepted had their hourly pay cut and their holiday entitlement reduced. Cleaners at an East London school were promised the same working conditions when the school opted out of local authority control if they resigned and took up employment with the new cleaning contractors. They were given yearly contracts, and when these were renewed after the first year their hours and pay were reduced.

A key equal-pay case, brought by three dinner ladies against North Yorkshire County Council, is currently challenging the notion of market forces as sufficient argument for cutting women's pay and conditions. When school catering was put up for compulsory competitive tendering, the council service won the first bid, meanwhile paying the same rates to its employees. But it lost the second bid to a private contractor paying much less to an exclusively female workforce. In order to win the remaining contracts, the general manager decided to cut his female employees' pay by 10 per cent, and to reduce their hours from twenty per week to fourteen. This brought their hourly pay below the lower earnings limit for national insurance contributions, and excluded the dinner ladies from employment protection. The women working for the council catering service were sacked, and re-employed on these new contracts; meanwhile the pay and conditions of male employees remained broadly the same. Given that the men mainly worked as managers, and that the majority of the catering staff were female, substantial cuts could be made to the overall costs of labour; subsequently the council catering service won the contract. The dinner ladies won their case, at an industrial tribunal in 1992. In the following year, however, North Yorkshire County Council obtained a divided ruling at an employment appeal tribunal, which said that the original ruling had not been clear in interpreting the law. The dinner ladies backed by their union, NUPE, will now be taking their case to the court of appeal.

The one protection formerly offered to the very low-paid was the wages councils. These councils were eliminated in the Trade Union Reform and Employment Rights Bill in 1993, even though there had been no such proposal in the government's election manifesto just a few months earlier. Britain's wages councils represented some 2.5 million people, comprising one in eight of the workforce, more than 80 per cent of them women. They guaranteed a minimum rate of between £2.60 and £3.20 an hour for employees working in retail, hotels and catering, in toy and clothing manufacturing, and in hairdressing and laundries. Employers caught paying below the legal minimum wage could be prosecuted; in fact they rarely were. In 1991, 5,205 establishments were found to be underpaying their staff, but only seventeen were prosecuted (Written Answers, 12 November 1992). Disturbingly, the wages councils' power was quietly depleted over the years, so that they could then be shown publicly to be almost useless. In 1970 they had 177 inspectors; by 1992 there were only fifty.

But though the rates guaranteed were low, and infringements rarely punished, at least there was a publicly stated minimum below which workers' pay should not fall. Some two-thirds of those employed in wages council industries were earning a little more than the minimum rate, which suggests that many employers not only knew of the law but wanted to abide by it. Minimum rates for those workers meant everything: they knew they could complain to their employer, and then to outside bodies for assistance, with the law on their side. Now they have nothing to rely on but the goodwill of their employer, and if low-paid workers could be treated badly while the wages councils were in existence, it is probable now that pay and conditions can only deteriorate.

The government had two unsophisticated and contradictory arguments for the abolition of the wages councils. Firstly, if so many employees were being paid above the legal minimum rate, then wages councils must no longer be necessary, their mere existence an 'anachronism'. 'The world of 1992 is very different to that of 1909. Low-paid workers are today covered by a vast array of benefits' (Conservative Research Department paper quoted in Parliamentary debate, 28 January 1993). The second argument was that wages councils were a barrier to employment – were indeed helping to increase unemployment – and that low pay was better than no job at all. No one has offered to explain how they can be redundant at the same time as fixing pay at an unacceptably high rate.

Political justification behind the scenes for their abolition was more pernicious yet. In a letter to the chair of the EOC, the then Secretary of State for Employment, Gillian Shephard, wrote, 'Most wages council workers work part time, contributing a second income to the family home' (Parliamentary debate, 28 January 1993). Why does Mrs Shephard, who had the job title of Minister for Women tagged on to her already busy schedule, think that working part-time makes these female workers less important? This suggests that a second income is considered less significant than the primary, male, income and therefore does not need regulation, whatever the minister's alleged support for principles of equal opportunity or the Equal Pay Act. Similarly: 'Most of the workers covered by wages councils are not poor,' according to a letter from the Minister of State at the Department of Employment to the Group Secretary of the Transport and General Workers Union. 'Many work part-time and live in households with two or more earners. Evidence shows that there is no close link between the wages rates of such workers and their household's total income.' Evidently you are still not poor when travelling to work and a sandwich at lunch time cost you two hours' wages. What is clear is that a woman's income is still not considered essential to the welfare of her family, even though for many families it is the earnings of the woman that lift them out of poverty.

It is because most low-paid workers are women that government allows rates of pay formerly covered by wages councils to be forced down. The matter of low pay has fallen between two stools, in the view of Chris Pond of the Low Pay Unit. The women's movement has largely ignored it, thinking, misguidedly, that low pay was a concern for the trade-union movement, 'while the trade unions have ignored the issue, because of their own blindness and misogyny. There has been little effective resistance other than over the amorality of the whole issue.' At the standing committee discussing clause 28, under which the wages councils were to be abolished on 28 January 1993, opposition MPs defended the councils' existence with reason, passion and vigour. Their proposition was to postpone the abolition at least until further research had been conducted on its likely effects. It is easy to destroy something, but so hard to fill the ensuing gap. At first government was only prepared to cite alleged effects on unemployment. But at length Angela Eagle MP asked Michael Forsyth, the Minister for Employment, 'Will the Minister tell me how low he is prepared to see wages fall? According to neo-classical economics and the equilibrium of pay and jobs there is nothing to stop wage rates falling to zero depending on where the demand and supply curves are drawn.' When she received no reply, she continued, 'I see that no Conservative member of the committee is prepared to stand up and say how low it is appropriate for wages to fall. We must assume, therefore, that Conservative members have no view on the matter and that, as far as they are concerned, wages can fall to zero. If they can find someone prepared to work for that rate, that rate can be paid. The logical extension of the neo-classic theory, which seems to be their motivation, would be slavery.' Michael Forsyth replied: 'The idea that, because we believe that wage levels and terms and conditions are best agreed between employers and employees as free agents, we are in favour of slavery, is absurd. The Hon. Lady appears puzzled by the notion that there might be jobs that people are prepared to carry out for no wage. She has only to look at the many volunteers, without whom our caring services would be lost.' Once again women can be relied upon to work for nothing, secondary citizens with a secondary, almost non-existent, wage. It insults not only those struggling on poverty wages, caring for the young, the sick and the dying; it's also dismissive of women's equal right to a reasonable income for the work they do.

There is nothing to show that in most European countries a minimum wage has led to greater unemployment. There is evidence, however, that its existence has helped to narrow the pay differences between women and men. Britain stands alone among European countries in its lack of a statutory minimum wage; it also has the highest earnings differential between the sexes. Under the wages councils, the lowest-paid manual workers had a difference in pay between the sexes of 12 per cent less than in other industries (*Narrowing the Gender Pay Gap*, 1993). It is interesting to contrast the clothing industry, covered by the wages councils, with the – unregulated – hosiery industry. In clothing the average hourly earnings of women were 82.5 per cent of the male wage, with average weekly pay at 80.2 per cent, whereas in hosiery the figures were 63.3 per cent and 71 per cent respectively.

The wages councils were never ideal, but they conformed utterly to principles of equal pay, rather than pay determined by segregation of sector. They also provided women and men, and organizations such as the Citizens' Advice Bureaux, with a place to air their complaints. By abolishing the wages councils we have destroyed the last refuge of retribution for the low paid. As Winston Churchill said in 1909 when arguing for the establishment of the Trades Boards, as the original wages councils, 'Where you have . . . no organization, no parity of bargaining, the good employer is undercut by the bad and the bad employer is undercut by the worst. Where these conditions prevail you have not a condition of progress but a condition of progressive degradation.'

Contracting out of services and the abolition of the wages councils both undermine the principle, enshrined in law, of equal pay for work of equal value. The pay of the three dinner ladies in North Yorkshire had been established initially as an equal rate under the job evaluation scheme. Nonetheless reducing their pay was not accompanied by cuts in the earnings of those few men also working within the catering section. The employers' argument for cutting the women's pay is that, if they lose their appeal, they will have to make all 1300 of their dinner ladies redundant. Why should it be the women who have to choose between lower rates of pay or no job at all, merely to indulge the notion of market forces? How too is the principle of equal pay so volatile that it can be so incidentally taken away?

Far fewer men than women suffer from the consequences of abolishing the wages councils. Removing them is a discriminatory act. If part-time workers have secondary status in law, as well as less pay than full-timers in proportion to the hours they do, and if the majority of those workers are women, such practices are potential discrimination on the grounds of sex, supposedly outlawed in Britain. We are living at a time when, at one end of the spectrum, personnel managers go on courses to learn how to get the best out of their staff or 'human resources'. At the other end, low-paid women are stripped of their dignity because they have no choice. The government's policy of negligible affordable childcare, and reducing the costs of flexible female labour, sit cosily hand in hand.

Barbara's husband came to pick her up one night from the local supermarket where she had been filling shelves with cans of pet food. This was arduous work, and he was shocked. 'Have you had to shift all that?' he said in disbelief. 'But that's nearly as much work as men do on a building site,' speaking with knowledge gained as a construction worker. He told Barbara that he wouldn't have done it, and that she should give it up: 'You're being exploited.' She said: 'But while I am being exploited, we

desperately need the money, and I suppose it's a bit of freedom.'
The difference is that Barbara's husband sees he has a choice,
while she knows that she doesn't.

It is true enough that women have to stand up and demand
what is rightly theirs. But institutional discrimination of this
magnitude renders many working women powerless. They are
the new victims, ignored and misunderstood by the very men and
women of the articulate middle classes who now claim that
equality of opportunity is with us, and who declare that it is only
a question of time before women in general can make it on merit.
A woman on low pay can ask for more money. But she is unlikely
to get it, and risks losing her job by doing so. There is always
another poor woman willing to fill her shoes, to squeeze in an
extra part-time job to pay that bill or buy her children new shoes
for the winter. The belief that part-time workers are secondary
has allowed employers to pretend that their needs can justly be
denied, when in their heart of hearts they know such employees to
be essential to their own increased wealth.

The work achieved by a part-timer is every bit as good as that
of a full-timer; they just work fewer hours and are punished for it.
Lyn Wainwright has worked for the Co-op bank in Manchester
for twelve years, running the office administration in the corporate lending division. She recently converted to part-time
work, three days a week, because of a serious illness. She is one of
the lucky part-time employees in this country who actually enter
the PAYE statistics, being paid the same pro rata salary as
full-timers, with the same terms and conditions. 'I do all of the
donkey work, wading through the paperwork and picking out
the information they require; and then someone else presents this
in a glossy package, and gets the credit for it. The work I do in
three days is of the best quality, better than someone who works
seven days a week. There's more to life than your job; and if you
do nothing but your job, you must be very narrow-minded, so
you can't be doing your job very well.'

It is time we removed the distinction between full- and part-time status. All sorts of people should be encouraged to work less, for the sake of greater equality of opportunity between men and women, and a more even spread of available jobs. We want fathers to be with their children for more than a few hours at the weekends, when they are almost too tired to read the newspapers. We need men and women to see each other for more than ten exhausted minutes at the end of each day if they are to maintain their relationship and give their children a sense of stability and continuity; for children need fathers, good fathers. Above all, natural justice dictates that people should be paid fairly for their work and enjoy equal access to benefits on a pro rata basis.

Women do not choose low-paid repetitive part-time work with no promotion prospects because they want to lead boring lives and be poor. They are vulnerable, especially when they have children, because new employment law and changing work practices actively encourage recruitment of a lump female flexible labour force. There is no reason why a skilled and talented woman should not enjoy the same pay, working conditions and promotion prospects as her full-time colleagues. As Dr Helen Mason of Cambridge University says, 'To improve the lot of part-time women is not positive discrimination, which we in Britain are so suspicious of; it is equal opportunities, which we say we already have.' She is echoed by an Industrial Relations Services study of pay and gender: 'Our research suggests that the use of flexible and market-based pay and the willingness of an organisation to adopt different approaches to the pay of different groups of employees has probably served to widen gender differences in recent years' (IRS/EOC, *Pay and Gender* . . ., 1992.) Overall a handful of well-paid women, working full-time in the male-dominated professions, marginally narrows the differential. They also disguise a widening of differences in pay between the sexes lower down the scale.

The wages councils had been in many ways potentially impotent before they were abolished. But they had been allowed to become that way through deliberate reduction of their resources, at a time when there were three times as many workplaces for their inspectors to investigate as there had been in 1979. If we can get rid of the wages councils so easily, what comes next for the chop? The right to compensation for unfair dismissal? The Equal Pay Act? Our equality legislation is made all the more precarious, as we shall see in the next chapter, by deep prejudice and an unnecessarily complicated set of regulations. The Equal Pay Act is one of the most important legal developments for women since they acquired the vote in 1918. It must not be allowed to run down to the point of uselessness and then disappear, in the same way as the wages councils. But perhaps it is already too late; for if the law of market forces does rule supreme, why attempt to bolster up women's pay when it can so effectively be pushed down?

chapter six

the
equality
industry

We have employment legislation which encourages low-paid part-time work, coupled with a lack of affordable childcare. We have a full-time work ethic which ostracizes mothers and ignores the needs of children. The number of women able to enter the higher-paid professions is also limited, by the proverbial glass ceiling, a barrier essential to a highly segregated work force in which women are paid less than men whatever job they do. All of this guarantees a cheap source of lump labour, so that it is hard to see how women will ever achieve economic independence. More than twenty years of equality legislation has done little to shift the substantial difference in men's and women's earnings. There has been no change in the gap between the gross average hourly earnings of men and women working in industry between 1983 and 1989, and while the average overall pay gap between men and women has narrowed a little, the difference between the pay of most men and women on average or poorer incomes has in fact widened. The Sex Discrimination and Equal Pay Acts are supposed to protect women's interests, but in practice these pieces of legislation are virtually unworkable. The majority of women in Britain are denied access to them, and those few who can pursue their claim for equal pay for work of equal value find their case hampered by unnecessarily complicated regulations.

A woman who presses a claim under the equality legislation must exert a superhuman effort to have even a hope of success. The statistics are shocking. In 1990/91, out of a total of 12,423 cases, just 319 sex discrimination and 198 equal pay claims went to an industrial tribunal. Such a low ratio could suggest that there is no discrimination any more. A closer look reveals that most women who could benefit from taking action either lack financial backing from their trade union or the EOC, or cannot afford to bring their own cases. There is no legal aid available for cases considered by industrial tribunal. In 1991, success evaded all but seventy-eight of the sex discrimination cases, and just ten of the claims to equal pay. By contrast, roughly half of all unfair dismissal cases are won. Nonetheless, 1991 was a good year, comparatively speaking, for in the decade since the Equal Pay Act was amended to include work of equal value there have been just twenty-two successful cases. Largely at fault is the rarity with which men and women work alongside each other in the same jobs. As it is, women are consistently underrated for the work they do, so that an Act is essential if equal pay for work of equal value is ever really to be enforced.

Our existing equality legislation is one self-defeating influence among many which box off 'women's' issues from the needs of society as a whole. Others include equal-opportunity policies and personnel, women's units, and quangos such as the Women's National Commission. An entire industry has mushroomed around the principle of equal opportunity; but rarely are the individuals working in it given the resources, or enough influence at the heart of decision-making within companies, to bring about any effective change. When these people fail, as they are often bound to do, women as a gender are blamed for neglecting to seize their apparent opportunity, rather than blame a system that refused to integrate them fully into working life.

It is easy to assume that unequal pay, discrimination on the grounds of sex, and dismissal for pregnancy have been eliminated at a stroke simply because such practices are now illegal. Only when women try to use the law do they discover how few rights they really have and how ineffective the laws and equal-opportunity policies to protect their interests actually are. Being new, the Sex Discrimination and Equal Pay Acts lack decades of precedent to clarify meaning and, by osmosis, to challenge old assumptions. We have laws as ancient as the Ten Commandments against murder and theft; but that doesn't mean no one gets killed or robbed, or that all perpetrators of these crimes are caught. But there is a popular conscience about such transgressions; they offend common morality, and committing them casts a person into social exile. Breaching the equality legislation comes at the bottom of the league table of wrongs. A great many people, particularly in middle age or onwards, believe in the survival of the traditional family unit, along with the new myths surrounding the rise of the working woman, namely that for each woman who works there is an unemployed man, and that a man's sole source of pride is his pay packet. Such falsehoods can mitigate the illegality of paying a man more than a woman, or of dismissing a woman because she is pregnant. Most people indeed do not clearly understand what it means to discriminate. The definition is woolly, and can easily be justified – in recruitment practices by 'we wanted somebody who would fit in', in promotion by 'there just aren't the women around to pick from', and in unequal pay by 'this is the market rate for the job'.

Cases under the equality legislation are judged by industrial tribunals comprising three members: a lawyer in the chair and a representative each from the CBI and the trades union movement. This system copies one set up to solve industrial relations disputes, but is not adequate in cases complicated by gender. The trades union movement, the CBI, or for that matter the legal profession, are not renowned for exemplary dealings with women employees, nor is there any statutory requirement for a woman to be part of the judging triumvirate. Tribunal members are often older, indeed retired, with limited understanding of issues today facing younger people; and they show a tendency to belittle the experiences of the women before them, on the assumption of a woman's work and income being secondary to those of a man.

The industrial tribunal system was set up to allow ordinary people access to justice without the prohibitive costs of legal representation, and in the absence of a right to legal aid. However, pay discrimination cases are particularly complicated. This is partly because of specific regulations governing equal value claims, but it's also because the employer has an unfair advantage in the number of defences available before the facts of the case are actually heard. It is extremely difficult to bring a protracted case under the equality legislation, let alone win one, without legal representation. In 1991, the EOC received 17,363 enquiries from the public; but provided legal assistance to only 161 cases. The commission was established with responsibility for 'enforcing, promoting and developing equality of opportunity between women and men' (*Annual Report 1991*). However, even that right was challenged by the appeal court during the EOC's recent attempt to remove the secondary status of part-time workers from the Employment Protection Act. The commission was told it had no right to bring a case of judicial review against the Secretary of State for Employment. Its correct role was to assist the cases of individual women through the tribunal system. The EOC has limited funds to do this; besides which, winning any such case does nothing to improve the lot of countless other women in the same position.

It is hardly surprising that the commission is careful to select cases for backing which will clarify or test the law by precedent. The EOC no longer backs pregnancy dismissal cases, even though formal complaints and a mass of anecdotal evidence suggest that ever more women are victims of this illegality. 'The legislation is supposed to be simple enough for men and women to take on board. If they can't do that without our help, then there is something wrong,' says Sheila Wild of the EOC's legal department. Something certainly is amiss, for proving a case of dismissal for pregnancy is so complicated that few are likely to succeed. The EOC now send out DIY packs to women who fear this is the reason why they have been dismissed. These packs contain the guidelines and requisite forms, with examples of the case law, written in legal jargon guaranteed to put off all but the most educated or angry.

The trades unions, like the EOC, have limited resources for litigation. They too select cases carefully, preferring to use the threat of litigation when negotiating terms and conditions that can quickly benefit large numbers of women. Employers know that unions are reluctant to dedicate dwindling resources to fighting one-off equality cases through the courts; in any case many working women do not belong to a trade union. Those most open to abuse and exploitation are also the women least able to seek justice from laws and a court system set up largely for their benefit.

Should a woman succeed as a result of her gruelling ordeal by litigation, compensation is minimal. Until the European Court of Justice ruling of August 1993, there was a statutory ceiling of £11,000 on compensation awarded by an industrial tribunal. In fact the average award in 1991 was £1,142 – roughly £700 below the equivalent recompense for race discrimination and unfair dismissal. Literally, it adds an insult to any figurative injury. The most an employer has to do is pay the fine and walk away. Many do not even offer that compensation, forcing the woman to instruct another solicitor to chase the money, this time at her own cost. The tribunal has no statutory powers to order the woman's reinstatement, or the avoidance of further abuse through training managers or monitoring staff ratios. One woman's success in proving discrimination at an industrial tribunal does nothing to set a wider precedent. All it does is prove that a particular individual has been wronged. The contrast with libel cases is irresistible. In compensation for the libel, so-called, of homosexuality, Jason Donovan was deemed to need £70,000. A woman who has undergone daily harassment, abuse or loss of earnings through thwarted opportunity at work must be content with £1,500. Cases in the UK have, however, been affected by pressure from the European Court of Justice to raise the statutory ceiling of compensation. Two women were recently awarded £33,000 and £22,000 against the Ministry of Defence for dismissal for pregnancy. Higher awards immediately made their stories newsworthy; they also highlighted the considerable costs potentially incurred through discrimination by the ministry and therefore by the taxpayer, given that thousands of women had already been blatantly dismissed from our armed forces when they became pregnant.

The threat of litigation could yet be an effective deterrent were compensation higher, not just for pregnancy dismissal, but for all cases involving discrimination, as it is in the United States where the maximum limit was recently raised to $300,000. This would also enable professional women who felt they had been wronged to hire their own lawyers, if they thought there was more to gain. Most women simply ignore or belittle their experiences, or move on to another job if they cannot tolerate their working conditions. At present only the saintly or the insane are likely to risk all to prove an injustice by going through the lengthy, stressful and often isolating experience of the tribunal system. They are also unlikely still to have, or want, the same job at the end of their ordeal.

Kathleen Wheeler has worked for the London Ambulance

Service since 1975, training drivers. She applied for promotion five times in five years and was regularly turned down. 'I was becoming a laughing stock, as I kept applying for promotion and never got it. It's not what you know, but who you know, that matters.' First she went through the standard grievance procedure. But the personnel manager went against her, for, as Kathleen says, 'He had to be seen as supporting his manager.' Then she went to the regional health authority. Their hearing also found in favour of management; it was concluded that she may have suffered some discrimination, but that men could be chauvinistic, besides which this was a minor issue. Then she rang up the EOC, who backed her case. The personnel department, meanwhile, told her they were proud of the fact that, although they had been taken to the industrial tribunal before, they had never lost a case. Kathleen was offered an out-of-court settlement of £500, which the solicitor advised her to accept as she might lose. She went back to work and put in for three subsequent promotions, none of which she got. When she asked why, she was told not to rock the boat as she might get the next one. She was pregnant when she applied for the subsequent promotion, and found the interview dates extended into the week before she went on maternity leave. The job was not offered to her; however, having gained confidence from her earlier experience of filing a case against her employer, she commenced proceedings of victimization and indirect discrimination, and finally won her case in April 1991 with damages of £1,700. This time she had been offered £6,000 to settle, but refused. 'I was there to see justice done. There's no money to be made from it.' The London Ambulance Service was also told to implement their equal opportunities policy, which had been in a draft form for the past twelve years.

When Kathleen Wheeler took her case, there were no female officers above her grade in her division, and only twenty-seven women out of 258 across all of the management grades. All her case proved, however, was that she personally had been victimized and passed over for promotion, because of her sex and because she had been labelled a troublemaker. While she was pursuing her case through the industrial tribunal, life at work eventually became too difficult and humiliating, and she applied for a job in another district, where she became a hospital ambulance liaison officer. 'I soon learnt who my friends were, and I was surprised by the number of men who supported me.' Kathleen now has two small children and a full-time job as quality assurance manager at the ambulance training centre in New Malden. She refused to gloat at her success over her former employer. 'It's shameful that I had to do it at all; it's down to bad management. Now I'm not as ambitious as I used to be. I would do it again if I didn't have kids, but your priorities change. I have little enough time with my children as it is. I don't want to spend my evenings going through paperwork.'

And there lies the kernel of the problem. How many women can be bothered? How many have the time? Kathleen's drive to prove that she had been the victim of discrimination inevitably comes second now that she has to commute from Crawley to New Malden five days a week, and wants to spend evenings and weekends with her children.

Pregnant women are even less likely to want the extra stress of pursuing a case for unfair dismissal. Employers could – and commonly did – dismiss a pregnant woman with impunity until the Employment Protection Act of 1975 deemed it unfair. The marriage bar had finally been eradicated a decade or so earlier, only to be replaced by the motherhood bar. Old habits die hard meanwhile. The attitude that pregnant women cannot and should not work is so deeply inculcated that often it is difficult to separate myth from truth, and the law currently reflects that confusion. Dismissal for pregnancy is commonplace in this country because the law has no clear attitude and because pregnant women are an easy target.

Are pregnant women sick? If so, can we compare their confinement to a prolonged period off work for a man, due to, say, a heart attack or a major operation? It's hard to imagine how the two are comparable, given that almost every woman goes through the former at some time, and that most people avoid the latter. Yet, until a landmark ruling from the European Court of Justice in July 1994, known as the Webb case, that is exactly what British women had to do if they believed they had been sacked simply because they were pregnant.

The principle of comparison with a sick man is exemplified by two employment appeal tribunal decisions in 1985, in the case of Hayes and Maughm. These held that if a man would not have lost the same job, the dismissal of the pregnant woman amounted to unlawful discrimination. Judges of such appeals are largely men, with little knowledge of pregnancy other than how unseemly and peculiar it has made their wives for a while. Accordingly the condition has to be likened to something that they have experienced personally or can more easily understand. Pregnancy, after all, isn't something that you catch by standing in a draught (although sometimes it does feel that easy), or develop as the body breaks down through stress and old age (although sometimes it feels as if it contributes greatly to these). But lacking acceptance of this fact of life, the courts make it even harder for a woman to bring a case, by forcing her to find an ailing comparator. They will even admit a hypothetical sick man if a real one can't be found, since so few women actually work with men.

Should a member of staff announce that he has to undergo open-heart surgery, followed by at least three months off, it is hard to imagine an employer saying, 'Tough luck, old boy; I'll find someone else to do your job.' It's also hard to picture that same employee being required to provide written notice, within twenty-one days of undergoing the knife, of when he intends returning to work. Yet a young mother is required by law to do this, even if she doesn't actually get her job back. Some employers' sick-pay schemes also exclude pregnancy, and many private medical arrangements, provided through insurance companies such as PPP, do not cover the consequences of pregnancy and labour unless there are complications. However, they do cover men and women who are undergoing open-heart surgery.

We express sympathy and make allowances for tragedies that can happen to anybody but affect only a few. Pregnancy, which is likely to affect most working women at least once in their lives and which should provoke celebration and a chorus of congratulations, requires women, in law, to compare themselves with sick men. Such is our respect for the rights of procreators. Carol Webb discovered that she was pregnant several weeks after she had been recruited to cover for the maternity leave of another employee. Her employers dismissed her because she would be unable to be there for the full period of maternity cover. The Industrial Tribunal, Employment Appeal Tribunal and the Court of Appeal dismissed Carol Webb's claim that she had been dismissed for pregnancy and upheld the need for pregnant women to compare themselves with sick men. Carol then took her case to the House of Lords who referred the decision on to the European Court of Justice who ruled in her favour in July 1994, thus finally overturning the legal nonsense of comparing pregnancy with illness. But what a haul! What unbelievable lengths this woman had to go through in order to establish an obvious prerequisite for Equal Opportunity between women and men; accepting that women have babies (while men don't) and that they need protection from dismissal while they do.

'Am I essentially the same as a woman, save for the odd differences I have in my anatomy, and some different social conditioning, or are the biological differences between men and women to be regarded as so fundamental that they must be recognized in law?' It is the answer to this question from the lawyer Michael Rubenstein that seems to leave interpreters of the law in a quandary. He himself is in no doubt. 'The philosophy – and it is very much a modern feminist philosophy – is that in order to be treated without discrimination, women must be permitted to be women; that means, a right to be a woman without being burdened by any discrimination on account of characteristics which are peculiar to her sex. An employer who treats a woman less favourably because of her pregnancy, discriminates against her on the grounds of her sex, since the less favourable treatment flows from a characteristic unique to the female sex. In other words, pregnancy discrimination is sex discrimination.'

Such fundamental differences between the sexes have to be recognized by the law if the law is to defend the rights of all citizens equally. The current confusion over fundamental truths comes partly from society's muddled reluctance to incorporate family life with work. Many people find aspects of pregnancy, birth and early motherhood so disgusting that they feel these should take place in private; also that, as women's business, they have nothing to do with the workplace. But if women are now paid employees it has everything to do with the world of work. Employers need to recognize this through a clear legal directive to stop women from being treated like lepers.

The Maze of Equal Pay Legislation

In the small number of jobs where both sexes worked together, the Equal Pay Act of 1970 when it became law did manage to bolster the earnings of a few women. It succeeded, for example, in destroying the widespread practice of three different rates for the job: unskilled, skilled and the woman's rate. It also helped to raise the average hourly rate of women's pay from 64 per cent of men's in 1971 to 74 per cent of men's by 1977 (Dale, 'Women in the Labour Market', 1990/91), although the pay differential has been roughly unchanged ever since. But as we know, most people don't work with members of the opposite sex in the same jobs. Consequently the effect of such an act is likely to be limited, as reflected by the drop in equal pay cases filed for tribunal from 1,742 in 1976 to thirty-nine six years later (Bourn, *Sex Discrimination Law*, 1992). It was only because of our entry into the European Community that the British government had to address itself to the principle of equal pay for work of equal value, as outlined in Article 119 of the Treaty of Rome.

In March 1981, however, the European Commission commenced proceedings against the UK government, alleging that Britain had not yet introduced measures enabling an employee to claim equal pay for work of equal value free of sex discrimination. Procedures were established by the Equal Value (Amendment) Regulations of 1983 for the handling of equal value claims by industrial tribunals. But these simply tagged the concept of equal pay for work of equal value on to existing legislation. The matter wasn't addressed afresh; it was simply adapted in order to comply in a haphazard way with the Treaty of Rome. Little consideration was given to how such amendments would work in practice, in spite of pressure from MPs to consider the implications for women. The lawyer and MP Robert MacLennan said in the Commons at the time that the Equal Value Amendment was likely to 'deter the maximum number of applicants from seeking remedy and to provide the greatest possible resistance to those who persist' (*Request to the Commission . . .*, EOC, 1993). How right he was.

Let's not mince our words – the Equal Value Amendment has produced the most complicated piece of legislation in Britain. From the inadequate, sloppy wording of the acts themselves, through the lengthy and apparently arbitrary industrial tribunal procedure, to the insultingly low settlement, should you be lucky enough (and it is largely luck) to win, the current equal pay legislation fails. 'It seems likely that job segregation is still acting to protect pay differentials. Therefore it is of acute importance that Equal Value legislation is made to function efficiently,' said the EOC. But it has prompted one leading QC to call it 'more like income tax than a human rights code'. Lord Denning remarked of it, 'Ordinary people ought to be able to read and understand the regulations. Not one of them would be able to do so. No ordinary lawyer would be able to understand them. The industrial tribunals would have the greatest of difficulty, and the court of appeal would probably be divided in opinion.' It is a legal labyrinth of Kafkaesque proportions.

Dr Pam Enderby began her case against Frenchay Health Authority in 1986. As head of a hospital department of speech therapy she found herself increasingly concerned by the numbers of women who were either leaving her own specialism for academia, or not coming back after career breaks. She was then earning £10,000, while heads of department in pharmacy or clinical psychology were paid £12,000 to £14,000. Speech therapy over Britain as a whole has a 98 per cent female staff; pharmacy and clinical psychology are 40 per cent male, of whom 80 per cent are in senior management, and they also have considerably less clinical and research work. The EOC backed Dr Enderby's case for equal pay for like work along with two other test cases in speech therapy. To make all three combined as representative as possible, the others were brought by a more senior and a more junior speech therapist. For the first two years the case bounced backwards and forwards between the industrial tribunal and the appeal court, while these bodies tried to clarify whether the NHS was exempt from the Equal Pay Act on the grounds that pay and working conditions were laid down by the Secretary of State for Employment. How many more cases would that have eliminated, given the numbers of women in teaching, nursing and other parts of the public sector?

The case was then taken by Dr Enderby to the High Court, where she sat for ten days' holiday leave listening to a philosophical debate, conducted at extraordinary expense and with highly interesting and erudite presentations, as to whether you should look at the cause of discrimination before the effect of discrimination or vice versa. 'Of course it was a case of covert discrimination. There was no big bad monster: what he wanted to do was to prove that if there is the effect of discrimination, then you should look at that situation to establish why. But the other side were insistent that since there was no big bad monster, there was no discrimination. We were all reasonably intelligent people. What I couldn't understand was why we couldn't sit down and sort it out in two hours over a cup of tea, instead of this legal chess that cost so much money that we could have given all the speech therapists a pay rise.' Eight years after beginning her case, the European Court of Justice ruled, on 27 October 1993, that the government's descriptions of how the differences came about in pay between speech therapists and pharmacists were not sufficient to justify that discrepancy.

Dr Enderby has not yet won her case. She hasn't even won the right to have it heard. She has merely succeeded, before the case opens, in removing one of several defences open to employers which prevent details of the jobs concerned from being considered, and which deny a woman access to justice and lost income for years. 'It's all to do with how the law works, rather than is speech therapy not paid appropriately and why are clinical psychologists paid more. These issues have not occupied more than five minutes in eight years.'

Less exceptional cases are quicker to get down to the nitty-gritty. But industrial tribunals seem keen to allow the employer every possible opportunity to prove, before a case is actually heard, that the dismissal/pay discrepancy/lack of promotion/

general bum deal is caused by something other than direct or indirect discrimination. The obstacles a woman has to overcome in order successfully to pursue her case are so formidable that it is worth describing them in detail. First, since an employer is unlikely to admit to discrimination in court, it has to be shown that 'but for her sex' a woman would have been treated more favourably. This means producing a male comparator who has not been subject to the same treatment. Even when such a comparator is available this is hard to prove, and involves subjective assumptions about the roles of men and women at work and at home. But the law also states that discrimination can be 'indirect' where a requirement that applies to both sexes indirectly discriminates against a woman. For instance an age restriction of 25 to 28 would affect a greater number of women at their prime age for childbearing. This definition of 'indirect' discrimination ought theoretically to allow for differences between the sexes. In fact it is even harder to prove in a court of law, notwithstanding evidence that appears logically incontrovertible.

If your employer has a 'job evaluation study' – a 'scientific' analysis of the demands of the job – and this study is found to be non-discriminatory, your case will automatically fail before any factual evidence has been considered. The Workplace Industrial Relations Survey shows that in 1990 26 per cent of Workplaces had a job evaluation scheme. However the overwhelming majority had either non-analytical schemes or they did not cover all of the different types of job within the establishment, making it almost impossible for the jobs of men and women to be compared (Millward, *Targeting Potential Discrimination*, EOC, 1995). To employers the existence of a 'job evaluation study' is an attractive protection from equal-value claims – so much so that many large occupational consultancies sell such systems to their clients. 'Mediquate' is being bought by the new health trusts, and 'Aquate' by the water companies; and any company or local authority who buys the Hay scheme knows that in the unlikely event of a challenge they will have the backing of the large company who produces the system. To the EOC's knowledge, no job evaluation scheme has been successfully challenged at a tribunal and shown to be discriminatory ('EC Law . . .', *Equal Opportunities Review* 39, 1991).

It is easy to understand how a technical stopper like this can develop. The regulations established a way of assessing a job before too much taxpayers' money had been wasted on judging it. But if a case automatically fails because the job evaluation scheme is found to be non-discriminatory, why doesn't it succeed in the unlikely event that the scheme is deemed discriminatory? This would allow the tribunal to proceed directly to the question of compensation rather than just to the next hurdle at the preliminary hearing. Why, as the EOC suggests, is the job evaluation scheme allowed to block the entire proceedings, rather than be submitted as evidence with other relevant papers?

If a job evaluation has been thoughtfully designed, from altruistic motives, it can indeed reveal inadequacies of existing pay differentials. But the tendency of job evaluation schemes is to reinforce the lower values traditionally placed on the work that women do. Frank Spencer, Head of the Pay Policy and Development Unit at the EOC, describes their inherent discrimination. 'Women are called supervisors, not managers; clerks, not administrators; operators, not technicians; and men's jobs can be consistently overwritten compared to women's. Skills and knowledge may be written in a way that emphasizes skills acquired through formal training, rather than skills acquired informally and on the job, to the benefit of men and detriment of women. Higher levels of demand may be illustrated with examples from men's work. Attention may focus on male responsibilities – supervising staff, responsibility for machinery, allocating budgets, and so on, but not female responsibilities— customers, patients, product quality, and so on. Physical effort may look at explosive lifting demands associated with men's jobs, but not repetitive lifting demands associated with women's jobs. Working conditions may be described in terms of heat, dust and fumes, rather than noise, pace of work or interruptions of task that are found in a busy office.'

The different values we place on the respective jobs that men and women do are based on years of assumption and prejudice. These cannot simply be eliminated by a system of numbering, especially when applied by people bringing their preconceptions to bear. Studies by psychologists show that women will consistently underestimate the value of what they do; also that business students, of both sexes, attach significantly lower ratings to jobs with a female-stereotyped job title (McShane, *Journal of Occupational Psychology*, 1990; Major *et al*, *Journal of Applied Social Psychology*, 1984). The older a job-evaluation scheme, the more likely it is to be inherently discriminatory. 'In such circumstances,' says Michael Rubenstein, 'job evaluation does not get rid of pay discrimination against women. All it does is make pay discrimination against women more subtle, more covert and more difficult to prove. You cannot maintain the status quo at the same time, and neither can you change pay relativities without altering the pay hierarchy.' In this way has the law of equal pay for work of equal value been made virtually impotent. The government's response, in July 1993, to the EOC's proposals for strengthening legislation indicates that they have no intention of removing the existence of a job evaluation scheme as a bar to an equal value claim. They also fail to acknowledge that a job evaluation scheme can in itself be discriminatory, and justify their position with the old excuse of avoiding unnecessary cost.

So ... You've got backing for your case, and you've jumped through the initial pre-hearing hoop, as there's no job evaluation study. But, sorry; your case can't be heard quite yet because the employer has deployed another blocking mechanism, known as a 'material factor defence'. If the employer can excuse himself by pointing out one of these, the case is dismissed unheard, and the plaintiff has to take her case to the Employment Appeal Tribunal. This is a bit like saying that you can get off if you convince the judge that you didn't steal the watch – it just happened to fall off the counter into your pocket – *before* the cases for the prosecution and the defence are presented.

The most common 'material factor defence' is this: 'Separate, non-discriminatory, collective bargaining.' This means that the woman's pay was determined by a process of collective bargaining with a different union to that of her male equivalent. Any sane being would assume that having the same employer as your equal pay comparator was enough. And how can you prove that the collective pay agreement wasn't in itself discriminatory, given the lack of women involved in negotiations over pay? For the three people in the industrial tribunal – a legal person in the chair, with one nominee from the TUC and one from the CBI – aspects of collective bargaining occupy much of their working lives. It is unsurprising that they should get drawn into considering details of this, rather than the case in question.

This was the excuse used by the Department of Employment to prevent speech therapist Dr Enderby from pursuing her case for pay equal to that of pharmacists and clinical psychologists. Dr Enderby's success at the European Court of Justice in October 1993 does now make it harder for employers and government to use so-called separate, non-discriminatory, collective bargaining as an excuse at the preliminary hearing. But it is likely that one or both of two other 'material factor defences' will be raised when Pam Enderby goes back to the industrial tribunal, once again preventing the facts of her case from being heard. These two defences are the 'red circling of male salary', where the comparator is said to have been moved from one job to another because of injury or extenuating circumstances but has been kept on the same pay, and the catch-all of 'market forces', where it is argued that the amount paid was the price for the job.

It is common for all three excuses to be raised at the preliminary hearing one after the other, if need be. Should these fail to get the case dismissed at the preliminary hearing *they can be raised again after the tribunal has found that the work is of equal value*. Is this justice? Is this fair to someone who has been found to be the victim of an injustice, who has suffered great stress getting her case through at all? The EOC monitored the outcome of cases filed under the Equal Value Amendment between 1984 and 1989. They won 19 of the 117 cases filed with their backing; 23 were withdrawn; 23 were settled; and 52 were dismissed, overwhelmingly on the grounds of the material factor defence.

So you're lucky enough to get the necessary backing, and your case has not been dismissed in advance. You've made it – your case can be heard (if you haven't dropped out in the meantime from frustration, or because your counsel has persuaded you to settle). The next stage is the appointment of an independent expert to investigate and analyse the demands of the job in question. This appointee is selected by the conciliation service ACAS, one of whose strengths is that they are independent, not being attached to either party, or there to present a case. Their report is the only one required before a final judgement can be made. The regulations require that this report must be written within forty-two days. According to EOC estimates, it takes an average of twelve months for the experts' report to reach the tribunal, largely because of hostile obstructions such as denial of access to employer's premises.

The actual outcome of successful cases, according to Alice Leonard's study covering 1980 to 1984 (*Pyrrhic Victories . . .*, 1987), reveals that over half the applicants found the most stressful aspect was the length of time the case took. It was less oppressive for those with recruitment cases, since they didn't have to come into contact with their employer until the day of the hearing. But for women with promotion or equal-value cases, relations ranged from finding oneself ignored to being 'subjected to an orchestrated campaign of victimization'. If witnesses have to be raised, you discover who your friends are. But you still have to live; and who else is likely to offer you another job, if they discover that you are taking your former employer to an industrial tribunal? If a woman does eventually prove that she has been paid less for work of equal value, the tribunal has no power to award her interest on the back pay lost through procedural delays. So long as employers control the lengthy process by introducing successive defences at the preliminary hearing and by blocking access to independent experts, the odds are stacked overwhelmingly in their favour and women continue to lose out financially.

The experts' report is submitted as evidence, and although it is not the role of the tribunal merely to rubber-stamp their conclusion, it is hard to see how a tribunal can be prevented from paying it undue attention as the only seemingly unbiased report available. Clearly the conclusion of the experts is important; but how is it reached?

The job is assessed under chosen headings such as 'responsibility', and 'skill, knowledge and experience'; and factors are listed under each for both the applicant and the comparator. The one with the most points wins, and as a rule of thumb the more factors listed the higher the score. 'Weighting' systems are used, which fail to refer to the reality of working in specific jobs, that if, say, you are a teacher in the London Borough of Hackney it helps to have both social work and army disciplinarian skills as well as the ability to teach maths. Instead these weighting systems increase analytically the number of factors under a particular heading, by breaking them down even smaller. This 'responsibility' can stand unchanged, or break down into such components as 'for own work', 'for work of others' and 'effect of efforts'.

There is no common guide or methodology. Investigation by Anne-Marie Plumer for the Industrial Relations Research Unit at

Warwick University (*Equal Value Judgements* ..., 1992) found that out of twenty-four cases the independent experts used nine different choices of how many factors to list, twenty-three weighting systems and eight methods of scoring. Even in broadly similar cases a variety of scores was produced. In three similar cases, comparing packers with labourers, the 'experts' listed three different numbers of factors, and three scores each arrived at by a dissimilar weighting system. One case was found to be equal by the tribunal, and the other two 'not equal'.

No one would deny the difficulties in assessing other people's jobs. But what hope is there of fairness if there is little consistency even in the methodology of the experts? The most dismaying aspect of Anne Marie Plumer's research is the lack of agreement it reveals between one tribunal and another on what constitutes equality. It seems hard to deny that the jobs compared are of equal value when the applicant's score differed from that of the comparator by only 1 per cent. But how similar is work of a 'broadly similar nature'? In the case of French *v.* Lloyds Bank the tribunal found the work to be of equal value when the claimant's score beside that of the comparator was 95 per cent. But not in Lawson *v.* Britfish Ltd, when the relative score of the applicant was 98 per cent. You can be forgiven for feeling like Alice in Wonderland on trial by the Queen of Hearts. Pursuing a claim for equal value is more like entering a lottery than exposing a small segment of society to public scrutiny for an assessment of inherent inequities between the sexes.

Given such an arduous process of assessment, it isn't surprising that most cases settle out of court. Settling does not mean succeeding. Carol Walker taught geography at a Catholic girls' school in London. She is a practising Catholic herself and has four children, the eldest of whom is severely handicapped. When Carol was pregnant with her third child, the headmistress allowed her back to her part-time contract with extreme reluctance. She was given a timetable that jumped about all over the place, and was ignored in her request for leave to be with her eldest child when he was not at his special nursery. The headmistress also insisted that she did not get pregnant for at least two years. When Carol became pregnant with her fourth child just one year later, the head decided that Carol should leave the school. It seemed four children, for a working woman, offended even Catholic standards. The head advertised Carol's job and gave her a leaving present at the end of term, causing an embarrassing scene when Carol said she wasn't leaving.

Because the school employing her was Catholic, Carol, backed by the National Union of Teachers, succeeded in pursuing two cases: against the local authority and against the school. The local authority was prepared to pay for a course in technology that she wanted to do, and guaranteed her job; but they stressed that she should use her best efforts to find work elsewhere. The school offered £1,500 in an out-of-court settlement, which Carol's solicitor advised her to accept as this was more than she would get if she went through the rest of the case and won. After years of humiliation Carol feels let down and angry. 'I feel as if I have no choice but to settle. The reason I've stuck with this for so long is not so much the job (although I need a job), but more to prove that the reason she did it was to give a clear message to the other staff and to the girls: that you can't have more than one or two babies and work there. For a mere £1,500, she doesn't have to go into a court of law and explain why she did what she did – she is therefore clearly above the law. I have no redress, and if I hadn't been in a union I'd have got nothing.'

Carol also considers an opportunity has been wasted because at the end of this debilitating battle 'the Diocese still have a rogue school in their midst, behaving in a totally unChristian way'. As things stand, her former employers can avoid public comment. Settling a case means that it cannot be written about without the potential threat of a libel charge. Consequently I have changed the teacher's name and omitted the name of the school. The discrimination has not been proved, Carol hasn't won her case, and her story is therefore potentially defamatory.

The lucky few who succeed in proving discrimination will have had to undergo immense stress. To begin with, most will have been unaware of how few rights they have, and how long it will take to reach a conclusion. Many will have feared the effect of the action on their career, and the reprisals from their employer or colleagues. There is also the dread of losing the case. Dr Pam Enderby describes the industrial tribunal itself as demoralizing. 'There's nothing positive about it, just an attitude of, "What are these whinging people wanting?" There's no common chat, no ordinary language; and my junior colleague found it completely intimidating. Because we haven't even got to the point where we can explain to the tribunal what speech therapists do, all of the references to my profession are not in context. The other side constantly throw out belittling one-liners, which imply that I am making more of an issue of it than is required, or that I am politically motivated.' She also expressed surprise at the speed with which she became known as a feminist striver, which she doesn't consider herself to be. It's more to the point that she has considerable achievements as a speech therapist, and is well known for research in her own field. 'People immediately assume that you are also a vegetarian, wear a donkey jacket, and visit Greenham regularly. It's very odd how you get categorized with things that you don't associate yourself with or necessarily agree with; and yet it is my speech work, and desire to raise its status, that is most important. I rate helping someone to overcome a speech impediment as far more important than fighting this case.' The rigours of attending the tribunal, and the length of time taken up by this extraordinary system of justice, demand considerable stamina from the applicant. For Pam Enderby it has been eight years; she jokes modestly that only complete inertia has kept her in the running. 'Meanwhile we wait with baited breath for the European Court to decide on the cause and effect of discrimination; and then it's back to the tribunal to see if they can decide.'

While Alison Halford has reached a conclusion and obtained a good settlement, she feels that she has failed to achieve a clear result. 'If the police could treat me so badly, with twenty-eight years of exemplary service, then how can ethnic recruits expect better?' As Britain's most senior woman police officer, on one occasion she received an invitation to meet John Major, the then new Prime Minister, at Number Ten. When she rang up to RSVP, she found that her invitation was void. The reception was suddenly oversubscribed, just as it had become public knowledge that she had been suspended pending legal action against her employers. Alison Halford's reputation and history were paraded through the witness box, where every attempt was made to blacken her character. The industrial tribunal heard how the papers written by Her Majesty's Inspector were 'categorically negative and full of personal criticisms which was not the same for her male colleagues'. But when it was the turn of the police to defend their actions, they pressed hard to settle. 'There was also an assumption made in my records that I could not cope in the witness box, which makes me smile because I was the one who stood in the witness box during my case, and they bottled out when it came to their turn. Treating staff fairly is an important tenet of good management, and we all need a jerk on the reins now and again. The police have to be more accountable and they also have to learn how to apologize. When a settlement was finally agreed, not one word of apology passed through the lips of the men who had made my life misery.'

Perhaps the most disturbing aspect of the legislative process is how little it actually changes anyone's circumstances. Catching a thief doesn't necessarily recover the goods, and the imprisonment of a child-murderer will not restore the victim to his or her parents. But we are talking here about trifles compared to murder, so in this field why can't the law be made to work? Of the seventy successful applicants in Alice Leonard's study (*Pyrrhic Victories* . . ., 1987) not one woman said her terms and conditions of work had improved because of her taking the case. If a court of law rules that an employer has been indulging in bad practices, why isn't that employer, and appropriate staff, required to undergo training; and why isn't he or she required to produce facts for the court about the rest of his employees? All the guilty party has to do is pay the fine and walk away. Why aren't they monitored after the ruling? Why isn't that employer induced to run a more efficient firm based on better industrial relations? What happens instead is that too often the threat of legislation forces those who discriminate to be more subtle, to learn what they should or should not say, while remaining essentially unchanged.

A woman who does win her case can become paradoxically more of a victim. Many find it hard to get another job once they are identified as troublemakers. Some even face hostility from friends and neighbours. In spite of shoddy treatment and inadequate compensation, which often remains unpaid, a staggering 61 out of 70 successful applicants in Alice Leonard's study said that it had been worthwhile. Fifty of these felt a matter of principle had been established; four said that winning had restored their confidence in their own capabilities. Some felt that it had helped others, and expressed satisfaction at knowing that the law could be used successfully against an employer. Women who take their employer to court for breaching the equality legislation don't do it for fun, and they certainly don't do it for money. They take action because they believe they have been the victim of an injustice and they hope to spare someone else from suffering in the same way. For some, like Pam Enderby, raising the value and status of their profession is the motive. She cared enough about her profession and the quality of its service to do something. 'I wouldn't mind if they found against me; what I want is a conclusion – we're still losing valuable people in speech therapy.'

At the level of everyday need, Decia, who has two sons with speech problems, knows that her children's impediments if untreated could lead to more intractable problems. She finally managed to get one of her sons into a school in another London borough with a language unit. But though both need help, 'speech therapists are like gold dust – hard to find'. As a playgroup leader she understands how important it is for children to be able to communicate. To multitudes like her, speech therapy is as important an aspect of health care as pharmacy or clinical psychology. But the government appear to think otherwise. In Dr Enderby's case Frenchay Health Authority would have settled, but the Secretary of State for Employment and the Treasury refused to allow this. They appear determined to fight this principle to the very end. When she asked why, she was told by her counsel that it was because the knock-on effects were so broad. 'Of course they are,' she says. 'But does that justify this kind of discrepancy?'

The Equal Value Amendment to the Equal Pay Act attempts to attack the very infrastructure of society by challenging occupational segregation. Dr Pam Enderby's attempt at raising the pay and status of speech therapists raises questions that are hard to answer. Why are speech therapists paid less than clinical psychologists, when there is little difference in the training and skills required? Why is one specialism considered to be more important than another to general health? If the Equal Pay Act were not so restricted by regulation we could see an immense improvement in the pay differentiation between men and women. The prejudices that keep the sexes working in different jobs would be more open to public scrutiny, and it would be harder to justify differences in pay before a court of law. But our equality legislation is not allowed any real bite, because government and employers fear an immense rise in labour costs, and believe this would result in increased unemployment. For more than twelve years the EOC has suggested amendments to our equality laws. In 1990, its proposals to strengthen the acts detailed the drawbacks of current legislation and recommended introducing one clear act. In spite of pressure from MPs, the response from successive ministers was that the EOC's proposals were 'under consideration'. The Secretary of State for Employment showed how high equal pay is on the government's agenda, when he finally got around to replying to the EOC's proposals after three years, in July 1993. He acknowledged that the government was prepared for minor procedural modifications in equal-value cases. However, he saw no major need to strengthen the legislation in order to allow more women to seek judicial remedies or to speed up the process of judging.

Recently the Equal Opportunities Commission tried to prove in court that the British government was in breach of European law, given the less favourable employment conditions of part-time workers as compared with full-time employees under the Employment Protection (Consolidation) Act of 1978. The EOC submitted that because 90 per cent of part-time workers are women, often with hours limited by family responsibilities, such differences in employment protection indirectly amounted to gender discrimination. Since it was the law that needed challenging, not an individual employer, and the Secretary of State for Employment could not be called to a tribunal to explain why UK law was not in line with that of Europe, the EOC applied for a judicial review within the divisional court rather than pursuing an individual case before an industrial tribunal. Rejecting this request for review, Lord Justice Nolan said '... employment opportunities in part-time work would be reduced by the imposition of additional burdens on potential employers. The administrative burden of organizing part-time employment of individuals is relatively greater than for full-time employees. If so, the fact that part-time employees do not have the same rights in relation to redundancy payments and claims for unfair dismissal would appear, at the lowest, to be a counterweight to the increased administrative and cost burden imposed on employers of part-time employees. Legislation to dispense with the qualifying thresholds would lead to an increased burden on employers and therefore to a reduction in part-time jobs available to those individuals who want them.' At its time, slavery, too, had its apologists.

Are these supposed 'ends' – the fear of job losses – justified by their 'means' – encouraging the use of women as cheap and more easily dispensable labour? Lord Justice Nolan argued that 'the time may come – may already be coming with the current recession – when part-time work will be carried out in much more equal proportions by men and women'. This ignores the fact that it is women who have to work part-time because they have primary responsibility for the care of the young and the old, and because gender differences in pay are effectively upheld by equal-value regulations. It is women who must work part-time once they are parents: since they earn less than men, and in the absence of a policy for affordable childcare, it makes economic sense for them to give up full-time employment. But even if it were true that the majority of women actively choose part-time work, should they be penalized for this in law?

While the EOC has won a number of small battles against the government, it has yet to win the war in persuading them that we need a major overhaul of our equality legislation in order to make it more effective. The Law Lords were finally persuaded in 1994 that part-timers should have the same redundancy rights as full-timers and pressure from the European Court has helped to raise the ceiling for damages should a woman succeed in proving that she has been unlawfully discriminated against. The media tends to present these small victories as major improvements and radical change when in fact all that has happened is that the EOC has persuaded the establishment to remove an obstacle to equality and a fairer distribution of wealth between the sexes which should never have been erected in the first place. While a greater number of women may have won the right to have their case heard, they still have to prove their case against overwhelming odds.

To convince the government that it is failing women, the EOC has decided to take it to the European Commission for failing to fulfil its obligations under the European Treaty and the Equal Pay Directive. If, through delays and the absence of legal aid, women are denied access to judicial remedy, the UK government has failed to implement the Equal Pay Directive which states that 'to implement the principle that men and women should receive equal pay contained in article 119 of the treaty . . . it is primarily the responsibility of the member states to ensure the application of this principle by means of appropriate laws, regulations and administrative provisions in such a way that all employees in the community can be protected in these matters' (*Request to the Commission . . .*, EOC, 1993).

The United Kingdom is also obliged by Articles 5 and 119 of the European treaty to take no measure jeopardizing attainment of equal pay. The EOC will argue that the government have done just that by abolishing the wages councils, since these were the only means by which national law protected a large number of women in sex-segregated industries from discrimination in pay. If this doubtless long and expensive case is ever resolved, the costs to both sides will be borne by the taxpayer. It would be interesting to compare those costs with supposed increased labour costs due to acknowledging equal pay for work of equal value as a prerequisite for justice.

*

Equal-opportunity policies and
women's units

Women at work face discrimination not as a separate, self-contained problem but as an essential aspect of the whole work ethic. The rise of the equal-opportunity policy can partly be seen as a failure to recognize this. Many companies have initiated such policies only as a protection from litigation, rarely backing them up with adequate resources or personnel, or serious commitment from the top of the company. Often the mere existence of an equal-opportunity policy lodged in some drawer enables a company to feel that they have dealt with the issue of sex discrimination, 'so we'll have no more bleating from now on, thank you'. Unjust work practices may simply be forced further underground, with managers and recruiters being more careful about their choice of language. Consequently many women dare not raise the possibility of discrimination, on the grounds that that sort of thing is not supposed to happen any more.

Though admirable in principle, equal-opportunity policies are rarely permitted to work; when they fail, women are blamed for not seizing the initiative and competing for the jobs now seemingly open to them. The most positive thing about equal opportunity culture is that it has helped persuade employers and government of a substantial shift in attitudes; they recognize that it is no longer acceptable to be seen to be perpetuating anachronistic practices and attitudes. A handful of employers pursue the philosophy with gusto. Littlewoods has developed a twenty-page code of conduct and a training programme for all line managers, set five-year targets, improved maternity provisions and introduced part-time working into management. They have also integrated their Equal Opportunities Unit into their general management, with senior line managers as well as personnel forming an equal opportunity committee which reports directly to the chief executive. IBM, Rank Xerox and the Civil Service have also adopted family-friendly policies and demonstrated a commitment to making their equal-opportunity policy work. Over a more general area, Opportunity 2000, a Business in the Community initiative, has had much publicity and open support from the government; but it still covers no more than roughly a quarter of the British workforce and can only do so much under current legislation. Opportunity 2000 focuses on individual success, on increasing the numbers of women within management and at the top, rather than on the poverty of working women within an increasingly segregated workforce.

Caroline Langridge runs the women's unit at the Department of Health. 'The fundamental reason for being part of Opportunity 2000 isn't because we're woolly liberals with airy-fairy notions of equality. It's because of the business case; we want to make the best possible use out of our resources.' Since training a doctor costs a quarter of a million pounds and a nurse £40,000, such an attitude is admirable. But it is doomed to failure, for nurses, who are after all low paid, and lack extensive subsidized childcare as well as a radical altering of the work ethic to introduce family-friendly schedules. It is hard to see how a mere PR campaign can do much to stop the brain drain. Caroline Langridge is proud nonetheless that since March 1992 women have been 40 per cent of top appointments. 'Women have been working in health for fifteen to twenty years, and they are now in a position to compete for some of the top jobs. But men feel that they have a God-given right to be in those jobs, so inevitably some are going to feel threatened. You do hear them saying things like, "You only get appointed if you wear a skirt." We help women to compete more effectively, but once they're in an interview they are entirely on their own. So to blame us is very silly; these women get there because they are the very best.'

As Equal Opportunities Director at the Midland Bank, another subscriber to Opportunity 2000, Anne Watts is also well placed to observe male resistance to the promotion of female colleagues. 'Men are now having to compete with women in a way that they never bargained for. Some assume that they will just be able to work their way up, and now see women coming back after maternity leave and being remarkably effective in their work. The competition is greater, and many men simply haven't adapted. We've worked at the cutting edge, but we still haven't changed the culture of the organization sufficiently because people are a product of the society in which they live; and although they may behave accordingly at work, they can go home at the end of the day and behave differently.'

While the effort of such women is commendable, it does little for those lower down the hierarchy – obliged for example to adopt flexible working in a 24-hour district service centre, where row upon row of women sit processing paper in factory conditions with next to no promotion prospects. In their PR material, the Department of Health choose not to mention the staff without childcare who have to opt for 'bank' nursing, or the large number of scandalously low-paid ancillary staff employed on flexible contracts by hospitals to do valuable cleaning and laundry.

As an answer to all of womankind's ills, invocation of 'equal opportunity' became fashionable during the late 1980s. In organizations concerned to appear socially progressive, individual women had begun pushing for change; there had also been the discovery of a 'demographic time bomb'. Statisticians had predicted a substantial drop, by nearly a quarter, in the numbers of school leavers able to enter the workforce simultaneously, with a huge increase in pensioners drawing benefits. Amid a flurry of public activity, every newspaper carried articles on how women were to provide commerce and industry with a new dawn, and how mothers were to be coaxed back into the workforce. Ironically, the gap that these workers were to fill had been caused by women having fewer babies, later in life, in order to lose out less on their career prospects. At last women felt needed and acknowledged. Issues such as childcare occupied media that had previously ignored the concerns of working mothers. Promises of childcare, more pay and flexible working arrangements were handed out like children's party bags. 'The 1990s, unlike the 1960s, will be a decade in which childcare becomes a substantial part of the pay package of working women, more important than health, insurance, mortgages or company cars . . . and employers will have to pay because the gun is pointing at their own heads,' said John Patten, the then chair of the ministerial group on women's issues in 1989 (*Guardian*, 2 January 1989). If the gun is still pointing, many working mothers would like to pull the trigger.

This was no conversion on the road to Damascus. Political rhetoric of the time never pretended to adopt a philosophy of encompassing women's distinct needs as a means to true equality. The reasons were purely economic. Just as women could be drawn into the workplace during a wartime shortage of male workers, they could also be persuaded into the labour force when changing birth patterns cocked up the national maths figures. During the Second World War, the government was suddenly able to provide 62,000 nursery places for children in England and Wales – double the number of places available in 1988. At the end of the war the British closed many of their nurseries, in contrast with the French, who decided to keep theirs open. British mothers were forced back into full-time parenthood, partly because of fashionable theories espoused by 'scientists' such as John Bowlby, who stated that children would grow up psychologically disturbed and delinquent if the mother was not permanently in their company from birth. Exhorted by government to foot the bill for childcare, postwar employers responded reluctantly. They were more interested in competing for the shrinking graduate market and making better use of their existing workforce, with older women recruited to the unskilled work previously done by teenagers. With the recession bringing graduate unemployment for the first time in history, the demographic time bomb was defused. Sighs of relief were heard throughout Westminster and British business as women ceased to be an 'issue'.

Several ingredients must be added to a recipe of good intentions for an equal-opportunity policy to succeed. There has to be outspoken commitment from the very top of an organization, with adequate investment in staff and management training, including the message, repeatedly given, that sexual equality is the responsibility of everyone rather than a concern of the equal opportunity officer alone. Staff ratios also need regular monitoring in order to keep sight of whether or not women employees are progressing. There is no statutory requirement for employers to introduce or implement an equal-opportunity policy. The Companies Act of 1985 does require shareholders to be informed, through annual reports, on the employment, training, health and welfare of employees; there is, however, no requirement to report on the practice or progress of an equal-opportunity policy. Of the equal-opportunity employers so described on their job advertisements in 1988, one in five could only provide a policy statement, with no evidence of implementation (*Equal Opportunities Review 22*, 1988).

In 1992 the EOC conducted a survey of health authorities. The NHS is the largest employer of women in Europe, and although almost every health authority said they had an equal-opportunity policy, nearly a third hadn't communicated it to their employees, three-quarters did not monitor their policy's workings, and 10 per cent hadn't even bothered to write it down. Application forms for nearly a quarter of health authorities still included potentially unlawful, discriminatory questions, and 22 per cent didn't train their staff in methods of recruitment and selection (*Equal Opportunities Review 45*, 1992).

Often an employer's commitment to fair dealing in matters of gender will stop with the appointment of an equal-opportunity officer. She – as this staff member usually is – then finds herself left to transform the entire culture of an organization, with little financial or staff resources and no access to mainline management. Most equal-opportunity staff are not involved in pay decisions, and are restricted to ensuring equality of opportunity at recruitment. Even then their power can be limited. Personnel often have little influence over line management, who like to recruit through their own networks and resent the bureaucracy imposed by the doctrine of equal opportunity.

Line managers are older and mostly male, and have an extensive knowledge of the production process. Personnel staff tend to be younger and female, and increasingly marginalized from central questions of recruitment. These women can find it hard to challenge discrimination at recruitment; they are usually in a minority of one at the interview panel and concerned to keep their own job.

Within larger companies most equal opportunity personnel are situated at head office, with little influence over the outlying reaches of an organization. When they do try to extend their influence they are seen as company policewomen, sticking their noses where they are not wanted. Also, as one such officer said of working in a higher education institution, 'People will behave while you are looking at them, but will regress once your back is turned.' If an equal-opportunity officer is employed to manage change, they are bound to be personally identified with its unpopular aspect. With change comes uncertainty; and there is bound to be antagonism if male employees in turn feel that their promotion prospects are being limited.

Some employers merely pretend to want change. Personnel staff sometimes admit to knowledge of major inequities or discrepancies in pay, particularly in relation to part-timers, but excuse their subsequent inaction on the grounds that they were 'under no pressure to do anything' or were 'apprehensive about opening a can of worms which might be too expensive to deal with' (*Pay and Gender . . .*, IRS/EOC, 1992). One personnel manager confessed that he didn't know how his company had managed to gain the description of an equal-opportunity employer. 'We've got a reputation which is not totally deserved. For example, in chain-store management, if I'm honest, I'd have to say that we discriminate. It took us until 1982 to appoint our first female store manager. We do discriminate; I know I shouldn't say that, but we do. Men can't bear children, and women are more likely to drop out for biological reasons.'

Among equal-opportunity personnel, one major survey showed that almost a quarter had no job description; a third did not have appraisal. Consequently it was often hard for them to ascertain exactly what they were expected to do (Kandola *et al*, *Equal Opportunities* . . ., 1991). Many of the women interviewed had entered these jobs because they genuinely want to help shift corporate culture. They found themselves pigeonholed, however, and under-resourced. Professional impotence often lowered their self-esteem, with officers blaming lack of results on their own performance. Ninety per cent of those interviewed showed higher than average symptoms of physical ill-health. Few equal-opportunity officers have sufficient staff; one third of those surveyed worked completely on their own. The nature of their work isolates them, which is inevitably a strain, but, as one officer commented, 'You cannot show the stress you are under. This would be seen as a sign of weakness and would ultimately be detrimental.' Brenda Wilkinson worked as women's officer for six years with Brighton Council, where she found her job inherently difficult. 'I had to work hard for the unit to be seen as credible. It was like talking two different languages. They needed to understand what they should be doing; but when I told them, they didn't understand. We were talking past each other the whole time, with everything resting on persuasion; and unless you give equal-opportunity advisors top-management status why should they listen?' During the six years that Brenda worked at Brighton, the council never introduced qualitative monitoring of their staff.

When high expectations are not met, these women are easy scapegoats. From within a special penned-off area, they are judged by the product of their work rather than incorporated into the mainstream process to bring about genuine change. Three-quarters of the women interviewed (Kandola *et al*, *Equal Opportunities* . . ., 1991) had no intention of staying in 'equal opportunity', let alone the same organization. And who can blame them.

Social engineering as a whole is no longer fashionable. Individual teachers who strive to monitor their own work and the behaviour of pupils are having to return to the tradition of the three Rs as if both approaches were not possible. Within local government generally the very idea of a women's unit is felt to reek of bra-burning activism; recession and substantial cuts have led in any case to their elimination. 'Cuts are being used as a reason for doing away with specific women's units, and committees that they do not like,' says Marilyn Taylor of the National Association of Local Government Women's Committees. Often the greatest resistance comes from the very women such departments aim to represent. Until she was made redundant on sick leave, Peggy Eagle worked for nine years in the women's unit of Greenwich Council. Approached by a group of women on the subject of sexual harassment, she conducted a survey, and wrote a policy for all staff. 'The women's unit was seen as a bit of a threat, as we were inevitably going into other people's departments and treading on their toes. It didn't matter how humble or ingratiating you were. When you went into another department and offered them training, you would still get flak from both the women and the men.' For drawing up the policy, on sexual harassment, the council women's unit was boycotted by the Transport and General Workers Union. 'It was seen as loony lefty stuff by both men and women. We had no post or phone calls for three months because the two full-time union organizers were men, and real charmers, with many of the women responding to them. Because they didn't like what we were doing, the cleaners, telephonists and postroom boycotted us, and many of them were women.'

Inevitably the recession has had an effect on equal opportunity. As Anne Watts, of the Midland Bank, diplomatically points out, 'If you're not recruiting, an organization becomes more static and therefore opportunities for promotion are more limited.' The banking union BIFU are more blunt in their interpretation. Women matter less. As an issue they have to wait. Where banks once guaranteed the jobs of women going on maternity leave, they now say that there 'is no business need for it at the moment'. Statutory maternity pay is all that any bank offers; none has occupational maternity schemes. The main problem for female staff, BIFU finds, arises from returning after maternity leave or a career break. When women come back on to part-time contracts and are then made redundant, their redundancy is calculated solely on their pay as part-timers. This by now common business practice has been challenged in the courts by the EOC but without success. The judiciary has accepted the government's argument that changing the system would involve unacceptably high administrative costs; also that it is not discriminatory, since it applies to men as well as women.

It takes just a few women to say, 'This is what happened to me when I went on a career break', for employees generally to mistrust their job security and take only the minimum statutory maternity leave. Given that most banking employees are female, of reproductive age at some stage of their employment, this is a pretty big apprehension to have actively compromising a large part of any workforce – and doing so in spite of the intense PR campaign generated by Opportunity 2000 and the bank's public commitment to gender equality. As fear of the consequences reduces the numbers of women opting for career breaks, employers can then point to the low take-up of such schemes as evidence that women do not really want them.

Threats of litigation or experience of the tribunal system have confronted many companies with equality policies, or who have subscribed to Opportunity 2000, as braver members of staff have sought to challenge them under the Sex Discrimination or Equal Pay Acts. Lloyds Bank, Sainsbury's, British Rail, the Home Office, numerous local authorities, the TSB and Mirror Group Newspapers are just some on a lengthy list compiled by the EOC. It would be naive to expect organizations to implement fairer policies for purely altruistic reasons. The object is to brandish an alleged conversion in the face of criticism, and to spout what has become established rhetoric about widening the opportunities for women at the top. In this way a smokescreen can be formed over the trends which are reducing opportunities for women lower down the hierarchy. Supermarkets, retailing, banking and the health service are all keen advocates of increased casualization, with lower pay and fewer genuine opportunities for progression excused by flexibility for working mothers. Such practices dramatically reduce costs for employers who all too often are also proud apostles of 'equal opportunity'.

Schooldays – who stays back,
who gets on

Contrary to the law's advertised aims, our schools also lack a national policy or commitment to equal opportunity, with foreseeable consequences for the workplace of the future. The Sex Discrimination Act of 1975 requires all educational establishments 'to give pupils of both sexes equal access to all subjects offered and to any other benefits and services'. While the law is theoretically applied, little is done to ensure that social conditioning doesn't dissuade either girls or boys from taking subjects which they feel to be unsuited to their sex. Until the introduction of the National Curriculum there was also no requirement for boys and girls up to sixteen to study the same subjects. There has been no specific teacher training on gender presumptions, even though a hive of research has shown that girls while at school are particularly vulnerable to neglect and a lowering of self-esteem. Teachers are apt to reflect society as it is, anachronisms of outlook and all. At a conference on 'Girl-friendly Schooling' organized by the EOC in 1984, nearly half the teachers present thought that boys were better than girls at technical problems, 42 per cent thought that a woman's career was not as important as a man's, and 29 per cent said that a woman's place was in the home. One third believed career choices were due to innate differences between boys and girls. Many teachers favoured equal opportunity in principle; but in practice they were less committed, arguing that they had to prepare pupils for 'society as it is'. Young girls are repeatedly shown to be vulnerable to social conditioning when at school; and we do them a grave disservice by not training teachers to appreciate their distinct and different needs. We pretend instead that young girls and boys have an equal start within our education system, and that it is inherent genetic difference that causes them to lead such different lives.

We have never even attempted a more equitable balance of men and women within the teaching profession. Our children see few women at the top of the hierarchy as headteachers or heads of departments. Notions of innate gender differences are thus reinforced, lowering girls' expectations. On the other hand, women dominate nursery and primary-school teaching. Younger children are for some reason thought easier to teach; indeed nursery staff have shorter training, less pay and even lower status than other teachers because their role is thought to be primarily that of caring rather than education. Recently it was proposed to recruit mothers as a new lower-status category of primary-school teacher with just one year's training. In this way policymakers confirmed their failure to attach importance to a greater balance of sexes within primary teaching; even fewer men will be attracted to the profession if it is seen to be principally 'mum's' work, and children will continue to associate only the female sex with teaching infants.

Gender differences are apparent to children from as early as nine months. At nursery school, boys tend to be preoccupied with construction kits and cars, while girls occupy the home corner and like drawing and painting. Unless teachers understand the need for balanced play in both boys and girls, they are unlikely to encourage all children in a wider range of activities. Research on children as young as five has shown them aware of activities or occupations as being particular to one sex or another. This is so even when a child has direct experience of both sexes occupying a similar role, such as, say, a teacher or a doctor. Fixing cars, woodwork, fire fighting, climbing mountains and the natural sciences are seen as male activities by both boys and girls, while cooking, and mending and washing clothes are perceived as female concerns (Smithers *et al, Gender, Primary Schools . . .,* 1991). One child on such a study associated sewing with his mother, even though his father was a tailor.

Stereotyping of this kind shows itself in older children by a marked difference in public-examination entries. In 1985 nearly three times as many boys as girls took O-level and CSE physics and O-level computer science, and boys formed 95 per cent of entrants for design, technology, woodwork and metalwork exams. The converse was true of entrants in English literature, modern languages, home economics, teaching and sociology. Boys still outnumber girls by four to one for entry to A-level physics; and roughly 40 per cent of all women in higher education study arts subjects, languages and education, as opposed to only 18 per cent of men (White *et al, Women's Career Development,* 1992). The subjects which boys study tend to lead to higher-paid jobs, while those taught to women often take them nowhere. The National Curriculum does now prevent pupils from dropping certain subjects as early as thirteen; its emphasis, however, is on uniformity, rather than on ensuring that boys and girls receive a broadly balanced education.

Science and technology are notably absent from most primary-school teaching; this too can disadvantage girls by withholding an early injection of enthusiasm. Far greater emphasis is placed on developing reading and language skills, at which boys are known to be slower during the infant stage of schooling. In many primary and secondary schools, classes are still divided into boys and girls rather than at random: alphabetically, by height, or according to the sizes of their noses. Registers and lining up are also organized with the boys' names read out first. Boys have been shown to get more of their teachers' attention, shoving their hands up more frequently to answer questions, and dominating the use of computers and science equipment, while the girls wash up the equipment. In class boys will occupy the centre of the teacher's field of vision while girls occupy the margins. This is largely a question of confidence, according to Sue Mison, who teaches maths at a school in Bath: 'But if you're not concentrating, because the boys are so much more pushy than the girls you select them more. You have to alternate consciously, asking girls even if they haven't got their hands up; and without someone monitoring you, it's very hard to know whether or not you are being fair.' Where an individual's teaching practice is adapted to show awareness of gender distinctions this is usually done on a personal initiative, rather than on the prompting of teacher training or a formal equal-opportunity initiative.

For every teacher like Sue there are thousands who believe boys to be better at maths, and generally more intelligent, and who therefore expect more from them. When girls make a mistake in class it is often attributed to lack of intelligence; boys in the same situation are thought to be either lazy or mucking about. The answers to problems are more readily given to girls, while boys are allowed to muddle through; in consequence girls give up on problems more easily. When boys believe themselves in the right they are much more willing to argue with their teachers; this draws them to staff who like pupils to respond, and boys are in turn more likely to have confidence in their own all-round abilities. Inevitably this translates into higher expectations and aspirations. For girls whose confidence has been knocked, whole subject areas such as maths and sciences can be eliminated from the field of vision forever. On end-of-term reports it has been found that girls receive more approval for their willingness to be nice, rather than for scholastic achievement. Such prejudicial assumptions inevitably enter into internal marking of exams, with girls' papers graded for neatness while boys are assessed for content and creativity.

While most primary schools teach PE to mixed groups, at secondary school the sexes are segregated: boys play ball games, which encourage a healthy attitude towards competition; girls are channelled into dance and gymnastics, where emphasis is less on social interaction and more on individual grace and appearance. Physically boys occupy more space in schools; they also tend to eat up more of the school's resources in terms of extra-curricular activities, pastoral care and teacher time. They dominate the playgrounds with ball games, while girls play more quietly, taking up no more room than the length of a skipping rope. A study of playground use at one junior school in Colchester found that though boys comprised only half the pupils, they took up two thirds of playground space. In a rare attempt at forcing boys to show consideration as a sex, this school has introduced a 'no-ball playtime' once a week to encourage the children to integrate and to give the girls more physical space.

At primary school, girls do as well as boys at a full range of subjects, including science, when it is taught. But their success rate drops dramatically at secondary school. This is precisely the time when their self-esteem also declines radically in response to problems of adolescence. It must be said that in recent years the GCSE pass rate for girls in maths and sciences has actually improved: between 1974 and 1984 the proportion leaving school with O-level physics almost doubled. Passes in chemistry also rose, by 91 per cent. In 1991 38 per cent of girls left school with maths GCSE and 36 per cent with a science GCSE, as compared in 1982 with only 26 per cent and 25 per cent respectively. But take this as a proportion of the school-leaving population as a whole. Three times as many boys as girls sit A-level maths; and only 9 per cent of girls passed O-level physics, compared with 22 per cent of boys. While the science curriculum focuses on such concerns as how cars work, and presents a macho image of engineering and industrial design, inevitably it will still attract more boys than girls. Science teaching is rarely related to daily experience, or to the lives that girls would like to lead. Dr Jill Clough, head of the Royal Naval Girls School in Haslemere, is passionate about the need to improve education for girls in this way. 'My cousin studied chemistry and is now a renowned restorer. She uses chemicals all of the time to restore old masters. It's all about alchemy; and if you tell that to girls, it makes science sound exciting and applicable to life.' For example, 'I'd like to cover the floor with oily mud and teach girls how to get it off, so that they can save birds covered in oil from slicks.'

A lack of female scientists or mathematicians as role models does little to encourage girls into similar professions. But many schools have been slow in gearing the curriculum to highlight such examples, or introducing talks from women who do work in those fields. Filling this gap has largely been down to WISE, Women into Science and Engineering, a small wing of the Engineering Council whose buses tour secondary schools to give girls the chance to use technology away from boys. The National Curriculum now has combined sciences taught to GCSE standard; but girls are nonetheless at the vulnerable age of fifteen to sixteen when they have to choose whether to continue with science-related subjects. At a time when they are anxious to be attractive to boys, many are reluctant to be seen choosing a subject perceived as unfeminine. Dr Helen Mason of Cambridge University feels that, because they are forced to choose so publicly at such an age, young women may well find themselves channelled into decisions which they later regret. 'They can't go back if they make a mistake; it's too late. It may well be a good argument for a broader-based education system, like the French baccalauréat, until eighteen. It is interesting that the French have more women scientists than we do.'

Pupils enter secondary school as children; they emerge as young adults. Boys and girls alike can exhibit disgusting behaviour at this difficult age; but it is above all the self-esteem of girls that plummets, with the development of paralysing self-consciousness about their appearance and abilities. Many become introverted and uncertain, and 'I don't know' becomes their most frequent answer to the simplest of questions. It is at this susceptible age that girls develop eating disorders, and take up smoking at a far higher rate than boys. The onset of periods and the possibility of pregnancy make them feel suddenly vulnerable, whereas for young men adolescence makes them proud of their increased physical prowess and eager to test it.

There is little counselling in our schools for the problems peculiar to teenage girls, and which are bound to affect their academic performance. Even basic sex education can be absent, replaced, at best, with bits of information picked up from magazines, or at worst with inaccurate information from fellow pupils. What sex education there is may cover only the basic biological functions, as if we were rabbits rather than emotionally complicated beings. There is little said on the use of contraception, or on how to get the most enjoyment out of sex. Of fundamental importance to all young girls is knowing how to stand your ground and get what you want; yet this is considered far too radical to be taught in schools. Where else will most children learn these things? From their parents?

In practical terms the basic biological information that is

available falls short. More than 12 per cent of girls have to suffer the shock of knowing nothing in advance about menstruation. When this is covered in class, emphasis is on the biological aspects of menstruation rather than on emotional and practical problems. This means that if young girls have heavy or distressing periods and experience mood swings, they are wrongly inclined to feel abnormal and isolated. Boys, meanwhile, grow up in considerable ignorance of menstruation and its effects, often up to a time when their knowledge of women has to stand the test of adult relationships.

When girls do suffer while menstruating, they are often reluctant to admit it, receiving little sympathy from teachers. Shirley Prendergast, a senior research fellow at Cambridge University, has interviewed some five hundred girls from different parts of Britain. 'It takes energy to plan everything. Keeping supplies hidden, but to hand. Not revealing that you're unwell or tired, and making sure that you won't show. Forty-five per cent of girls claimed they suffered lack of concentration, so it seems likely that many are underachieving.' Half of all school lavatories intended for these girls were locked during lessons; when open, half had no locks or toilet paper, and even more lacked soap and adequate disposal facilities. Privacy and even the means of keeping clean are minimal. Many schools no longer have individual lockers for pupils, so that girls have to carry sanitary wear around with them. A common form of harassment is to turn out a girl's bag so that her most embarrassing possessions can be flung around the classroom.

Though the intricacies of sex are often brushed under the carpet, this doesn't reduce sexual activity, whatever the risk of accident or disillusionment. Two-thirds of 13- to 14-year-olds surveyed in 1991 had not been taught contraception at school; only half of 13- to 16-year-olds had had any education about relationships; and one third did not know at what point in her cycle a woman was most fertile. Yet it is the girls who are likely to take a severe knock, by undergoing an abortion or a teenage pregnancy or finding themselves suddenly sexually inhibited. Interviewing sixth-form girls at a school in Chippenham, I was staggered by the weight of problems they had to bear. Given their inexperience and age, with no one to talk to but each other, they were unlikely to share much concrete advice or assistance. Many spoke for the first time about their isolation or unhappiness, and several burst into tears. All of the girls bar one had had full sexual intercourse; all feared pregnancy. In the changing rooms the most talked-about subject was whether or not they were on the pill; and although all of them pretended to enjoy sex, when questioned further most had little idea how good good sex could be. One had an alcoholic mother; another felt friendless, and betrayed by a boyfriend who had left her for another girl in the school. One girl, seriously taken advantage of by an older man, was too frightened to go out with anyone else and just relieved not to be pregnant. She reproached herself for going out with the man, rather than blaming him for assaulting a minor, and up until that point had been unable to confide in any adult.

Careers advice offered to either sex in schools is often basic to the point of irrelevance. Girls, however, are likely to suffer an extra degree of negligence. One of the pupils I interviewed in Chippenham said that she wanted to go into PR. It transpired that a teacher had recommended this because she liked talking to people (I could almost hear him thinking, 'and you're pretty'). But when asked what the job entailed, she didn't know; the teacher hadn't bothered to tell her. Often girls are dissuaded from pursuing certain career paths, especially in sought-after professions where women nonetheless are few. Sometimes advice is prejudicial to the point of downgrading perfectly capable women. One young black woman, now a primary-school teacher, was told to opt for something easier. 'At school, I wanted to teach. But I was put off by the careers officer, who said that I ought to try another career that would be easier to get into. He also said that I should sit CSE rather than GCE. I went on to do nursery school training; and it was only when I went to night school, studied, sat my exams and went on to teacher training, that I realized I could always have become a teacher if he had not persuaded me out of it.'

Choosing marriage over a career is no longer seen by most young women as a possibility. But though they know that they have to earn their own living, most are unaware of how difficult this is likely to be, especially once they have children to raise. Society, too, expects young women to work yet few teachers or careers officers will tell them the best way to go about it. They grow up believing that they have equal opportunity and that the law protects their interests; yet they have little idea how ineffective any legislation or anti-discrimination policy is, and they are unaware of the additional sacrifices that they will have to make, over and above those their mothers made for them. The journalist and newscaster Julia Somerville says that when she is asked to give talks she has two standard lines. 'When I talk to schoolgirls, I say that you can have it all. But when I talk to working mothers, I talk about the set of compromises that we have to make, and how often we seem to end up feeling that we are not doing both well.' For young women properly educated about life as they will find it, such a distinction would not be necessary. By excluding young women's specific needs from their education, we force them either to behave more like boys if they want to succeed, or to believe that they have weaknesses, whereas in fact they have only biological differences.

Only single-sex secondary schools can ensure that girls are able to excel academically without having their self-confidence battered. In the absence of boys there is less distraction from the work in hand, as well as less anxiety about being attractive. In single-sex classes, for example, girls do better at least until the third year; they also get better marks in the subject if their teacher is female. Yet girls-only education is distinctly unfashionable; in the state sector such schools have been radically cut, from 3,000 thirty years ago, to just 240. 'The whole issue of girls' independent education is so political,' says Jill Clough. 'People are so suspicious – anxious – about giving girls priority over boys. It's as if they feel that there's something unnatural about all of those girls together.' This, despite all the evidence that girls so taught are more likely to make it to the top of their chosen field, will more readily assume they have every right to occupy the job they do, and will continue working in greater numbers after they have had children. Out of the ten female members of the Institute of Physics, seven attended single-sex schools, a tendency confirmed in every survey of successful women's education. 'In mixed schools the emphasis tends to be on exams,' says Dr Clough, 'whereas girls' schools encourage women to think for themselves and do what they want to do.' Her students at Haslemere's Royal Naval Girls School attend management-training-type sessions, where they have to work in teams to complete a task. 'The girls really love it; they thrive. It brings out leadership, teamwork and creativity.' Of one prospective head girl Dr Clough remarks, 'When I asked her what her hobbies were, she said needlecraft, cookery and mountain climbing; a combination of traditionally male and female activities. But it was the mountain climbing that gave her the edge, for you don't talk a lot in mountains other than to give exact precise instructions – there's too much at stake – and that brought out her qualities as a leader. Employers recognize that quality in women when they find it; but they don't know what to do with it.' Jill Clough's school aims to equip girls for life with an all-round education; unfortunately it is only available to those whose parents can afford the fees. In a majority of schools, meanwhile, girls are being asked to sacrifice the one educational advantage they had, in the controversial hope that their presence will civilize the boys.

Underfunding, complex and toothless regulations, and a general suspicion of social engineering – all combine to thwart our equality legislation and related policies. Some after all are born more equal than others. Women's concerns are either neglected, or boxed off. Only when somebody remembers to ask them do bodies such as the Women's National Commission and the ministerial group on women's issues write up policies, carry out research and comment on bills going before Parliament. It was in this arbitrary way that women's refuges were successfully exempted from the now defunct Poll Tax after the WNC pointed out that violent husbands would be able to track down their aberrant wives via addresses that were made public. If women's 'issues' really mattered they would be central to policymaking rather than on the periphery. Women's officers in trades unions and local government and equal-opportunity personnel in business would be allowed genuine power, whereas their current efforts are mostly as effective as substituting sticking plaster for radical surgery.

Have women deliberately been allowed to fail? At times I hear the bogeyman say, 'We've tried to do the best for you. We've designed laws and policies to help you; therefore it's not our fault if you women haven't seized your opportunity.' More probable is the chaos theory of history, according to which differing interests cajole or crash into each other until a solution emerges along the path of least resistance. From whatever motive, however, the former, more malicious result is the one achieved. Men and women alike are fooled into believing we have equal opportunity, and then marvel that there are not more women in positions of influence. Men can assure themselves that they no longer discriminate and therefore cannot be challenged; and women attribute their failures to inherent weaknesses of their own.

Complacency notwithstanding, equal-opportunity policies, women's units and our hard-won equality legislation have to be a good thing. Merely knowing of their existence can empower women to seek retribution for an injustice. If collectively they do fail, it will not be through their own or their users' fault, but as a result of inadequate official funding or a lack of other support. A disquieting precedent has already arisen: women's units and equal opportunity policies have started to disappear, or are presented as redundant, when they have never properly been allowed to function. The same device, of reducing to the point of impotence, could threaten the very existence of our equality legislation. The law can change cultural values; but only if it is enabled to work, through mechanisms such as effective financial deterrent and training. The danger otherwise is that our equality legislation would be labelled redundant or benignly displaced, so we'd be told, by the pitch-and-shove of market forces. Without it Britain would be a very dark place indeed.

chapter seven

the myth
of
the sex war

'How I hate the word feminism.' Dr Helen Mason, of Cambridge University, is dedicated to improving the science education of girls. She is also keenly aware of the general disadvantages that women face. 'I wish they could think of another word. It's not about hating men, but about recognizing women's value.' But feminism never was about hating men; it has merely sought to right the balance tipped so distinctly in men's favour. Feminism is nothing more than an intellectual tool enabling men and women to understand how preconceptions of masculine and feminine behaviour have shaped our lives and disadvantaged women. Acting on its ideals is at times exhilarating, and often depressing; but it was never going to solve the world's problems. Yet now it is blamed for not doing so overnight.

'Feminist' has become one of the most loaded and ill-defined words in the English language. Almost every woman interviewed for this book, when asked if she was one said, 'That depends what you mean by feminism.' All believed in the principles of equal opportunity, and recognized that women faced distinct problems as a result of their sex. But the word 'feminism' has been so successfully defined as man-hating, aggressive, anarchic and lesbian that few were prepared to stand tall and claim it for themselves.

The term 'postfeminism' is consequently used to imply that the women's movement is dead. In fact it is alive and obstreperous, focusing on smaller areas to exact change. Groups such as the Women's Medical Federation, Women in Dentistry and Women in Publishing serve members of the professions. There is a well-run, if poorly funded, childcare lobby, with organizations such as the Daycare Trust and the Working Mothers' Association making recommendations on childcare to employers, lobbying politicians and filling an essential gap in advising the public on where to find daycare for their children. The national network of playgroups and afterschool clubs was set up by a group of women dissatisfied with the statutory provision. The voluntary efforts of all these organizations do at least help to fill the chasm left by the state's blindness to the needs and welfare of mothers and children. Their imagination, innovation and sheer dedication show just what could be done if there was the political will.

But this energy is rarely harnessed, let alone subsidized, by the state. It is seen, not as crucial in enabling women to work, but as an extension of the tradition of female voluntary labour, in which for example women make cakes and organize jumble sales in order to raise money for their child's school. The Women's Aid Federation provides advice and refuge through 120 local groups to the victims of violent men. But these groups are poorly funded and the refuges overcrowded; often they have to turn women and children away because there is simply no room for them. Where else are battered women to go? How are they to live without economic independence? Often they don't have enough money for a bus fare, let alone shelter. Such is the value placed on their important work by a state happy to confine their efforts to the underfunded voluntary sector.

Because we now have laws against discrimination, there is

one message that has got through, namely that you mustn't actually be seen to discriminate. Where once discrimination was overt, now it has been forced underground. Employers realize that they cannot advertise solely for a man or a woman; but they also know they can stick the words 'we are an equal opportunities employer' on the bottom of their advertisement and then recruit whom they like. They can indicate through the wording and the salary (or lack of it, 'commensurate with experience') that they would prefer a man, or communicate their preference verbally to employment agencies or head hunters. If a woman fails repeatedly to get promotion she can no longer say, 'It's because I'm a woman, isn't it?', once a company has circulated an equal-opportunity policy.

Men have been allowed to adopt the language of feminism without altering the practices of a lifetime. Too many still think it enough to say, 'It must be so marvellous being a woman', or, 'I'm a feminist', and then promote or recruit men over women because they still see a woman as a risk. The man who will declare, 'I have the greatest respect for women', will also blame all women for their own secondary status on the grounds of not being sufficiently confident or assertive. Often the existence of an equal-opportunity policy allows men to become even more inconsiderate. Sandra Brown, a check-out assistant at Sainsbury's, feels that men interpret equal opportunity as not opening a door for a woman. 'But all that stuff is just common politeness; you should do it; for anyone. My brothers are lazy, so I cop all the housework; and then at work the men like to watch the women doing the heavy work. If you ask someone who's passing to take the rubbish away he'll say no, you do it, you want equal opportunity. It just allows them to be lazy.'

Feminism itself is partly to blame for alienating men, for forcing them to pretend they have shed sexism overnight when often all they have done is to change chameleon-like in response to a new environment. Largely at fault is the suppression of supposedly sexist language. Leigh Watson, a botanical research technician, describes a conversation with a colleague, 'who was prepared to say that he felt intimidated by homosexual men. If you can say that, then you haven't got a problem; but if you harbour those thoughts then you definitely have. The same is true for equality issues. You have to acknowledge prejudice rather than pretend that it doesn't exist.' However, feminism itself has been denigrated from outside with spectacular success. Pushed into its own box, it has been spuriously linked to the lunatic revolutionary fringe in such a way that few women want to be associated with it. Those who consider themselves equal citizens with men, dismiss feminism as no longer relevant to their own lives. Some are wary of being labelled a troublemaker; others don't care to be dismissed as a token, catapulted to the top not on merit but to placate some equal-opportunity policy. The very thought of a mediocre woman at the top is dismissed as intolerable by both men and women, although it is baffling how they fail to see the number of male mediocrities up there.

While feminism has done much to highlight the discriminatory fabric of Britain, it has done little to alter it. A storm of controversy and debate has been stirred up as it challenges archaic attitudes and enters into the souls of young people who have never been to a women's group or read of feminist theory. Beverley Andrews, a young dental nurse, looked blank when I asked her what she understood by the word feminism. But she was quite clear about the fact that she wanted both to have a baby and to continue with her career. Margo Taylor, a tennis coach in her late twenties, had no idea what feminism meant and expressed no interest in finding out. 'I'm independent, and my being financially independent has to be important to the person I'm involved with and end up marrying.' Women who have grown up unaware of being influenced by feminism and an improved education nonetheless take heightened expectations with them wherever they go. Feminism is not an ideology which is put on and taken off like a new outfit. It enters the heart of one's being and influences everything a woman suffers or does. In universities, female academics, interested as women, have turned to researching how aspects of their specialisms have affected their own sex. Often this kind of research gets hived off into a part of academia far from public view. It becomes categorized as 'sociological' and therefore secondary to the supposedly more scientific and analytical research conducted by men. Despite such dismissals, across the media female revisionists persist. As more women enter publishing and television they commission books and programmes looking at the female perspective as well as a male view of things. Having once entered management, business or advertising, they have likewise shoved their foot in at a door that was formerly locked and barred. They are catalysts of change simply by being there, even if their high visibility does make them more vulnerable. In the short term, it is true, each female failure helps entrench prejudice, as the entire gender is blamed for the faults of one woman. But an ever shorter time passes before there is another talented, ambitious young woman to fill her shoes.

When the actress Juliet Stevenson worked for the Royal Shakespeare Company she felt that by not having a female director of any production a rich area of interpretation was excluded. 'Shakespeare is more concerned with gender than any other writer. *As You Like It* is all about what it is to be male and what it is to be female. Productions are constantly trying to find ways of making Shakespeare relevant to today, and it seemed to me foolish never to do Shakespeare from a female perspective.' She became increasingly preoccupied with this; realizing at length that it would never be debated internally, she and other actresses opened up a discussion in the press. The company's then director was furious. 'First he sent me a letter saying something like, you can't be a guerrilla in an establishment institution – meaning, don't rock the boat; and then he summoned all of the actresses to a meeting, and said that we could have a slot at the Barbican the following year to do our own thing – a woman-only event. This was terrifying. We had no access to management and no resources. We had responsibility without power, and it also implied that there was a consensus amongst all of the actresses.' After a series of exhilarating and tortuous late-night meetings, they decided to do *Heresies* by Deborah Levy which in due course was staged to a mixed critical response. 'It was a one-off event which would either stand or fall at the end, but it did nothing to alter the process by which things are done. It's the process, not the product. No one is saying that women directors are better than men.'

Women have been sidelined by the treatment of their suggestions or complaints as if these were somehow distinct and separate from the real world of men. Appointing women to deal with 'women's issues' in companies merely allows men to consider these contentions dealt with. Although we have boxed women into their own compartment through our equality legislation and equal-opportunity policies, they are not an ethnic minority group. Nor in most other ways are they homogenous, with similar needs and concerns. As individuals they vary increasingly now that their careers beyond mothering extend in so many directions. They are half of the human race and an essential balance to the other sex. True equality of opportunity means society altering its base sufficiently to accommodate the needs of both sexes rather than dispensing panaceas whose quackery predestines them to fail.

The idea of a sex war perpetuates images of men and women making a battle of their relationships. In reality, as individuals they mostly try not to see the worst in each other, but diligently to seek the best. A woman who has been let down by a man may feel sore for a while, but most are intelligent enough to see the opposite sex as something more varied than a pack of cards. Even personal distrust going back a generation to an inadequate father is not invincible. Kirsty Wild is a primary school teacher, pregnant with her third child. 'I come from a strong matriarchal family and I had to be careful not to be off men. There were five generations of women who were still alive, while the men all died off, or disappeared, or got kicked out. So I went into my twenties thinking, I've got to reassess all this, not because men are wonderful but because I'm holding a very biased standpoint here. My expectations came from a father who was a bit of an arsehole really . . . men would let you down, and weren't worth an awful lot. Yesterday I went to the hospital for a check-up. The midwives had all told me that the baby's head had engaged; and the male consultant comes along, feels around and says, "I think it might be breech." I thought, "What does he know? He's only the male consultant – all these midwives know. *They* know everything." But he was right. At the end of the day, he was the only one who had picked up that the baby was breech. One can expect too much of women and too little of men.'

Women who nurture a hatred of the entire male gender are so few as to be invisible. Yet their influence has been exaggerated prodigiously by journalists who love a good story and by gynaephobic, feeble men who interpret every criticism as a swipe at their genitals. Most who dare to call themselves feminists do not hate men; they merely wish to help women achieve equality. All the women interviewed for this book have expressed feelings of exclusion from the male world, from the very powerful, such as the Director of Public Prosecutions, through to the poorest mother on an inner-city housing estate. Countless women at work felt confined to the wings, while men proceeded with the real agenda; mothers at home with young children felt excluded completely from the only milieu which appears to matter, the world of work. Yet nobody expressed the hatred towards men which is often implicit when the word 'feminist' is spat out as a term of abuse. Many women acknowledged that they had developed sufficient confidence to compete only because fathers or lovers had encouraged them to do so. Others pointed out that they were in their present job because a man gave it to them. Women need to get on with men and to have their approval in order to progress and feel connected to the real world. When women complained it was about men's laziness and their inability to understand completely the female perspective, rather than to express an attitude of 'all men are bastards'.

Women want to work with men, not against them. Even personal experience of physical and psychological torture can be followed by reasoned forgiveness. One night Janet Gardener ended years of abuse by stabbing her boyfriend with a kitchen knife as he smashed her head against a wall. While she was serving a prison sentence for the offence, her daughter got married. Janet said on her release that though she could not see herself having another relationship, her son-in-law was 'a lovely man, not a bit aggressive'. Time puts a new perspective on many women's anger with individual men. Ivy Simpson, a former trade union negotiator, is still an active campaigner on equality issues. With her male partner she has set up a consultancy advising companies on how to implement equal-opportunity policies. She is happy to see the man-hating dogma which fuelled so much feminist debate in the 1970s – female equals good and male equals potential rapist – as an anachronism. 'I was very angry with men as a whole. But now, when I look back on my life, I realize that the most important people who really looked out for me were men, and that the most difficult relationship of my life was with a woman.' Freed from doctrines of sexual hostility, men and women can begin to view each other more as individuals and less as gendered beings. There is no gross natural imbalance in the equation between the sexes; many of the women interviewed for this book have expressed as much uneasiness in relying on their sex as in trusting men.

Dishearteningly, it will sometimes appear that nothing has

altered, whereas a great deal has in fact changed. We have only to look back thirty years to the time when marriage rather than motherhood was the bar to work; sixty years to when the expectation of the female sex was of nothing but motherhood; or ninety years, to contemplate a time when women's views were considered so unimportant as not to justify a political vote. Growing up more independent than before, younger women expect as much from life as boys do – until, that is, they encounter discrimination at first hand. Bruising though this disillusionment can be, it tends not to come from individual misogyny, but from the diffuse, impersonal weight of a society that has yet to adapt itself to its citizens' changed expectations. Individual young men and women want to form relationships with each other and to find a way of doing so, in spite of the supposed 'sex war'. This fact is not wasted on older women who struggled for most of their lives over equality issues with few apparent results – but who now see their children adapting to great change. Brenda Wilkinson worked for many years as an equal-opportunity officer with a local authority before joining the EOC. She has a son in his early twenties of whom she says, 'When I listen to him talking with his friends, I can't believe sometimes how much has changed in the understanding in relationships between boys and girls. They say things to each other that previous generations were never able to say. That gives me great hope, as I know that there is no going back.'

In no way do our children's developing views of the opposite sex conform to the black-and-white theory of non-sexist child-rearing. Instead they take account of the many intermediate shades that represent the evolution of human society. Girls are still girls, different from boys in more ways than we may ever know. Gail Rebuck of Random House describes how she finally gave up pandering to non-sexist methods of child-rearing and bought her daughter a Barbie doll. 'Now there are twenty in the house. What am I meant to do?' she exclaims. 'On the other hand, she's happy in a dress and going to ballet classes, but she also talks about what she is going to do when she grows up; she assumes that she is going to fulfil herself in some way. She is aware at six that she can do what she likes. I wasn't, at her age. You got married and had children, and my brother was the one who went off and did things.'

As girls grow up demanding more from life, they force boys to expect more from them. Vicky Berger has taught at a primary school in rural Staffordshire where she ran workshops, both with girls and boys together and separately, on gender stereo-typing. In one session on the subject of maleness she asked a group of boys to design a poster depicting what interests men. 'While one less able group drew chunky watches and typical macho images, another drew a young woman dressed nicely, rather than in tarty clothes, who they imagined to be their future partner – "If you've got that, then you've got everything," said one young boy. It means you really can get through to them.'

In reassessing relationships with their fathers, once they become parents themselves, an increasing number of men seek to break the former pattern of absence and distance. They want to be involved in their children's upbringing. David Jenkins, who cares for his own son full time, recalls that his father 'slogged his guts out for thirty years to keep us fed and shod, and precious little respect he got for it. Because he was never there, we never knew how hard he worked; and then when he left we thought, what a bastard. He had that element of sacrifice that so many men have – whatever happens I'm going to stick to this job and bring home the bacon – and eventually he felt that he wasn't getting the respect for it that he deserved. That happens to so many men; they shoulder the blame for a broken marriage, and then shuffle off into the night. And a long lonely night it is too.' David would prefer not to have a career if it meant losing his relationship with his son. 'I would rather that he grew up with some kind of relationship with me – manhood

that is not to be feared or to be overly proud of: there's just me.'
David may be unusual in that he is a full-time carer while his
wife, a consultant anaesthetist, is sole breadwinner. But his
concern for a fuller relationship with his child is no longer out of
the ordinary. Albeit in small numbers, more men are prepared to
insist on leaving work early to meet an obligation to a child, like
attending sports day or collecting him or her from school. No
more than a generation has passed since men were rarely in the
habit of picking up their children and holding them, let alone
changing their nappies or providing affection or solace when
they were upset. Now the borderline between roles has softened.

Accusations of 'new man-ism' or 'political correctness' are
now sometimes levelled at the attempts, often valiant, of individual men and women to understand one another and live within
a more equitable partnership. Accusation would be better
thrown at the very fabric of a society that claims allegiance to
equal opportunity while at the same time ensuring that at every
turn women have a secondary status. The myth of a sex war
deflects attention from the most fundamental inequities – that
women form the majority of the poor, and that premeditated
policies keep them economically dependent on men. Men and
women may well consider themselves individuals, with certain
freedoms in how they choose to live, and with whom. But the
state still views us as members of family units comprising breadwinners, who pay tax, and their dependants, who live on hand-
outs, with the giver, usually a man, having priority in everything
over the taker.

This assumption, automatically perceiving women as the
second sex, pervades every aspect of Britain's organs of power.
In Parliament it influences policymaking, and is manifest in
government's repeated neglect of childcare, its avoidance of
political hot potatoes such as abortion, its enshrining of legislation which allows secondary status and lower pay for part-time,
mainly female, workers, and its refusal properly to empower our

equality legislation. It runs through the heart of our welfare state, whose payment of a state pension and unemployment benefit is based on regular contributions from those in work, and which takes no account of the fact that the mothering responsibilities of working women often leave them with a broken record of employment. It tyrannizes the world of work, which takes for granted unlimited dedication on the part of male employees, absent from home all hours while their wives look after the children, and which sees female employees as merely biding time until they can fulfil their true vocation of motherhood. It is ingrained in every aspect of the economy, with women almost invariably paid less, in whatever sector they work, because their income is presumed to be less needed.

So long as whole areas of employment are segregated by gender, the average pay of women can be held down without breaking the tenuous law that 'guarantees' equal pay between the sexes. From behind the fig leaf of equal-opportunity policy, government and employers can make patronizing promises of good intent without ever having them put to the test. Such policy remains only a sop, a public relations exercise with no substance, while tagged on to a structure which only allows women access to power provided they behave like men. Apprehension and loathing can still stalk women in response to their reproductive abilities, and ambush many in the form of a choice between motherhood and career. Such is the reluctance of Britain's political and economic infrastructure to make allowances for our biological differences and so accept us on genuinely equal terms.

In the face of institutionalized discrimination, individual men and women can only strive so far towards a more equitable relationship. 'I feel anxious about the way we reinforce the fact that it is up to women,' says Julia Somerville. 'Children see women, not men, bringing up children. The worry is that we may be raising a new generation of sexists who see their father

out at work all day long and exhausted at the weekend ...
Many men have a hard life. They want more time with their
children. The twentieth century's work ethic is totally counter-
productive. When I joined ITN there were roughly 1,300
people. Now there are less than 700, and the emphasis is on
fewer people doing more hours. That can't help women with
children, and it doesn't help men. Why hasn't the male revolution started?'

Janet Cohen, director of Charterhouse Bank, echoes Julia's
longing for a world where women and men work less hard. 'I
now feel that at 51 I have the confidence to kick the world
around. But imagine what we could do if we could transfer some
of that confidence to our early thirties. None of us manage to do
that. I see chaps staggering around who have obviously been up
all night with the baby. If they could only drop their heads on to
their desks and say, "I'm sorry, but I need a week off." Pro-
ductivity wouldn't necessarily fall, and everybody would have a
nice time. We overcompete. You need to be a director here by
the time you are 34; but you can't do that and have babies. But
what the hell does it matter if you're not a director until 37?'

Full-time working women can often feel as if they are toiling
just to pay the childminder and keep the bairns shod. But as an
alternative to their hard-earned gains, full-time housewifery,
and less economic power, are no longer acceptable. Women
with years of training behind them are aware that to give up
work would be professional suicide, whatever the temptation to
exchange the exhaustion of juggling work and motherhood in
return for a life of jam-making. Elinor Parker, a successful
dentist with teenage children to raise, sometimes wishes her
husband had earned more money, so that she didn't have to
work so hard. 'But if that had been the case, I know that I
wouldn't have this independence and confidence. I think that's
something that feminism has to keep reinforcing.' From Malay-
sia, where they lived when the children were small, she and her

family returned to England, to find her husband was out of a job. Elinor accordingly became the breadwinner. 'He put on weight, got very clingy, and kept asking me whether I loved him, just like women do when they are in that situation. It was an interesting lesson in role reversal. I used to feel that I should be able to get home from work, and put my feet up with the newspaper; and he used to feel that I didn't talk to him. Now that we both have full-time jobs, there's balance in our relationship.' David, as an actor who looks after their young son while his wife is the main breadwinner, has developed similar traits, and feels he understands the plight of millions of other housewives. 'Although we've reversed roles, the roles themselves haven't changed. The fact that I'm a man doesn't make any difference – she's the breadwinner and I'm the housewife, and we both suffer from the problems that are inherent in those roles: I'm taken for granted, nothing I do is right, my time is taken up with domestic trivia. There is little in the way of intellectual stimulation, and there is nothing at the end of the day that I can feel satisfied about.'

It is easy to forget that in the traditional marriage, where the wife is entirely supported by the husband, the imbalance of power can provoke mistrust. Sally Roberts is entirely supported by her husband, and has two children. She does not need to work for the money; nonetheless, the lack of an independent income or identity through work of her own means that she feels vulnerable. Her husband's solid sense of identity, gained through his work, moves her to resent him; so too does the fact that he will not tell her how much he earns. While she knows that by average standards he is rich, she has no idea precisely how well off he might be. 'It implies a lack of trust that I'm not taken seriously, that I'm not part of his business. It means that his money is not my money. If I don't know how much it is, how can it possibly be mine. He has a concept of women as spending, untrustworthy, frivolous . . . and that really pisses me off.'

Within her marriage Sally feels it is fear of the unknown world beyond, and her own vulnerability through lack of work, that holds her in place. 'My parents kept up a marriage, that was quite obviously not a good one, for years and years. What that's given me is the concept that you can have an unfulfilling marriage, rather than a real concept of loving which is what they hoped it would give me. That kind of fraud perpetuates itself . . . I'm now doing it; it was handed down.' There are, of course, many happy marriages where the wife does not work. But the potentiality for vulnerability is always there. People and marriages change. Should the husband leave for a younger woman, divorce is likely to bring a life of poverty. If a woman is fortunate in finding a husband, and a father to her children, who is not abusive, violent or simply neglectful, she is still susceptible to abuse and neglect from a society which sees the needs of women and mothers as secondary to those of men.

Only in a three-way alliance between the individual, employers and the state can equal citizenship for women be sought and won. The divide has become irrelevant between the private, once female, world of family and the more public, formerly men-only, world of work. We cannot pretend home life has nothing to do with work, when the majority of women now enter both worlds, and when men increasingly seek to spend time with their children. Nor can we maintain the fiction that home life is separate from the state, when country is nothing but the sum of its people. Without the family there is no context; no emotional support for each worker and no market to sell to. At some point in the future these pretences must give way, and changed attitudes, expectations and lifestyles are bound to alter the fabric of the British state. Tolerance is needed in the world of work towards the needs of children and their parents, who should be welcomed into the workplace rather than viewed with dread. If families need good fathers then good fatherhood must be encouraged by public policy. Removing the secondary status of pay and conditions for part-time workers would encourage more men to join them and spend time with their children. Removing downward pressure on women's pay in a segregated labour market would raise the status of their skills. High-quality national childcare would help men and women alike to better meet their serious responsibilities as parents. Child-rearing does not take a lifetime; we should recognize that mothers now need to work, to provide for their children as well as to preserve their own sanity. It is working women, rather than isolated depressed housewives, who make good mothers. They have more to offer their children, not only economically, but in understanding better how the world works. The punishment of motherhood continues meanwhile, whether through derisory maternity provisions, dismissal for pregnancy, or exclusion from career progression because working mothers have less time to engage in extracurricular politics. It is time to stop the loading on of guilt, for we just don't need it.

Cost is the main argument used against righting the institutionalized imbalance, in favour of women. Official rhetoric denies that we could ever afford such changes. In reality we cannot afford to resist them. By extending full citizenship to women in fact as well as in law, we would spare ourselves a world of loss, as individuals and as a society. We would also show, rather than just say, that women matter; they matter as much as men. The private salvations of friendship and family life cannot come about in a vacuum. They depend utterly upon the workings of the world at large. Living in that world on an equal basis with men, not only would women feel better esteemed; our children would grow up valuing them more because society would publicly have stated an allegiance to them.

Centuries of patriarchy notwithstanding, misogynist presumption and prejudice do indeed find themselves in retreat. If it is a process as irresistible as glaciation, it does sometimes appear as slow; and the frustration comes in wondering if we will all be dead first. There is neither merit nor success to be had from just sitting back and hoping that one day justice will prevail, without helping to push change in the direction that women want. As Barbara Castle, whom we have largely to thank for the very existence of the Sex Discrimination Act, has pointed out, there is no point in striving to change the manifestations of prejudice when the very core is rotten. 'If you fight battles for little things, the men will give you the little things and never the big ones. Don't be distracted by the trivia; go for the jugular' (*Guardian*, 2 March 1990).

So many improvements in the female lot have come from the continued efforts of women pleading or screaming their case until men are forced to listen. The balance of power can be shifted so that both halves of citizenship, male and female, are equally served; and the tedium, for women, of banging on decade after decade about these issues must surely one day become redundant. We are interested in other things; we have so much else to offer. In time to come, the numbers of educated and qualified women will duly swell within the ranks of influence and reduce the discrimination which still lives at the heart of our culture. Sooner or later we must build a society founded upon the strength of true equality of opportunity where difference between the sexes is respected and welcomed. We have everything to gain from such a civilization. I just hope that I live long enough to see it.

bibliography

A Balanced Workforce? Achieving Cultural Change for Women: A Comparative Study, Ashridge Management Research Group, 1991

Abdela, Lesley, *Breaking Through the Glass Ceilings*, Metropolitan Recruitment Authorities, 1991

Acker, Sandra (ed), *Teachers, Gender and Careers*, The Falmer Press, 1989

Action Towards Equality for Nursing Staff, Midwives and Health Visitors, Nursing and Midwifery Staffs Negotiating Council, 1992

Adler, Sue, Jenny Laney and Mary Packer, *Managing Women*, Open University Press, 1993

Allen, Isobel, *Any Room at the Top?*, PSI, 1988

Allen, Sheila and Carol Truman (eds), *Women in Business*, Routledge, 1993

Ashburner, Lynn, 'Men Managers and Women Workers: Women Employees as an Underused Resource', *British Journal of Management*, Vol 2, 1991

Baxter, Marilyn, *Women in Advertising*, Institute of Practitioners in Advertising, 1990

Beechey, Veronica and Tessa Perkins, *A Matter of Hours*, Polity Press, 1987

Beechey, Veronica and Elizabeth Whitelegg, *Women in Britain Today*, Open University Press, 1986

Bevan, Stephen, *Staff Retention in the Inland Revenue*, IMS, 1991

Bevan, Stephen and Marc Thompson, *Merit Pay, Performance Appraisal and Attitudes to Women's Work*, IMS, 1992

Bock, Gisela and Susan James, *Beyond Equality and Difference*, Routledge, 1992

Bourn, Colin, *Sex Discrimination Law: A Review*, Institute of Employment Rights, 1992

Brannen, Julia and Peter Moss, *Managing Mothers*, Unwin Hyman, 1991

Breen, Dana (ed), *The Gender Conundrum*, Routledge, 1993

Business Case and Action for Women in the NHS, Dept of Health Women's Unit, 1992

Cameron, Ivy, *Equal Opportunities for Women: A Challenge for the Finance Industry and BIFU* (BIFU), 1989

Campbell, Anne, *Men, Women and Aggression*, Basic Books, 1993

'Case Studies in Equality Training', *Equal Opportunities Review 39*, Sept/Oct 1991

Castle, Barbara, *Fighting all the Way*, Macmillan, 1993

Chambers, Gerry and Stephen Harwood-Richardson, *Solicitors in England and Wales: Practice, Organisation and Perceptions*, Second Report: The Private Practice Firm, Research Study no 8, The Law Society, 1991

Clarke, Karen, *Women and Training: A Review*, EOC Research Discussion Series, 1991

Cockburn, Cynthia, *In the Way of Women: Men's Resistance to Sex Equality in Organisations*, Macmillan, 1991

Coe, Trudy, *The Key to the Men's Clubs: Opening the Doors to Women in Management*, BHS/Institute of Management, 1992

Cohen, Bronwen, *Caring for Children: the 1990 Report*, Family Policy Studies Centre

Cohen, Bronwen and Neil Fraser, *Childcare in a Modern Welfare System*, IPPR, 1991

Collinson, David L., David Knights and Margaret Collinson, *Managing to Discriminate*, Routledge, 1990

Conway, Jean (ed), *Prescription for Poor Health*, Maternity Alliance, 1988

Crompton, Rosemary and Kay Sanderson, *Gendered Jobs and Social Change*, Unwin Hyman, 1990

Bibliography

Dale, Angela, 'Women in the Labour Market', *Social Policy Review*, 1990/91

Dale, Angela and Heather Joshi, *The Economic and Social Status of British Women*, Paper for conference in Berlin, 19–21 Feb 1922

De Lyon, Hilary and Frances Widdowson Migniuolo, *Women Teachers: Issues and Experiences*, OUP, 1989

Dex, Shirley, Steve Lissenburgh and Mark Taylor, *Women and Low Pay: Identifying the Issues*, EOC, 1995

Dex, Shirley, *Women's Attitudes Towards Work*, Macmillan, 1988

Dex, Shirley, *Women's Occupational Mobility: A Lifetime Perspective*, Macmillan, 1987

Dex, Shirley and Lois B. Shaw, *British and American Women at Work*, Macmillan, 1986

Dixon, Pat, *Making the Difference: Women and Men in the Workplace*, Heinemann, 1993

Dyson, Roger, *Changing Labour Utilisation in the NHS Trusts: The Re-profiling Paper*, University of Keele, 1992

'EC Law: Reaching the Parts UK Law Cannot Reach', *Equal Opportunities Review 39*, Sept/Oct 1991

Employment Gazette, Dec 1991

Employment Gazette, April 1992

EOC Annual Report 1991

EOC Annual Report 1992

EOC *Black and Ethnic Minority Women & Men in Britain*, 1994

EOC Workforce Employment Agency Ltd, *Report and findings of a formal investigation*, 1995

Equality Management: Women's Employment in the NHS, EOC 1992

Equal Opportunities Review 22, Nov/Dec 1988

Equal Opportunities Review 31, May/June 1990

Equal Opportunities Review 36, March/April 1991

Equal Opportunities Review 42, March/April 1992

Equal Opportunities Review 44, July/Aug 1992

Equal Opportunities Review 47, Jan/Feb 1993

Equal Opportunities and the School Governor, EOC, 1985

'Equal Opportunities in the Legal Profession', *Equal Opportunities Review 45*, Sept/Oct 1992

The Equal Pay Legislation: Recommendations for Change, EOC, Northern Ireland, 1990

Equal Pay for Work of Equal Value, The British Psychological Society, March 1991

Equal Pay for Men and Women: Strengthening the Acts, EOC, 1990

An Equal Start: Guidelines on Equal Treatment for the Under-Eights, EOC, 1992

Ermisch, John F., Heather Joshi and Robert Wright, *Women's Wages in Great Britain*, Birkbeck College Discussion Paper, 1990

Ermisch, John F. and Robert E. Wright, *Entry to Lone Parenthood: Analysis of Marital Dissolution*, Birkbeck College Discussion Paper, 1990

Evandrou, Maria, *Challenging the Invisibility of Carers: Mapping Informal Care Nationally*, LSE Welfare State Programme, 1990

The Everywoman Directory 1991–92, (Everywoman)

Eyer, Diane E., *Mother–Infant Bonding: A Scientific Fiction*, Yale University Press, 1993

Facts and Figures about Abortion, NAC Education, 1992

Family Planning Association Annual Report 1990/91

Family Policy Studies Centre Bulletin No 6, winter 1989

The Farley Report 1992

Ferris, Paul, *Sex and the British*, Michael Joseph, 1993

Firth-Cozens, Jenny, 'Sources of Stress in Women Junior House Officers', *BMJ*, Vol 301, no 6743, 1990

Firth-Cozens, Jenny (ed) and Michael A. West, *Women at Work*, Open University Press, 1991

Ford Motor Company 1991: Equal Opportunities Report, March 1992

Forty Years On: The CUWAG Report on the Numbers and Status of Academic Women in the University of Cambridge, Cambridge University Women's Action Group, Sept 1988

French, Marilyn, *The War against Women*, Hamish Hamilton, 1992

Bibliography

Gardner, Jo, *No Offence*, Industrial Society, 1993

Gender and the Criminal Justice System, The Home Office, 1992

General Household Survey 1991, HMSO, 1993

Girls and Boys, Moving Towards Equal Opportunity at School, Editions Infor Jeunes, Brussels, 1988

Gomulka, K. and W. Stern, *The Employment of Married Women in the UK 1970–83*, LSE, 1986

Goss, Sue and Helen Brown, *Equal Opportunities for Women in the NHS*, Office for Public Management/NHS Management Executive, 1991

Halford, Alison, *No Way up the Greasy Pole*, Constable, 1993

Haste, Cate, *Rules of Desire*, Chatto, 1992

Health and Personnel Social Services Statistics for England, HMSO, 1992

Health of Half the Nation, Royal College of Nursing, 1992

Hennessy, Eilis, Sue Martin, Peter Moss and Edward Melhuish, *Children and Daycare: Lessons from Research*, Peter Chapman Publishing, 1992

Henwood, Melanie, Lesley Rimmer and Malcolm Wicks, *Inside the Family: Changing Roles of Men and Women*, Family Policy Studies Centre, 1987

Hewitt, Patricia, *About Time: The Revolution in Work and Family Life*, Institute for Public Policy Research, 1993

Hirsch, Wendy, Sue Hayday, Jill Yeates and Claire Callender, *Beyond the Career Break*, Institute of Manpower Studies Report no 223, 1992

Holtermann, Sally, *Investing in Young Children*, National Children's Bureau, 1992

Holtermann, Sally and Karen Clarke, *Parents, Employment Rights and Childcare: The Costs and Benefits of Improved Provision*, EOC, 1993

Howell, Sara, Jill Rubery and Brendan Burchill, 'Gender and Skills', *Work, Employment and Society*, Vol 4, no 2, 1993

Howell, Sara and Jill Rubery, *Employers' Working Time: Policies and Women's Employment*, EOC, 1992

Hughes, Sally, *The Circuit Bench – A Woman's Place?*, Law Society, 1991

Huws, Ursula, Jennifer Hurstfield and Riki Holtmaat, *What Price Flexibility? The Casualisation of Women's Employment*, Low Pay Unit, 1989

Huws, Ursula, *The New Homemakers*, Low Pay Unit, 1984

Incomes Data Services Study 472 on Childcare, Dec 1990

Incomes Data Services Study 476 on Maternity Leave, Feb 1991

Incomes Data Services Study 521 on Childcare, Jan 1993

Janus, Samuel S. and Cynthia L. Janus, *The Janus Report on Sexual Behaviour*, Wiley, 1993

Job Insecurity, Citizens' Advice Bureaux, March 1993

Joshi, Heather and Hugh Davies, *Pension Consequences of Divorce*, discussion paper no 550, Centre for Economic Policy Research, 1990

Joshi, Heather, 'Changing Roles of Women in the British Labour Market and Family' in *Frontiers of Economic Research* by Phyllis Deane (ed), Macmillan, 1990

Jowell, Roger, Lindsay Brook and Bridget Taylor, *British Social Attitudes: the 8th Report*, Social and Community Planning Research, 1991

Jowell, Roger, Lindsay Brook, Gillian Prior and Bridget Taylor, *British Social Attitudes: the 9th Report*, Social and Community Planning Research, 1992

Kandola, R. S., D. Milner, N. A. Banerji and R. Wood, *Equal Opportunities Can Damage Your Health*, Pearn Kandola Downs, May 1991

Kennedy, Helena, *Eve Was Framed*, Chatto and Windus, 1992

The Key to Real Choice, EOC discussion paper, 1990

Kiernan, Kathleen and Malcolm Wicks, *Family Change and Future Policy*, Family Policy Studies Centre, 1990

King, M. B., A. Cockcroft and C. Gooch, 'Emotional Distress in Doctors: Sources, Effects and Help Sought', *Journal of the Royal Society of Medicine*, Vol 85, Oct 1992

Kinnock, Glenys with Fiona Millar, *By Faith and Daring*, Virago, 1993

Bibliography

Labour Force Survey, HMSO, 1990

Lawson, Annette, *Adultery: an Analysis of Love and Betrayal*, Blackwell, 1988

Lawson, Annette and Deborah L. Rhode (eds), *The Politics of Pregnancy; Adolescent Sexuality and Public Policy*, Yale University Press, 1993

Leonard, Alice, *Pyrrhic Victories: Winning Sex Discrimination and Equal Pay Cases in the Industrial Tribunals 1980–1984*, HMSO, 1987

Link-up Group Research Survey on Men and Women at Work, 1993

Lister, Ruth, *Women's Economic Dependency and Social Security*, EOC, 1992

Lone-Parent Families: Report of an Ad Hoc Working Group, Women's National Commission, 1989

Lunneborg, Patricia, *Abortion: A Positive Solution*, Bergin & Garvey, 1992

Maddock, Su, 'Women's Frustration with and Influence on Local Government Management in the UK', *Women in Management Review*, spring 1993

Maddock, Su, 'Gender Cultures', *Women in Management Review*, (autumn) 1993

Macdonald, Fiona, *The Women's Directory*, Bedford Square Press, 1991

'Making the Invisible Visible: Rewarding Women's Work', *Equal Opportunities Review 45*, Sept/Oct 1992

Mansfield, Penny and Jean Collard, *The Beginning of the Rest of Your Life*, Macmillan, 1988

Martin, Jean and Ceridwen Roberts, *Women's Employment – A Lifetime Perspective*, Dept of Employment, 1980

McLoughlin, Jane, *Up and Running*, Virago, 1992

McRae, Susan, *Maternity Rights in Great Britain: The Experience of Women and Employers*, PSI, 1991

Millward, Neil, *Targeting Potential Discrimination*, EOC, 1995

Morris, Jenny (ed), *Voices of Single Mothers*, Women's Press, 1992

Narrowing the Gender Pay Gap: How Wages Councils Work for Women, Pay Equity Project, 1993

National Commission on Education: Briefing No 8, Nov 1992

The New Review no 13, Low Pay Unit, Dec 1991

Nicholson, John, *Men and Women: How Different are they?*, Oxford, 1993

O'Grady, Frances and Heather Wakefield, *Women, Work and Maternity*, Maternity Alliance, 1989

One-Parent Families: Benefits and Work, National Association of Citizen Advice Bureaux, July 1989

One-Parent Families, Fact Sheet 3, Family Policy Studies Centre

Opening Doors to Equality in Education and Training for Girls, Fawcett Society, 1986

Parker, Hermione (ed), *Citizens' Income and Women*, BIRG Discussion Paper no 2, 1993

Parliamentary Debate Standing Committee: Trade Union Reform and Employment Rights Bill, 28 Jan 1993

Pay and Gender in Britain 2, IRS/EOC, 1992

Payne, Joan, *Women Training and the Skills Shortage*, Policy Studies Institute, 1991

'The Pensions Gender Trap', *Equal Opportunities Review 43*, May/June 1992

People Who Care: A Report on Carer Provision in England and Wales for the Cooperative Women's Guild, 1987

Plumer, Anne-Marie, *Equal Value Judgements: Objective Assessment or Lottery?*, Industrial Relations Research Unit at Warwick University, 1992

Poor Britain: Poverty, Inequality and Low Pay in the Nineties, Low Pay Unit, no 56

Poverty in Pregnancy: The Cost of an Adequate Diet for Pregnant Mothers, Maternity Alliance, 1988

Proctor, Jackie and Christine Jackson, *Women Managers in the NHS*, NHS Women's Unit, 1992

Public Appointments: A Handbook for Women's Organisations, Women's National Commission, 1992

Bibliography

Public Bodies 1992, HMSO, 1993

Quest, Caroline (ed), *Equal Opportunities: A Feminist Fallacy*, Institute for Economic Affairs, 1992

Randall, Vicky, *Women and Politics: An International Perspective*, Macmillan, 1991

'Redundancy and Discrimination', *Equal Opportunities Review 37*, May/June 1991

Rees, Teresa, *Women and the Labour Market*, Routledge, 1992

Regional Trends 92, HMSO, 1992

Request to the Commission of the European Communities by the EOC of Great Britain in Relation to the Implementation of the Principle of Equal Pay, EOC, 1993

The Report of the Hansard Society Commission on Women at the Top, 1990

Roberts, Bethan, *Minority Ethnic Women: Work, Unemployment and Education*, EOC, 1994

Robinson, Margaret, *Family Transformation through Divorce and Remarriage*, Routledge, 1991

Roll, Jo, *Babies and Money: Birth Trends and Costs*, Family Policy Studies Centre, 1986

Rubenstein, Michael, 'Understanding Pregnancy Discrimination: A Framework for Analysis', *Equal Opportunities Review 42*, March/April 1992

Rubery, Jill, *The Gender Pay Gap: Some European Comparisons*, paper for conference on women, minimum pay and the wages councils, 1993

Rubery, Jill, *The Economics of Equal Value*, EOC, 1992

Seccombe, Ian and Jane Ball, 'Motivation, Morale and Mobility, A Profile of Qualified Nurses in the 1990s', Institute of Manpower Studies, no 233, Oct 1992

Seward, Margaret and Elizabeth McEwan, *The Provision of Dental Care of Women Dentists in England and Wales in 1985*, Dept of Oral and Maxillofacial Surgery, the London Hospital Medical College Dental School

Shiftworking – What Price Flexibility?, NUPE's evidence to the pay review body for nursing staff, midwives and health visitors, Oct 1991

Singer, Elly, *Childcare and the Psychology of Development*, 1992

Skordaki, Eleni, *Judicial Appointments*, Research Study no 5, The Law Society, 1991

Smith, Joan, *Misogynies*, Faber, 1993

Smith, John M., *Women and Doctors*, Atlantic Monthly Press, 1992

Smithers, Alan and Pauline Zientek, *Gender, Primary Schools and the National Curriculum*, NASUWT and the Engineering Council, 1991

Smithers, Alan and Pamela Robinson, *Technology in the National Curriculum*, The Engineering Council, 1992

Social Trends 22, HMSO, 1992

Spitze, Glenna, 'Women's Employment and Family Relations', *Journal of Marriage and the Family*, Aug 1988

Spurling, Andrea, *Report of the Women in Higher Education Research Project, 1988–1990*, Kings College, Cambridge, 1990

Statistics of Elective Admissions and Patients Waiting: England at 31 March 1992, Dept of Health

Stress on Women: Policy Paper on Women and Mental Health, Mind, 1992

Stuart, Spencer, *Point of View 17*, Women in Management, 1993

Tannen, Deborah, *You Just Don't Understand: Women and Men in Conversation*, Virago, 1992

Thomas, Helen, *Equal Opportunities in the Mechanical Media*, Goldsmiths College, University of London, 1992

Thorne, Barie, *Gender Play: Girls and Boys in School*, Open University Press, 1993

Towards Equality: A Casebook of Decisions on Sex Discrimination and Equal Pay 1976–1988, EOC, March 1989

Training Trends 8, The Industrial Society, 1993

Violence against Women, Women's National Commission Report

Walton, Pam, *Job Sharing: A Practical Guide*, Kogan Page, 1990

Ward, Clare and Angela Dale, 'Geographical Variation in Female

Labour Force Participation: An Application of Multi Level Modelling', *Regional Studies*, Vol 26.3, 1991

Ward, Clare and Angela Dale, 'The Impact of Early Life-course Transitions on Equality at Work and Home', *The Sociological Review*, 1992

White, Barbara, Charles Cox and Cary Cooper, *Women's Career Development: A Study of High Flyers*, Blackwell, 1992

Whittingham, Vivienne, *Full Marks for Trying: A Survey of Childcare Providers*, Daycare Trust, 1991

Who Cares?, Women's National Commission conference report, Sept 1990

Wilkinson, Brenda, 'Equalities, Work and Organisational Development', unpublished dissertation, 1991

Wilkinson, Frank, *Why Britain Needs a Minimum Wage*, Institute for Public Policy Research, 1992

Williams, Sarah and Jennifer Hann, *Gender Issues in Industrial Design*, Coventry Polytechnic, 1989/90

Winefield, Anthony and Helen R. Winefield, *Growing up With Unemployment*, Routledge, 1993

Without Prejudice: Sex Equality at the Bar and in the Judiciary, TMS Consultants, Nov 1992

Women and Men in Britain 1991, EOC, 1991

Women and Men in Britain 1992, EOC, 1992

Women and Men in Britain 1993, EOC, 1993

Women Doctors and their Careers: Report of the Joint Working Party, Dept of Health, 1991

'Women, Flexibility and the Service Sector', *Work Employment and Society*, Vol 6, no 3, Sept 1992

Women in the Architectural Profession 1978, a report on a survey conducted by the RIBA and PSI

'Women in Engineering', *Equal Opportunities Review 34*, Nov/Dec 1990

Women in the Labour Force: A Statistical Digest, Employment Equality Agency, Dublin 1986

Women in Management Journal, Vol 7, no 1, 1992

'Women in the Transport Industry', *Equal Opportunities Review* 46, Nov/Dec 1992

Women's National Commission: Annual Report 1990/91

Women's Organisations in the UK 1991–92, Women's National Commission

Women Returners: Employment Potential, Women's National Commission, 1991

Women, Work and the Family: Enabling the Double Contribution, University of London Conference Report, 1/2 Oct 1987

Work, Employment and Society, Vol 5, no 3, Sept 1991

Working for Equality: A Summary of the NUT Guidelines on Countering Sexism in Schools, NUT

The Working Parents' Handbook, Working Mothers' Association, 1992

Wright, Robert E. and John F. Ermisch, *Male–Female Wage Differentials in Great Britain*, Birkbeck College Discussion Paper, 1990

index

Index

Index